Lecture Notes of the Institute for Computer Sciences, Social Informatics and Telecommunications Engineering 93

Nalini Venkatasubramanian
Vladimir Getov   Stephan Steglich (Eds.)

Mobile Wireless Middleware, Operating Systems, and Applications

4th International ICST Conference, Mobilware 2011
London, UK, June 22-24, 2011
Revised Selected Papers

 Springer

Volume Editors

Nalini Venkatasubramanian
University of California, Department of Computer Science
2086 Donald Bren Hall, Irvine, CA 92697-3435, USA
E-mail: nalini@ics.uci.edu

Vladimir Getov
University of Westminster, School of Electronics and Computer Science
115 New Cavendish Street, London, W1W 6UW, UK
E-mail: v.s.getov@wmin.ac.uk

Stephan Steglich
Fraunhofer FOKUS
Kaiserin-Augusta-Allee 31, 10589 Berlin, Germany
E-mail: stephan.steglich@fokus.fraunhofer.de

ISSN 1867-8211   e-ISSN 1867-822X
ISBN 978-3-642-30606-8   e-ISBN 978-3-642-30607-5
DOI 10.1007/978-3-642-30607-5
Springer Heidelberg Dordrecht London New York

Library of Congress Control Number: 2012938028

CR Subject Classification (1998): C.2, H.4, D.2, H.5, H.3, I.2

Typesetting: Camera-ready by author, data conversion by Scientific Publishing Services, Chennai, India

Printed on acid-free paper

Springer is part of Springer Science+Business Media (www.springer.com)

Preface

The fourth edition of the International ICST Conference on Mobile Wireless Middleware, Operating Systems, and Applications (MobilWare 2011) was held June 22–24, 2011, at the University of Westminster, London. The development of mobile computing has revolutionized contemporary society and greatly influenced its economic and social progress in the last decade. Nowadays, the rapid emergence of innovative hardware and software products in this area is due to the diligent work of both researchers and practitioners and the great synergy in research and implementation across disciplines and geographical boundaries.

MobilWare 2011 was a three-day event with several high-quality technical and scientific papers that emphasized many aspects of mobile computing ranging from communication infrastructures, networks, to societal scale mobile applications and their impacts. The conference featured two keynote addresses on topics of emerging relevance to the field of mobile computing. Lajos Hanzo's keynote on "Shannonian Lessons for Wireless, the 'World-Wide Wait' and 'Green' Radios" contrasted lessons from theory with the practical constraints imposed on state-of-the-art multimedia communicators. Gordon Blair's keynote on "Revisiting Interoperability: The Case for Emergent Middleware" discussed interoperability challenges in enabling dynamic connectivity at run-time to match current context and requirements of heterogeneous devices and applications. There were regular tracks of technical paper presentations in relevant topic areas including mobile sensor networks, SoC for mobile applications, networking platforms, mobile distributed systems, and mobile frameworks. Highlights of the conference included a special session on mobile systems in education organized by Daphne Economou, a panel on "Novel Infrastructures and Applications for Mobile Computing" (featuring views from experienced researchers) and a poster session. The rich and diverse program provided new perspectives on research in mobile computing. It was particularly positive to see research efforts of a number of young researchers included as papers in these proceedings and in the associated Posters Session.

We would like to take this opportunity to acknowledge some of the volunteer leaders. We are all deeply indebted to Aza Swedin's all encompassing support in every aspect of conference planning and organization. Publicity Chairs Carlos Becker Westphall and Panagiotis Chountas together with our excellent Web Chair Carlo Giannelli provided substantial help for the publicity of Mobilware 2011. We are also indebted to our Local Chair Alexander Bolotov for his support and enthusiasm for the local arrangements. Also, I wish to thank all the reviewers for contributing their time and expertise and thus providing invaluable help in the selection process. I would like to thank the Organizing Committee members, Special Session Chairs, the Technical Program Committee members, and all reviewers who contributed immensely toward the success of this event.

Finally and most importantly, thanks are due to all of the authors for their high-quality research work, results, and papers that we are proud to publish in these proceedings.

We very much look forward to another successful conference in 2012 in Italy with MobilWare 2012, and in the forthcoming years.

Vladimir Getov
Stephan Steglich
Nalini Venkatasubramanian

Conference Organization

General Chairs

Vladimir Getov   University of Westminster, UK
Martin Sauter   WirelessMoves, Germany

Steering Committee

Paolo Bellavista   University of Bologna, Italy
Carl Chang   Iowa State University, USA
Imrich Chlamtac   CREATE-NET, Italy
Thomas Magedanz   Technical University Berlin, Germany

Technical Program Committee Chairs

Stephan Steglich   Fraunhofer FOKUS, Germany
Nalini Venkatasubramanian   University of California, Irvine, USA
Qinghua Zheng   Xian Jiaotong University, P.R. China

Publicity Chairs

Carlos Becker Westphall   Federal University of Santa Catarina, Brazil
Panagiotis Chountas   University of Westminster, UK

Web Chair

Carlo Giannelli   University of Bologna, Italy

Conference Coordinator

Åza Swedin   ICST

Local Chair

Alexander Bolotov   University of Westminster, UK

Technical Program Committee

Nick Allott   Wholesale Application Community, UK
Jean-Marie Bonnin   Telecom Bretagne, France
Cristian Borcea   New Jersey Institute of Technology, USA

Mathieu Boussard   Alcatel Lucent Bell Labs France, France
Jiajun Bu   Zhejiang University, China
Djuradj Budimir   University of Westminster, UK
Marcos Caceres   Opera, Norway
Cai Cai   Iowa State University, USA
Jiannong Cao   Hong Kong Polytechnic University, Hong Kong
Liang Cheng   Lehigh University, USA
Dan Grigoras   University College Cork, Ireland
Isabelle Demeure   Telecom Paris, France
Sudhir Dixit   HP, India
Olaf Drögehorn   Universität Kassel, Germany
Daphne Economou   University of Westminster, UK
Matthias Faeth   TNO, The Netherlands
Andreas Fasbender   Ericsson, Germany
Xinwen Fu   University of Massachusetts Lowell, USA
Christian Fuhrhop   Fraunhofer FOKUS, Germany
Anastasius Gavras   Eurescom, Germany
Nektarios Georgalas   British Telecom, UK
Giovanni Giambene   Università degli Studi di Siena, Italy
Mesut Günes   FU Berlin, Germany
Roch H. Glitho   Concordia University, Canada
Cristian Hesselman   Novay, The Netherlands
Robert Hirschfeld   Hasso-Plattner-Institut Potsdam, Germany
Stefan Holtel   Flensburg School for Advanced Business
                                 Research, Germany
Feng Hong   Ocean University of China, China
Ajit Jaokar   Futuretext, UK
Yang Ji   BUPT, China
Theo Kanter   Mid Sweden University, Sweden
Ralf Kernchen   University of Surrey, UK
Johan Koolwaaij   Novay, The Netherlands
Steffen Krüssel   Deutsche Telekom, Germany
Wei-Shinn Ku   Auburn University, USA
Martin Kurze   Deutsche Telekom, Germany
Sven Lachmund   DOCOMO Euro-Labs, Germany
Peter Langendoerfer   IHP Microelectronics, Germany
Xiuqi (Suze) Li   University of North Carolina, USA
Yan Li   Huawei, China
Xiaolin Li   University of Florida, USA
Mahi Lohi   University of Westminster, UK
Roberto Minerva   Telecom Italia - Future Centre, Italy
Klaus Moessner   University of Surrey, UK
Tamer Nadeem   Old Dominion University, USA
Christian Nord   Sony Ericsson, Sweden
Hiroyuki Ohsaki   Osaka University, Japan
Andre Paul   Fraunhofer FOKUS, Germany

Joachim Quantz   ART+COM, Germany
Mohammad R. Shikh-Bahaei King's College London, UK
Dave Raggett   W3C, UK
Nishkam Ravi   NEC Labs, USA
Gruia-Catalin Roman   Washington University in St. Louis, USA
Alfons Salden   Almende, The Netherlands
Roland Schwaiger   Deutsche Telekom, Germany
Francois Spies   University of Franche-Comte, France
Weiwei Sun   Fudan University, China
Javid Taheri   The University of Sydney, Australia
Xianping Tao   Nanjing University, China
Andrzej Tarczynski   University of Westminster, UK
Anand Tripathi   University of Minnesota, USA
Matthias Wagner   DOCOMO Euro-Labs, Germany
Xiaodong Wang   National University of Defence Technology,
                            China

Guangtao Xue   Shanghai Jiao Tong University, China
Yanmin Zhu   Shanghai Jiao Tong University, China
Franco Zambonelli   University of Modena and Reggio Emilia, Italy

Table of Contents

Mobile Systems in Education

SOC for Mobile Apps (SOC)

Networking Platforms (NW)

Mobile Execution Frameworks (MFW)

Mobile Cloud (MC) and Distributed Execution

Mobile Sensor Networks

A-VIEW: Context-Aware Mobile E-Learning for the Masses

Kamal Bijlani[1], Shivsubramani Krishnamoorthy[2],
Venkat Rangan[1], and Ranga Venkataraman[1]

[1] Amrita E-Learning Research Lab,
Amrita Vishwa Vidyapeetham, Amritapuri Campus, Kerala, India
{kamal,venkat}@amrita.edu, rangasv@am.amrita.edu
[2] MIND Lab, University of Maryland, College Park, MD 20842 USA
shiv@cs.umd.edu

Abstract. Developing countries typically have large populations in rural areas with inadequate resources for quality education. Concurrently, low-cost mobile devices are becoming quite popular in rural areas. The trends in the mobile industry show that a variety of mobile devices and choices in connectivity are becoming available and affordable. Synchronous e-learning is also starting to show immense potential with expert instructors being available to train teachers in other areas. The combination of these factors is unfolding a new era in mobile e-learning where the ubiquity of connected mobile devices has provided a tremendous potential for knowledge to reach large numbers of learners in rural areas.

In this paper, we present a case study in a large developing country like India where a major national initiative has been undertaken for providing e-learning to the masses. This program is addressing issues like nation-wide connectivity, affordable mobile devices and high-quality online content. As part of this program, we contribute a highly scalable framework called A-VIEW (Amrita Virtual Interactive E-Learning World) that provides live interaction between expert trainers and large number of learners. A-VIEW is designed to be context-aware, thus addressing the practical needs of a variety of users in various strata of society according to their available infrastructure, connectivity, bandwidth, local language and mode of learning.

Keywords: mobile learning, A-VIEW, m-learning, mobile UI, ACE.

1 Introduction

Developing countries face significant challenges when attempting to make learning more accessible by using Internet technologies for poorer populations [1]. The availability of new technologies like mobile devices has improved access from developing economies to the world market, but they have done little to help deprived groups gain access to educational opportunities. Limited Information Technology (IT) infrastructure has been a major hurdle in developing countries. There is a need to

N. Venkatasubramanian et al. (Eds.): Mobilware 2011, LNICST 93, pp. 1–14, 2012.
© Institute for Computer Sciences, Social Informatics and Telecommunications Engineering 2012

focus on and provide basic educational infrastructure to support low-cost, higher quality access in rural and deprived areas. This is important not only for equal access to learning, but also so that different groups may have the opportunity to contribute to the development of global knowledge.

In this paper, we present a case in India where a national program NME-ICT (National Mission on Education via ICT) is being implemented for providing mobile education for the masses. This project is a billion-dollar initiative for providing e-learning to the masses under the Ministry of Human Resources Development (MHRD), Government of India and is described on the website, www.sakshat.ac.in. The NME-ICT project has several facets for higher education. These include developing affordable mobile device, national connectivity, online content consisting of recorded lectures and other associated material like simulations, quizzes, and several other supporting projects.

As part of this NME-ICT program, we contribute a highly scalable framework called A-VIEW [2, 3] that provides live interaction between expert trainers and large number of learners. The context-aware model of A-VIEW helps a variety of users with different levels of access to IT infrastructure and connectivity to work in a collaborative manner with other participants in the education process.

In the next section, we describe the situations in developing and developed countries with regards to the education system and the potential of mobile technologies in these nations. We show that affordable basic IT infrastructure is necessary to dilute the digital divide between the rich and the poor. We discuss the issues in using mobiles in large and developing nations. In Sections 3, we present the A-VIEW framework and architecture, and show that it is able to address the needs of a wide variety of users, irrespective of their hardware and connectivity. We show that the context-aware capability of A-VIEW provides a custom solution and thus it is highly beneficial to a large variety of users. The synergistic approach of the A-VIEW server architecture with the national private educational network provides a strong foundation for making e-learning and m-learning practical and affordable to every learner in India. Initial user feedback from a survey of 300 professors around the country shows that A-VIEW is almost as good as a real class and easy to use.

2   Mobile Technologies in Developing Nations - A Potential Platform

In this section we discuss about how developing nations can benefit from mobile technologies. In developing countries the penetration rate of mobile phones surpasses that of desktop computers. The number of mobile internet users especially in developing countries has grown nearly five times in the last five years. For example, India has emerged as the second largest consumer of mobile Internet, after the US. India, with its 35+ million mobile internet users, ranks No.2 in the world. Around 14 billion web pages were viewed by Indian mobile internet users in February 2010. The number of new data connections added globally this year will be higher on the mobile than on the PC. According to industry estimates total internet penetration in India is about 7%-8% and out of that 4-5% internet is accessed through mobiles. Experts claim that mobile internet usage in India will touch 250+ million by 2015. By 2013, mobile phones will overtake PCs as the most common Web access device worldwide. According to Gartner's PC installed base forecast, by 2013, the combined installed base of smart phones and browser-equipped enhanced phones will exceed 1.82 billion units and will be greater than the installed base for PCs thereafter [4].

The numbers in Table 1 show how internet usage through mobile devices is high in developing nations, even when compared to the developed nations [5].

Table 1. Percentage of mobile web only users

Country	Percentage mobile-only	Country	Percentage mobile-only
Egypt	70%	Indonesia	44%
India	59%	Thailand	32%
South Africa	57%	China	30%
Ghana	55%	US	25%
Kenya	54%	UK	22%
Nigeria	50%	Russia	19%
Source: On Device Research (December 2010)		Survey group:15,204	

The aim of mobile e-learning in developing countries is different from those of developed countries. In developed countries, motives to widen participation and lifelong learning for non-traditional learners are closely linked to the development of a strong knowledge economy. In contrast, developing countries' motives for m-learning are to provide basic and literacy education to large numbers of poor people [6]. The so-called 'digital divide' between rich and poor countries remains unchanged. Despite significant improvements in the developing world, the gap between the Information and Communication technologies (ICT) haves and have-nots remains.

A number of factors are responsible for the low academic achievement in developing countries like India. Inequalities in access to education continue to pose major barriers in the developing world, and the delivery of cost-effective and quality education remains a persistent problem. Higher drop out ratios is being witnessed. Retaining students is an uphill task due to high teacher absenteeism, lack of adequate number of staff and low teacher motivation. There is also a lack of adequate training for teachers. Educational surveys have revealed that teaching activities are often limited to reading from textbooks, keeping children busy with written exercises, making them read aloud or memorize passages leading to student's poor performance. Most government schools lack basic amenities like electricity, drinking water and toilets, proper furniture, playgrounds or adequate lighting and ventilation in classrooms. The availability of resources is mainly concentrated in the urban regions. A mechanism that enables the rural population to tap these resources will be highly worthwhile.

Apart from the aforesaid, it's crucial to have a study into the following information. There are 2351858 primary schools, 534 universities [7], 6014 non-technical colleges [7] and 669 technical institutions in the country. In spite of this statistics, Indian education sector face the grave challenge of imparting right education to children. There is lack of adequate Infrastructure to meet the need of 26 million babies born in India each year. The enrolment ratio is 7 % in higher education. Moreover, India needs 2000-3000 universities in next 10 years. NKC puts the requirement to 1500 universities by 2015 to increase the enrolment ratio from 7 to 15%. In total, the need for educational institutions has quadrupled.

In the attempt to find viable solutions to these challenges, much hope has been placed in new information and communication technologies (ICTs), mobile phones being one example. Of the many different forms of ICTs, taking account that the vast majority of mobile phones support Internet browsing in local mode, mobile Web services have grounds to flourish; mobile phones are thought, for several reasons, to be a particularly suitable tool for advancing education in developing regions. Mobile devices now allow teaching institutions to experiment with bringing distance teaching and learning to even more remote audiences. Mobile phone, the most prevalent ICT in the developing world, are an especially good 'leap frogger' since they use the radio spectrum and has to its credit greater user population and market potential. In addition to voice communication, mobile phones allow the transfer of data, which can be particularly useful for delivering educational content over long distances, even on a real time basis.

Table 2. India's current situation on the availabilities of mobile devices based on the strata of society

Different strata in society	Mobile device	Cost in INR (Rs.)	Language	Bandwidth
Upper class	High definition mobiles such as Smart phones and high end 3G Mobiles.	15,000-35, 000	Speaks English, and other Indian languages also.	High Connectivity. 512Kbps-7 Mbps
Middleclass	Middle range 3G Phones and Edge supported phones.	4,000-15, 000	Speaks, local language but often English.	Medium connectivity. 56Kbps-2 Mbps
Rural class	Low-range mobile phones	600-4,000	Speaks only local language.	Low connectivity. 28 Kbps

Another assuring trend in developing countries like India is that mobile devices are becoming more affordable, thus becoming common even in the rural areas. Table 2 shows the current situation in India on the kinds of resources that are available on a mobile device to the masses in the different strata of the society. Based on Table 2, a graph has been plotted, Fig. 1. It shows estimation about an exponential increase in the number of smart phone users. The NME-ICT project described earlier has an objective of providing a mobile wireless tablet device to a large number of learners at a subsidized rate. If the price of this device is brought down, millions of learners will be able to afford such a smart mobile device. Along with connectivity and good bandwidth, this will bring e-learning knowledge resources to a large number of learners. Thus mobile e-learning approach will definitely prove effective.

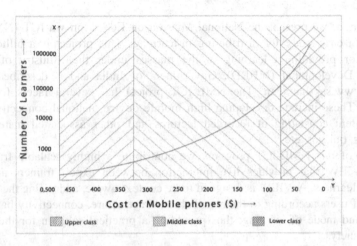

Fig. 1. Graph showing cost of mobile phones v/s number of learners in different strata of society

2.1 Challenges

Unlike developed countries, developing countries see an evident divide between the rural and urban areas in the different strata of the society; there are few critical challenges that need to be addressed.

Display. With different kinds of mobile devices available today, a different challenge of user interface is also to be addressed. Tablets and smart phones have different screen resolutions and the user interface needs to adapt to the available space and provide the education content most effectively.

Bandwidth. Urban areas have the luxury of high bandwidth connectivity. Urban India is seeing the surge of broadband connectivity with the availability of 3G networks. But the rural areas are yet to catch up. Therefore, a mobile learning system should not only be able to leverage upon the availability of high bandwidth but also should be able to perform efficiently in a low bandwidth situation.

Language. India possesses diversified languages similar to Europe. Therefore, to implement mobile learning in a country like India we have to first take up the gauntlet of localization of mobile learning content. Information can closely be knitted to the native language reading level or learning style of the user and could tailor programmed information into the handheld device.

3   A-VIEW: Synchronous Collaborative E-Learning Framework

In this section, we present the National Mission on Education via ICT (NME-ICT) project as a case study for distributing m-learning. This project is a billion-dollar initiative for providing e-learning to the masses under the Ministry of Human Resources Development (MHRD), Government of India and is described on the website, www.sakshat.ac.in. The NME-ICT project has several facets for higher education. These include developing high mobile device, national connectivity, and online content consisting of recorded lectures and other associated material like simulations, quizzes, etc.

As part of this NME-ICT program, we contribute a highly scalable framework called A-VIEW that provides live interaction between expert trainers and large number of learners. A-VIEW is designed to be context-aware, addressing the needs of a variety of users according to their available infrastructure, connectivity bandwidth, language and mode of learning; thus providing a practical solution for the various strata of society.

With its live teaching platform, A-VIEW delivers knowledge in a collaborative environment. In this framework, we target a set of nodes or places that are physically distant to be connected by an eLearning network. It consists of a set of tools that are provided for Live Lectures. The assumption is that the class can be transmitted simultaneously to a set of nodes. Several tools are provided for the instructor to use in a live lecture. The instructor has the ability to interact with the students, and there are tools for testing the awareness and basic understanding of the students during the class. During the live lecture, each receiving node becomes a live virtual university. The instructor can interact with each location, and they can share resources. The instructor node and all the student nodes together form the virtual world during the live lecture.

A-VIEW is based on a mapping between a real and virtual classroom. It includes all the entities used in a classroom like teacher video for a real teacher, whiteboard for blackboard and documents for textbooks (with real-time automatic synchronizing feature). Apart from this, using A-VIEW, lectures can be recorded and viewed later.

3.1   A-VIEW Client-Side Architecture

Fig. 2 shows the client-side architecture for A-VIEW. This is the overall process for synchronous live interaction between the instructor and the learners. The instructor video is processed and encoded at multiple bitrates. This can be received by the learners at different bandwidths depending on their available infrastructure. For example, the high-quality stream can be received by a large class room or seminar hall in which multiple large displays are available to be handled independently. The four major display components are the instructor video, the whiteboard, the presentation slides and an interaction window for chat and hand-raise facility. These four components can also be combined together as a single display. Figure xxx shows how the components can be viewed in multiple displays. The single display can be viewed on a desktop, laptop, tablet or a mobile phone. The A-VIEW system provides adaptive bitrates according to the available bandwidth. Thus, the image quality is dynamically adjusted so as to achieve optimum performance.

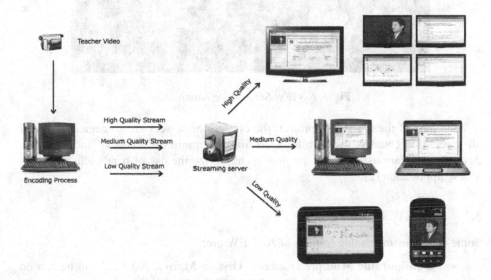

Fig. 2. A-VIEW Client-Side Architecture

3.2   A-VIEW Server-Side Architecture

The ACE (Architecture for Collaborative Environments) framework that is discussed in our previous work [8], is implemented based on a distributed client-server architecture, primarily consisting of two server clusters (active and passive servers as shown in Fig. 3), that communicate among each other. The active cluster consists of live media servers and content servers, while the passive cluster consists of database servers and content servers. Users who are logging into A-VIEW get connected to passive servers and download all the needed files (e.g. 2D/3D graphics and documents needed for the session); after successful downloading, they are connected to active server. In short, the active cluster serves the live users and the passive cluster initializes the newly logged in users. This provides a practical way for load-balancing the servers. As the content in the active servers get updated by the live users, it is incrementally transmitted to the passive servers. Thus, the passive servers maintain an updated copy of the multimedia content.

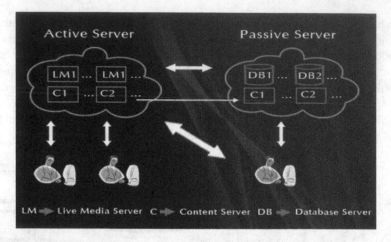

Fig. 3. A-VIEW Server-Side Architecture

As a part of the NME-ICT project, the clusters of servers are strategically placed all over the country to provide accessibility, minimize latency, and improve throughput. Various heuristics are used to minimize the use of bandwidth in the A-VIEW application [2].

3.3   A-VIEW and Its Features

Some of the distinguishing features of A-VIEW are:

- **Configurable Multiple Displays (One to Many).** A-VIEW can be run on any number of displays/screens based on the need of the user.
- **Adaptive Bandwidth Usage (56k to 2MB).** Depending on the available bandwidth, video quality will be adjusted automatically
- **No Proprietary Hardware:** A-VIEW uses existing hardware that is available like desktop, webcam, microphone
- **Crystal Clear Live Document Sharing.** Documents or presentations can be shared with the available best quality at real time
- **Multi Device Compatible Whiteboard.** To share users' annotations with other users using mouse or writing pads
- **2d/3d based animation/collaborative elements.** To share animations (2D/3D) preserving their quality at real time

3.4   A-VIEW on Mobile Devices

A-VIEW has been designed to work in a variety of devices like desktop, laptops, tablets and mobile phones. Irrespective of the device on which A-VIEW is used on, it imparts the same experience to the users. One important aspect of A-VIEW is that it takes into consideration the context of the user and the device used for running the same. Fig. 4 shows A-VIEW running on an Android Tablet.

Fig. 4. A-VIEW in Tablet (Android)

2D, 3D based contents & animations can be given as a complete package of collaborative elements which can be customized for the different versions of mobile in an effective approach which could serve mobile learning in a better way. Fig. 5 shows a 3D model of human brain in mobile A-VIEW; it helps students to have a 3-dimensional look and feel of the brain.

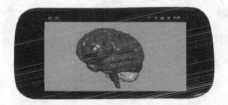

Fig. 5. 3D animation content (human brain) on Mobile A-VIEW (Android)

3.5   Mobile Quiz (On Simple Mobile Device)

Students can answer a quiz using desktops or mobile phones with internet connection or through SMS(Short Message Service). Mobile Quiz enables students to answer a quiz even when students are not present in their classrooms/centers. The student has to use the same number given during the initial registration process of A-VIEW. This feature helps the students in rural areas to attend the quizzes from their home or school on a simple mobile device, where internet connectivity is not provided.

The list of quizzes that the student has enabled as part of their course will appear on the client display once the teacher has done the settings for the same. The quiz can be answered through online or offline, through SMS. The application will evaluate responses to the quiz questions online & will display results at the end of the session, along with correct answers. For teacher, it also shows the number of students that have marked the correct answer, which can be used for knowing the level of understanding o the students about that particular course or topic.

Fig. 6. Quiz on simple mobile using SMS

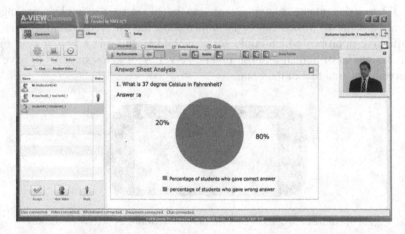

Fig. 7. Answer sheet analysis: A feature of quiz module which provides the percentage of students who gave the correct answer

3.6   Mobile User Interface

Designing user interfaces for various devices of different sizes poses a challenge. When the overall space available for the user interface is minimal, like a mobile device, the traditional design for user interface may not be effective. We completely abide with the *Visual Info seeking mantra: Overview First, Filter and then Details-on-Demand,* as proposed by [9].

Fig. 8. Cluttered conventional UI of A-VIEW in mobile phones

Using this paradigm the A-VIEW user interface has been designed exclusively for mobile phones. The overview is provided first; for example every feature like video, chat, whiteboard, document sharing etc can be viewed as a separate window with a single movement on the icons. The idea behind this simple User Interface is to save space and give better accessibility. Also the details are given as needed.

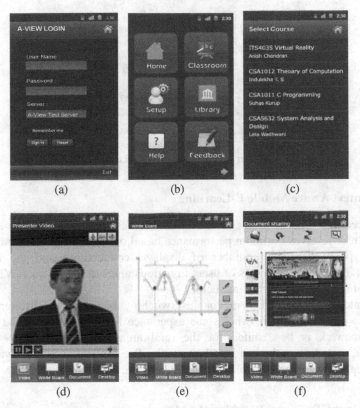

Fig. 9. Screen shots of the redesigned user interface of A-VIEW for MOBILE: (a) Login screen; (b) Home Screen; (c) List of Courses Screen; (d) Video Screen; (e) Whiteboard Screen; (f) Document Sharing Screen

3.7 Multiple Language Support

India possesses diversified languages similar to Europe. Therefore, to implement mobile learning in a country like India we have to understand localization of mobile learning content. Information can closely be knitted to the native language reading level or learning style of the user. The user interface controls can be made available in different languages. Also, the content is made available in different languages.

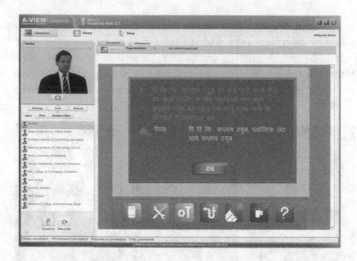

Fig. 10. A teacher taking classes in Hindi using A-VIEW

3.8   Context-Aware Mobile E-Learning

As described in the previous sections, A-VIEW is designed to be context aware so that every user receives optimum performance based on their available infrastructure like the type of hardware, number of displays, connectivity and the available bandwidth. This allows all types of users in various areas to access an A-VIEW live and interact seamlessly with the instructor.

The context-aware mechanism enables switching between the different media modalities to provide a more wholesome experience for the end-user. The context-aware framework is best suited for the rural areas with the *adaptive bit-rate mechanism*, according to the bandwidth available. The application is also available in different regional languages such as Hindi, Malayalam, etc....

3.9   Train the Trainers: Reaching the Masses

The A-VIEW network can be used by an expert trainer for imparting professional training in any field to the novice or inexperienced trainers. For example, the Teacher Empowerment program was initiated by IIT- Bombay for improving the quality of teachers. The vision for this program has been provided by Dr. Deepak Phatak. Over 1000 college teachers from around 500 professional institutions gathered at 32 nodal centers across the country and attended a 2-week online workshop from 13th to 22nd December 2010. The session was led by Dr. Sudarshan, IIT Bombay Professor and a renowned author of the standard international textbook on Database Systems. These 32 remote centers used the A-VIEW (Amrita Virtual Interactive E-Learning World) system developed by Amrita University.

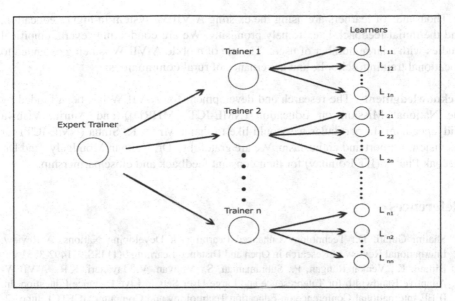

Fig. 11. "Train the Trainers" can result in large number of trainees

4   Conclusion and Future Works

Previous works have indicated that lack of proper IT infrastructure is a major hurdle in providing e-learning for the masses. In this paper, we presented a case study in a large developing country like India where a large national initiative has been undertaken for providing e-learning to every interested learner. This program is addressing issues like nation-wide connectivity, affordable mobile devices and high-quality online content. As part of this program, we contribute a highly scalable framework called A-VIEW (Amrita Virtual Interactive E-Learning World) that provides live interaction between expert trainers and large number of learners. A-VIEW is designed to be context-aware, thus addressing the needs of a variety of users according to their available infrastructure: hardware, connectivity, bandwidth, language and mode of learning; thus providing a practical solution for the various strata of society.

Although cheap mobiles are getting very popular in developing nations, affordable smart mobile devices and connectivity are also needed so that m-learning can be effective. Expert teachers are few in number, yet, synchronous e-learning is starting to show immense potential with 'Training the Trainers' type of programs becoming practical with distance and location no longer being a barrier. In this regard, the role of context-aware ubiquitous mobile devices is pivotal to tap into the pools of global knowledge and quench the thirst of education in the large numbers of learners in rural and deprived areas in developing countries.

Thousands of learners are using the existing A-VIEW system in higher education, and the initial feedback is extremely promising. We are conducting several empirical studies with a large number of users. The use of mobile A-VIEW is being extended to vocational training, schools, and governance of rural communities.

Acknowledgments. The research and development for A-VIEW has been funded by the National Mission on Education (NME-ICT [MHRD]) and Amrita Vishwa Vidyapeetham. In particular we would like to thank Mr. N.K. Sinha (NME-ICT) for his vision, support and enthusiasm. We are grateful to Dr. Kannan Moudgalya and Dr. Deepak Phatak (IIT Bombay) for their constant feedback and close partnership.

References

1. Shalini Gulati, D.: Technology Enhanced Learning in Developing Nations: A Review. International Review of Research in Open and Distance Learning 9(1) ISSN: 1492-3831
2. Bijlani, K., Venkat Rangan, P., Subramanian, S., Vijayan, V., Jayahari, K.R.: A-VIEW-Adaptive Bandwidth for Telepresence and Large User Sets in Live Distance Education. In: IEEE International Conference on Education Technology and Computer (ICETC), June 22-24 (2010)
3. Bijlani, K., Guntha, R., Pai, C.S., George, S.: Talk to a Teacher- Ecosystem for Synchronous Online Interaction with a large set of Students, IC4E, Mumbai, India (2010)
4. Gartner, Inc.: IT research and advisory company,
   http://www.gartner.com/it/page.jsp?id=1278413
5. MobiThinking: Research and Web marketing company,
   http://mobithinking.com/stats-corner/
   global-mobile-statistics-2011-all-quality-mobile-marketing-
   research-mobile-web-stats-su
6. Zhang, K.: China's online education: rhetoric and realities. In: Carr-Chellman, A.A. (ed.) Global Perspectives on E-learning: Rhetoric and Reality, pp. 21–32. Sage Publications, London (2005)
7. University Grants Commission (UGC),
   http://www.ugc.ac.in/pub/stategies/HEIstategies.pdf
8. Bijlani, K., Venkat Rangan, P., Jayahari, K.R., Sreejith, K.H., Narayan, K.: ACE-Architecture for Collaborative Environments. In: IEEE International Conference on Computer Science and Information Technology (IEEE ICCSIT 2010), July 9-11 (2010)
9. Shneiderman, B.: The Eyes Have It: A Task by Data Type Taxonomy for Information Visualizations. In: Proceedings of the IEEE Symposium on Visual Languages, pp. 336–343. IEEE Computer Society Press, Washington (1996)

Mobile Augmented Reality for Cultural Heritage

Anastassia Angelopoulou[1], Daphne Economou[1], Vassiliki Bouki[1],
Alexandra Psarrou[1], Li Jin[1], Chris Pritchard[2], and Frantzeska Kolyda[1]

[1] School of Electronics and Computer Science, University of Westminster,
W1W 6UW, United Kingdom
{agelopa,D.Economou1,boukiv,psarroa,L.Jin02,kolydaf}@wmin.ac.uk
[2] PortablePixels
SW4 6DH, United Kingdom
chris59david@yahoo.co.uk

Abstract. This paper introduces an approach of using mobile Augmented Reality (mobile-AR) in cultural organisations, such as museums and archaeological sites, for information provision and enhancing the visiting experience. We demonstrate our approach by presenting a mobile-AR educational game for iPhones that has been developed for the archaeological site and the exhibition area at Sutton Hoo. This pilot aids visitors' understanding of the site and its history via an engaging and playful game that connects the site with the British Museum where the objects that have been excavated from the site are exhibited. The paper discusses stakeholders' requirements, the system architecture and concludes with lessons learned and future work.

Keywords: Augmented Reality, smartphones, mobile-AR games, cultural heritage, ARToolkit.

1 Introduction

In recent years, mobile phones and particularly smartphones, have developed into an ideal platform for AR applications. This is significant because the widespread adoption of smartphones means that this platform could be one of the dominant platforms for AR applications in the near future. Mobile AR has been named as one of the top 10 emerging technologies by MIT [1]. The potential of AR is huge, particularly in the mobile space where research firm ARCchart forecasts that by 2015 2.2 billion AR-enabled phones will be present in the market [2]. That growth has opened up a plethora of new possibilities in learning, teaching, and the creative sector.

Current technology allows researchers and visual artists to investigate a variety of application possibilities using mobile-AR in domains not commonly associated with computer technologies. Such domains are cultural heritage, and performing arts [3,4,5,6,7]. The current study investigates the possibilities offered by mobile-AR in cultural organisations like museums and archaeological sites without necessarily investing in buying hardware infrastructure, but taking advantage of devices own by the visitors. A survey in Europe showed that 35% of

N. Venkatasubramanian et al. (Eds.): Mobilware 2011, LNICST 93, pp. 15–22, 2012.

museums have already incorporated Virtual Reality (VR) and AR presentations to enhance their exhibitions [5]. While some projects are at an initial stage, the rapidly growing number is an indication that museums start to understand that AR can be an effective way to build user interest in museum collections and exhibits by engaging users and prompting their participation within an exhibit. Studies also, have shown that AR could provide an alternative mean for navigation, interaction and orientation in a museum especially when museums do not have the space and resources required to exhibit their whole collection or the nature of some of the objects prevent the museums to make them available to the public.

While most of the studies in museums have been conducted indoors, there is little literature involving outdoor mobile-AR without the use of fully embodied and wearable systems [8,9]. It is more challenging to move an AR application outdoor, into archaeological places and excavations where interactive storytelling and environmental conditions could play a significant role in the user's experience. Such a system would require an intuitive human-computer interface based on metaphors, hotspots, logical clues, and portable technology. The users should be able to interact with digital content naturally and get augmented information of the excavated objects. Furthermore, the system should provide solutions that enable the comparison and identification of artifacts, in different historical periods, found in the specific archaeological place.

This paper presents an example of a multi-user mobile-AR educational application for the Sutton Hoo site, a group of Anglo-Saxon burial mounds, for SmartPhones. The site combines indoors and outdoors points of interest that need to be connected. The AR tour is delivered in the form of a team-oriented puzzle game. A number of teams of children visitors, age between 11 and 16, are cast into the role of investigators trying to solve a number of puzzles that involve finding specific exhibits from the excavation site. Every real excavated object is augmented by its virtual counterpart in its physical environment with the use of mobile-AR. The information space embeds all exhibits into the game storyline and carries visitors along the Sutton Hoo site in an exciting way.

The remainder of the paper is organised as follows. Section 2 discusses the potential of mobile-AR game-based in learning. Section 3 presents the Sutton-Hoo case study. Section 4 discusses the interface aspects of mobile-AR and the system architecture of the application, before we conclude in Section 5.

2   AR-Mobile in Education

One of the most promising aspects of AR is that it can be used for visual and highly interactive forms of game-based learning as presented in this paper. Learners are provided with a new tool that allows them to enhance the existing environment by augmented it with extended knowledge. Learning activities can follow different pedagogical approaches. The theory of Flow has been introduced in game-based learning approach which addresses the issue of focusing in a learning activity and examines the issue of immersion. The psychologist M. Csikszentmihalyi [10] defined the optimal learning experience in the Flow theory which aims to achieve clear goals, concentration, a loss of feeling of self-consciousness, distorted sense of time, immediate feedback of the current activity, balancing of ability level against challenge, a sense of personal control, a motivated rewarding activity, and high level of involvement in the proposed activity. This theory has been applied to video games but also to educational activities [11].

The mobile-AR application discussed in this project incorporates: conventional game-play mechanisms including interactive narrative and setting; master goal divided into subtasks; choice and collaboration through which are intended to enhance historical content interpretation; user engagement and inspiration. In addition, novel pervasive game features are introduced to it with three types of expansion: temporal, spatial, and social [12]. Temporal expansion defines game sessions as possibly unlimited actions without explicit start or stop. Spatial expansion reflects the impact of the real world as a 'playground' in the game environment. Social expansion takes into account multi-players that share the playground. By integrating with these game-play features, dynamic simulation, rich media datasets, and augmented content can be brought into a learner's personal space at a scale and in a form easy to understand and work with others at a social level through the mobile platform for communication and collaboration.

Thanks to these innovative features, it is seen that mobile-AR system can be used to enhance various types of learning practices for Technology Enhanced Learning (TEL) in terms of the creation, distribution, and access of learning resources, collaboration and interaction, time and location independency, role changing, and achievement of learning outcomes. In a broader context of education, mobile-AR is appealing because it aligns with pervasive learning by offering the technological innovations to the learner and their learning environment that can support the delivery of flexible, seamless and personalised learning activities to learners.

3   Sutton Hoo Case Study

The Sutton Hoo archaeological site is widely known about the burial ship which is believed to be of an Anglo-Saxon King. However, what the site is really about is a group of Anglo-Saxon burial mounds overlooking the River Deben in southeast Suffolk, England containing artefacts from various periods of time, the most important of which containing a sand-impression of a 27 metres ship which is positioned around the 599 to 625AD and is believed to be the burial ship of an Anglo-Saxon King. In the middle of the ship a burial chamber was found with a deposit containing over 260 artefacts. The treasure includes weapons, symbolic objects, gold and garnet jewellery, Byzantine silver, personal items, and objects associated with music and feasting, a king's helmet. However, when the visitors arrive at the site they do not see a burial ship and any of the aforementioned artefacts. After the completion of the excavation the mounds were closed and only one has been reconstructed to its original 7th century size. Most of the artefacts found at the site are on display in the British Museum and only very limited objects and replicas are on display at an exhibition area at the site.

For the visitor to appreciate the importance of the site, information needs to be provided about various periods of times, such as the medieval period, as well as the early 20th century when the excavation took place. Three places need to be connected: the Tranmer House (Edith Pretty's house the land owner who initiated the excavation); the archaeological site; and the exhibition area that consists of limited original objects found at the site, series of photos that provide information about the excavation, replicas of objects and explanatory material and a reconstruction of the Anglo-Saxon King burial chamber. There are also certain characters that are important for the cultural heritage of the site such as: Mrs Edith Pretty, the owner of the Sutton Hoo Estate; Basil Brown, a local archaeologist who began the excavation of the largest mound on the site; Charles Phillips, the archaeologist that coordinated and completed the excavation. So there is a requirement for connecting the three points of interest and British Museum and augmenting information over the real environment in order to aid the visitors understanding about the site.

The application targets key stage 3 and 4 children (11 − 16 years old) visiting in groups, or with their parents. The application can be downloaded at visitors' iPhones and involves them in a scenario where they have to use the application to explore the site and discover objects that are offerings to the "Dead King". The application consists of two versions: a standalone that can be played by individual ad-hoc visitors and one which is multiplayer and is based on the fact that organised groups of visitors participate at the same time at Sutton Hoo and at British Museum.

In the standalone scenario the navigation starts at the reception area, the visitors take the role of Basil Brown who has been invited by Mrs Edith Pretty to start the excavation of the mounds. The application guides the visitors to the Tranmer House to meet Mrs Pretty. Then Mrs Pretty directs them to the dinning room where by pointing their iPhone on markers placed on the bay window the visitors see the mounds as they used to be before the excavation (see Figure 1). The visitors are then guided to the excavation area and are directed to start the excavation at mound 2. The users are provided with a basic archaeological toolset that contains: a hand shovel; a trowel; a hand brush; and a find bag that plays the role of a repository of objects that have been found. The visitors pick up a tool and start digging. Tapping on the screen indicates the duration of the particular action with the selected tool. After several taps an artefact is partially revealed and the application indicates the user to choose the appropriate tool to fully reveal the object of importance. Markers placed at wooden stitches on a fence that surrounds the archaeological site help superimposing multimedia content on top of a phone's camera feed of the real environment. This content is photographs that show how the site looked during the excavation and after continuing the tapping on the screen with a different tool selected, such as a brush, a $3D$ reconstruction of artefacts is being revealed. Then the application involves the visitors in series of quizzes and puzzles about the objects that have been found in order to help them decide if the objects found could be offerings to the Dead King. Once all the objects of a particular mound have been excavated, then the application guides

Fig. 1. A sample view of superimposed information with location and direction to the next mound. The inventory at the bottom of the screen displays the artefacts found in this mound. Location of next mound is shown on top corner.

the visitors to the next mound to be excavated. Once the visitors have finished the excavation and based on the information they have collected so far they have to decide which of the collected objects are offerings. Then the visitors are guided to the exhibition area with the reconstruction of the burial chamber to offer those to the Dead King. Once the visitors reach the exhibition area they can walk through the reconstruction of the burial chamber and then it is revealed to them if the objects that they found are offerings or not.

The networked version of the application connects with the British Museum and is based on the fact that at least two groups of visitors participate simultaneously at both sites. The visitors are involved in a treasure hunt scenario where the ones at British Museum are more knowledgeable and guide the ones at Sutton Hoo to find the required objects via a list of clues that they give them. The visitors at British Museum use a web based application that provides information about the visitors at Sutton Hoo location, the objects that they have found and feed from their phone's camera. The application allows the remotely located groups to communicate with each other by instant messaging. The visitors at Sutton Hoo use their phones to get instructions, directions and clues. The tools for the excavation and the augmented content are the same for the ones provided by the standalone application.

The winners of the game in both the standalone and the networked versions of the application are the ones that identify correctly the objects that are offerings to the Dead King in the shortest period of time. To increase competition the application provides some information about the stage of other groups that have started playing the game at the same time.

4   System Architecture

Tracking rectangular fiducial markers is one of the most widely used tracking solutions for mobile-AR applications. In recent years, many researchers have worked towards the development of different APIs for mobile devices with the most widely used the ARToolkit API [15]. Originally, the ARToolkit was designed to run only on standard PCs but AR researchers like Wagner [13] and Henrysson [14] extended the ARToolkit tracking library to different phone platforms.

For the Sutton Hoo mobile-AR project (SHMAR) the iPhone 4 is used, since its wide screen and OpenCL technology for high performance computing, makes it ideal for high resolution object visualisation and real-time game interaction, especially in an outdoor environment. The proposed system uses the ARToolkit for iOS development platform, and the location-based educational game is written in Objective-C. OpenGL ES, which is a subset of OpenGL made for mobile phones and other embedded devices, is used for the $3D$ rendering. For marker tracking and pose estimation, a software development kit called Studierstube Tracker (StbTracker) is used for the creation of multiple markers. Figure 2 presents an example of multiple markers on the left, with virtual objects projected on the markers on the right. The system incorporates a database server for the information space, providing the multimedia content on demand, making it scalable to a large number of visitors. The multimedia database is stored along with attributes that relate each artefact to the geographic position. GPS information extracted from the image tags, allow us to augment the images with navigational

Fig. 2. Virtual objects superimposed on different markers

arrows and direct the visitors to the different mounds. The communication is extended to include different place sharing of information, so that a number of new collaborative interactions are enabled, for example, guiding users to the different mounds and confirming object selection from the excavation site. A basic workflow of the SHMAR project at run-time is outlined in Figure 3.

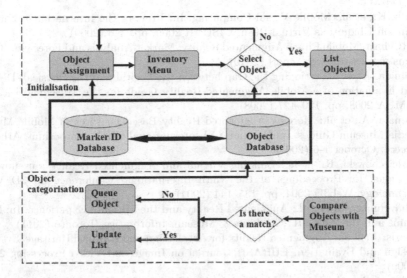

Fig. 3. Architecture of SHMAR visualisation system

5 Conclusions and Future Work

In this paper we present an approach for designing mobile-AR applications to enhance the visiting experience at cultural sites by providing information and interpretations about the sites objects of interest. We demonstrate this by presenting a mobile-AR educational game for iPhones that has been developed for aiding visitor's understanding about the archaeological site and the exhibition area at Sutton Hoo. The paper presents the combination of various technological advances, such as mobile wireless technologies, AR, multimedia and game technologies that have all been brought together in a cultural context to provide meaningful information in a playful and engaging way. The application demonstrates that mobile-AR technology offers great opportunities to cultural organisations for providing added value to their visitors experience by investing in developing applications for hardware owned by their visitors.

Currently the networked version of the project is developed. Once this part of the project is completed a study on site with real users will provide evidence about the effectiveness of the application in improving the visitors understanding about the site, enhancing the visiting experience and addressing the visitors' and the cultural organisations' requirements.

Acknowledgments. We would like to express our deepest gratitude to Sutton Hoo National Trust for the provision of archaeological data, content, and access to the site.

References

1. Pulli, K., et al.: Mobile Visual Computing. In: Proc. of the International Symposium on Ubiquitous Virtual Reality, ISUVR 2009, pp. 3–6 (2009)
2. ARCchart. Mobile Phone Augmented Reality: Market Analysis and Forecasts. Telecoms market research report (2010)
3. Damala, A., et al.: Bridging the Gap between the Digital and the Physical: Design and Evaluation of a Mobile Augmented Reality Guide for the Museum Visit. In: DIMEA 2008, pp. 120–127 (2008)
4. Damala, A., et al.: Merging Augmented Reality Based Features in Mobile Multimedia Museum Guides. In: Proc. of XXI International CIPA Symposium, Athens, Greece, October 1-6 (2007)
5. Wojciechowski, R., et al.: Building Virtual and Augmented Reality museum exhibitions. In: Proceedings of the Ninth International Conference on 3D Web Technology, Web3D 2004, pp. 135–144 (2004)
6. Schavemaker, M., et al.: Augmented Reality and the Museum Experience. In: Museums and the Web 2011. Archives & Museum Informatics, Toronto (2011)
7. Caarls, J., et al.: Augmented Reality for Art, Design and Cultural Heritage–System Design and Evaluation. EURASIP Journal on Image and Video Processing 2009 (2009)
8. Kolsouzoglou, A., Veneris, Y.: Studying Antikythera Mechanism in Mixed Reality. In: International Conference on Decoding the Antikythera Mechanism - Science and Technology in Ancient Greece (2006)
9. Schmalstieg, D., Wagner, D.: A handheld augmented reality museum guide. In: Proc. IADIS International Conference on Mobile Learning (2005)
10. Csikszentmihalyi, M.: Flow: The Psychology of Optimal Experience. Harper Perennial, London (1990)
11. Chen, J.: Flow in games. Communications of the ACM 50(4) (2007)
12. Astic, I., et al.: A Ubiquitous Mobile Edutainment Application for Learning Science through Play. In: Museums and the Web 2011, Philadelphia, PA, USA (2011)
13. Wagner, D., Schmalstieg, D.: ARToolKitPlus for Pose Tracking on Mobile Devices. In: Proc. of 12th Computer Vision Winter Workshop, CVWW 2007 (2007)
14. Henrysson, A., et al.: Face to Face Collaborative AR on Mobile Phones. In: Proceedings of the 4th IEEE/ACM International Symposium on Mixed and Augmented Realitym, ISMAR 2005, pp. 80–89 (2005)
15. Wagner, D., Schmalstieg, D.: First Steps Towards Handheld Augmented Reality. In: Proc. of the 7th International Conference on Wearable Computers, ISWC 2003 (2003)

WMIN-MOBILE: A Mobile Learning Platform for Information and Service Provision

Daphne Economou, Alex Keable-Crouch, Vassiliki Bouki,
Arti Basukoski, and Vladimir Getov

School of Electronics and Computer Science, University of Westminster,
115 New Cavendish St, London W1W 6UW, United Kingdom
{D.Economou@,a.keable-crouch@my,basukoa@,
boukiv@,V.S.Getov@}westminster.ac.uk

Abstract. Educational organisations hold lots of valuable information and material in different forms that needs to be communicated to people with different profiles anytime, anywhere. Mobile phones offer great opportunities of accessing such information and services by using hardware owned by Educational Organizations' members. This paper studies the requirements for such mobile learning (m-learning) tools for information and services provision to support learning and teaching and enhance student experience and satisfaction. To demonstrate this it uses the WMIN-MOBILE project as a case study. The WMIN-MOBILE is a prototype that provides general information about the School of Electronics and Computer Science (ECS) at the University of Westminster (UoW) and services like announcements, timetable and lab facilities and availability. The paper justifies the educational value of such m-learning tools and reports requirements for developing such tools. It further describes the WMIN-MOBILE system design and architecture and concludes with lessons learned and further work.

Keywords: m-learning, educational mobile, market analysis, web services, J2EE, JDBC, SOAP.

1 Introduction

Over the last decade information and communication technology have transformed the way in which we communicate, interact and learn as a community to our own sense of personal space, time and privacy. New forms of learning have emerged like e-learning which is the most recent development of computer-supported collaborative learning (CSCL) [1] – one of the most promising innovations to improve teaching and learning with the aid of modern information and communication technology. Networked communication systems serve as specific media to support e-learning processes [2]. E-learning applications and processes include Web-based learning, computer-based learning, virtual classroom opportunities and digital collaboration. The content which is disseminated to support e-learning has the form of text, images, animation, streaming video and audio.

N. Venkatasubramanian et al. (Eds.): Mobilware 2011, LNICST 93, pp. 23–33, 2012.
© Institute for Computer Sciences, Social Informatics and Telecommunications Engineering 2012

Mobile devices and wireless technologies nowadays offer a number of important characteristics including: increasing portability; functionality; multimedia convergence; ubiquity; personal ownership; social interactivity; context sensitivity; location awareness; connectivity and personalisation [9], that makes them attractive from an educational perspective and expand on e-learning. Those capabilities of mobile and wireless technologies support new models of learning, that are provided "just-in-time, just enough, and just-for-me" [3]. The use of mobile and handheld IT devices, such as personal digital assistants (PDAs), mobile phones, laptops and tablet PC technologies, in teaching and learning is known as mobile learning (m-learning). M-learning has always implicitly meant mobile e-learning and its history and development have to be understood as both a continuation of conventional e-learning and a reaction to this conventional e-learning and to its perceived inadequacies and limitations [3].

However, despite the almost ubiquitous ownership of mobile phones, the adoption of mobile technologies in higher education is still in its infancy. Given the current financial climate it is decisive for educational organizations to make use of hardware owned by students to deliver content and services, rather than investing in procuring equipment. What needs to be understood thought is how students want to use m-learning and deliver against their needs.

The remainder of this paper is organized as follows in order to investigate ways of providing mobile applications and services to enable communication and collaboration among university students, faculty and staff to support education, learning and teaching and enhance information provision, communication and improve student experience and satisfaction. In Section 2 the benefits of m-learning are discussed. In Section 3 a marketing analysis is provided that demonstrates that there is a substantial market that possesses the technology based on which m-learning services can be provided and to justify the directions towards which m-Learning applications and services should be developed in order to satisfy student needs. In Section 4 a review of current m-learning platforms is provided, while in Section 5 the WMIN-MOBILE prototype is described as a means of evaluating user and technical requirements. Finally, Section 6 presents the conclusion and proposed future work.

2   Market Analysis

2.1   Mobile Phones Marketing Analysis

Analysis of student IT services surveys conducted amongst various UK universities during the last 5 years shows that all students own increasingly sophisticated mobile phones [10]. In particular, approximately 80% of students have smart phones, 80% can access the Internet, 96% have a camera, 86% can record video and 80% can record audio. A US market survey showed that an average of 50% of students access email, Facebook and Twitter through their mobiles several times a day [12]. Research by Kaiser Family Foundation conducted within 2010 reported that children in the US spend approximately 8 hours a day using media, 20% of which is using cell phones. Those numbers are by much larger in Eastern countries. Those figures indicate that there is a valuable audience that processes the required technology, has the technical skills and would be willing to use mobile technology as a means of communication with the university environment to get information related to their study and work literally on-the-move, anytime, anywhere, without the need to carry special equipment or being fixed in an environment with particular settings and get the required information "just-in-time, just enough and just-for-me".

2.2   User Requirements for Effective M-Learning Tools

In March 2010 the Edinburgh University Information Services undertook a survey of approximately 2000 students to gather student requirements for developing a pilot "Mobile Campus" set of applications [1]. The survey asked the students what type of devices they owned, what they used them for and which University Information Services they would mostly prefer to see delivered on a mobile platform. The survey indicated that the top three University services which students would most like to see becoming available to their mobiles would be:

- course information , like deadline notices, messages about courses, etc.;
- exam and course timetables;
- PC availability in open access labs.

In November 2010 the Information Systems and Library Services (ISLS) of the UoW performed a similar online student survey that showed that 99% of the students would like to use dedicated applications and 96% of the students have or plan to get a smartphone whilst at the University. The survey also showed that the most desirable applications for students would be the following:

- Blackboard access   96%
- Library search   83%
- Timetable   80%
- Email/calendar   79%
- Notifications   62%
- Staff directory   61%
- Events   57%
- PC availability   51%
- News feeds   50%
- Student handbook   50%
- Course Directory   45%
- Maps   39%
- Find a friend   36%
- Social networking   28%
- Video   24%

Those results indicate that there is great demand for developing m-learning applications and services for information provision, dissemination of material and communication supporting different user profiles and mobile platforms and devises. This means that there are two important issues to be addressed:

a) developing student centric m-learning applications to aid higher education studies, improve retention, engagement and outcomes;
b) bring together existing information in various platforms and formats and presenting it in existing technology that students use for their own communication and entertainment.

An administrative statistics report for Blackboard usage created in March 2011 for modules registered for one of the four campuses of the UoW helped into understanding which are the most desirable services provided by this widely used amongst universities e-learning tool [13]. The report showed that 5420 modules have been set up for the New Cavendish campus only. From those:

- 4396 have at least 1 student registered meaning that 1024 modules have been set up but there are no students registered with 81.10% of the modules with at least one student;
- the course content area is populated in 2354 modules;
- announcements are used in 2005 modules;
- online tests are used in 108 modules;
- assignments area is used in 130 modules;
- wikis are used in 98 modules;
- external links are used in 501 modules;
- forum posts are used in 149 modules;
- forums are used 350 modules.

The difference between 'forums' and 'forum posts' seems to indicate that although a forum has been set up in a module, there are no posts on this. Actually there are forum posts in 149 modules out of the 350 modules where forums have been set up – this means that less than half of the forums are used as 42.57% of the forums have forum posts.

The following percentages saw the usage of different areas and facilities on Blackboard out of the 4396 modules that have at least one student. Apparently the other modules are not used:

- the course content area is populated in: 53.54%;
- announcements: 45.60%;
- online tests: 2.45%;
- assignments: 2.95%;
- wikis: 2.22%;
- external links: 11.39%;
- forum posts: 3.38%;
- forums: 7.96%.

From the above analysis, it becomes apparent that the 'course content area' is the most popular area of Blackboard and 'announcements' is the second most popular tool. Tools that facilitate interactivity and communication among students and among students and lecturers (such as forums, forum posts, wikis) are used in few modules. The most popular of these tools is 'forums', used by only 7.96% of all modules and the least popular of all tools is 'wikis' with only 2.22% of all modules to use it. This is quite remarkable. It seems that Blackboard is mainly used as a static tool where lecturers can upload information for students in the form of 'course content' or 'announcements' but it is not used for students to express their opinions or to interact with the rest of the class. The communication seems to be in one direction only: from lecturer to students.

3   The Benefits of M-Learning

Education is being constantly transformed with possibilities offered by technology. It is the new technology that allows educators to explore and improve new teaching and learning processes as well as different pedagogical methodologies. Several e-learning platforms (such as Blackboard and Moodle) and applications (such as test builders) have been developed and offered learners a different learning experience.

Research has provided clear evidences that e-learning applications have positive impact for learners. Learners become more engaged in the learning process and learning goals accomplished more successfully. Several studies have shown that the use of e-learning leads to better results for students: pass rates are increased and failure rates fell [5, [6].

The main advantage of these applications that makes this possible is that they allow students to personalise the learning process according to their needs and abilities. Learning process becomes really learner-centred. An e-learning application could serve this goal by allowing learners to personalise their learning experience while it offers them the chance to discover and build the knowledge by themselves.

Furthermore, knowledge is socially and individually constructed on the basis of experience. e-learning applications and especially m-learning applications facilitate students to networking and communicate.

In the last few years, it became more apparent the need of mobility: learners should have access to learning material regardless of time and place. The focus shifted to m-learning platforms. A large number of universities – initially in the US – provided their students with portable and mobile devices where they can download specially formatted versions of lectures [7]. The development of m-learning platforms was the next step. The first step in this direction was the transfer of original web pages to mobile screen and also the incorporations of new modules such as feedback and quiz for mobile devices [7]. M-learning has all the advantages of e-learning: personalisation of studies; better engagement of students; communication. In addition, m-learning provides mobility and the possibility of delivering applications and services on students mobiles that address the learners' needs. At the same time m-learning tackles the issue of financial tighter funding opportunities for higher education as it provides the opportunity of using existing hardware infrastructure.

4   Status and Trends

There are various products and platforms that offer the infrastructure of providing campus information and services on-demand. Research incorporating over 40 of the UK's leading e-learning companies and a number of other organizations and individuals across Europe and North America, reported recently that European e-learning market enjoys strong growth and that the UK remains the largest market within the continent [16]. The report estimates that, in 2010, the UK e-learning market will grow approximately 4.76% on the 2009 figure, which shows that there is a valid market to justify research and development towards this direction.

The current mobile learning market has been driven by consumers and healthcare buyers, who spent more on mobile learning technologies despite the recession. However, academic institutions still contributed to the growth. Campus technology noted that Blackboard's Mobile Learn [14] was cited as "the most significant product in terms of a market catalyst", something which indicates that Blackboard access is one of the most desirable services for students. Students and faculty require to be provided with opportunities to experiment with new forms of informational, social and media access to next-generation digital platforms including Android, BlackBerry, iPhone, iPad and other smart phones.

From another view point platforms like Blackboard Mobile Central [14] and CampusM [15], give students, faculty, and alumni information related to campus life and library access. There exists significant potential of further increasing this type of mobile services and support by engaging new forms of social and media communication paradigms. One such example is the Mobile Campus Assistant (MCA) software, which is a part of the MyMobileBristol project, that provided students with time and location sensitive data, like: where is there a PC available; when is the next bus to a certain destination; what events are happening today and so on. This in turn creates some questions and requires scalable solutions about the integration of these new services and infrastructures with the existing university systems in such a way so that the upgrade comes at the lowest cost and requires minimum disruption.

5   WMIN-MOBILE Case Study

5.1   WMIN-MOBILE Requirements and Specifications

Experience at the UoW showed that various centralized ISLS services are very difficult to be managed and updated and do not always deliver the required information. Thus various schools have adopted home solutions to serve their needs. For example the ECS is using their own timetable services, which is more reliable and customized to the schools needs. The WMIN-MOBILE prototype application is targeting in providing information and services initially to students and staff at ECS, at UoW in order to study the ways m-learning tools could deliver effectively and efficiently information and services that address directly user requirements, support education, learning and teaching, enhance communication and improve student experience and satisfaction. It is also an exercise that allows understanding the technical implications of adopting an off the self solution or developing an m-learning platform from scratch.

The WMIN-MOBILE application focuses in delivering initially the following information and services:

- information about the ECS, like location;
- information about courses offered by ECS targeting current students, like modules per course level, short description, semester of delivery, module leader;
- events at ECS;
- timetable;
- lab location, availability and facilities;
- social networking by participation in a blog.

The following section provides a technical description of the system architecture.

5.2   WMIN-MOBILE System Architecture

Faced with a fast changing mobile market (Android, Apple, Microsoft) and rapidly evolving technologies, the WMIN-MOBILE system strives to be as platform neutral as possible. To achieve such platform neutrality there must be a separation of concerns between the data model, data access, and user interface. Such an approach enables each domain to be developed independently, and assists in the adoption and evolution of the prototype to new technologies.

The WMIN-MOBILE system follows a typical service-oriented architecture (SOA) and is comprised of three distinct elements: an external database; a web-service; and a mobile web-service client (see Fig. 1).

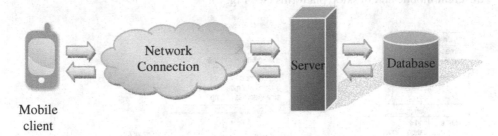

Mobile
client

Fig. 1. WMIN-MOBILE system architecture

A web service is essentially a standardised way of communicating with web-based applications that share data and/or application logic over a network. In order for a mobile application to access the network, a client-server relationship between the web service and application is required. As such it is typical for mobile applications to act as a consumer (client) and the web service act as a provider (server). The mobile Web-service client is the actual WMIN-MOBILE application that is being installed locally on a mobile device. This locally installed application functions as the web-service consumer, and requests and receives application data over a network connection such as WiFi or 3G. The web-service retrieves and serves data from the database, to the installed WMIN-MOBILE application as and when required.

The database contains the course data that is provided by the application. Other data is being accessed via the Google API and other web services as necessary. It can be located on the same or a separate server to the web-service. Web-services also allow the system to be scalable since the web-services are essentially standardised enterprise applications that are hosted on publicly accessible servers. This means that the web-services can theoretically be used by thousands of users at a time, on a wide range of mobile and desktop platforms (for example Windows, Mac OS, Linux, Unix, Android, BlackBerry and iPhone OS).

For the locally installed application Google's Android platform has been chosen mainly due to minimal development cost. The targeted android versions is 2.2 and above, however earlier versions can be supported if there is a demand for it. Because of the Google maps integration in the application, the Google API needs to be present in the android version in order to be able to run the application.

Android applications are essentially a mix of XML and Java which is converted into android bytecode that is eventually executed by the device. To port the application to iPhones the user interface can be implemented using Objective-C. The database and web services can then be accessed in a similar manner.

The enterprise server environment for the current application is hosted on the UoW glassfish server that is administered by the ECS School. The web-service is a J2EE application that receives a request from the locally installed application, and responds with the required data. Communication between the mobile application and the web service uses the Simple Object Access Protocol (SOAP). A SOAP message that is transmitted over a network connection is an standardised XML document. This standardised web-service protocol is what allows the web-services to be consumed by different mobile and desktop platforms (see Fig. 2).

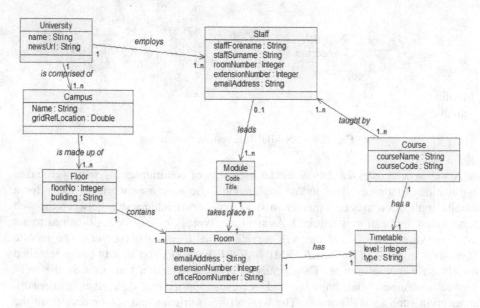

Fig. 2. WMIN-MOBILE system data flow diagram

Unfortunately all of the mainstream mobile programming languages (including Android) do not offer any libraries for making web-service calls using SOAP. This means that the programmer has to create this functionality or use a set of third party libraries. In the case of the prototype WMIN-MOBILE application the 'KSOAP2 for Android' libraries are being used in order to provide the programmer with a convenient and effective way of making web-service calls using SOAP.

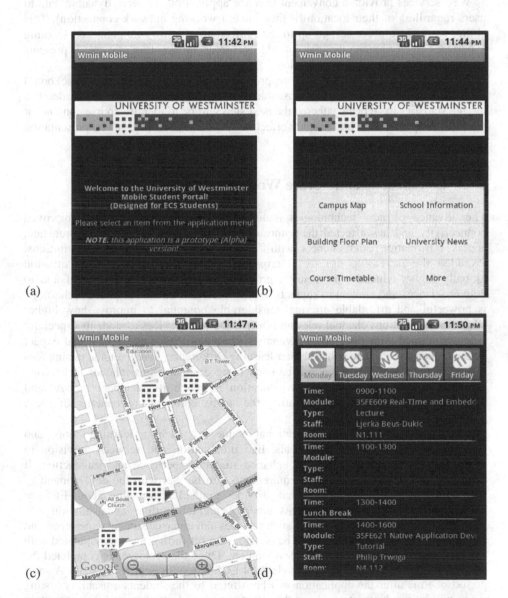

Fig. 3. Example screen shots of the WMIN-MOBILE application: (a) main screen; (b) main menu; (c) map Screen; (d) timetable screen

The web-service interacts with a MySQL database that resides on the UoW database server that is administered by the ECS school. The initial data model is designed to meet the main needs mentioned in Section 5.1. A secondary aim was to make it fully customisable so it can easily be adopted by other Universities. Any interaction between the web-service and database server is done using the appropriate Java Database Connector (JDBC) and using the structured query language (SQL).

Web-services provide a convenient way for applications to serve dynamic data to users regardless of their location (if they have a working network connection). This ability to retrieve accurate and up to date information allows an enhanced learning experience by reducing the risk of old incorrect information. Figure 3 presents example screen shots of the application.

The aims of the prototype were to provide for the most often used Blackboard functionality in order to deploy a useable system for further study. Once adequate useage statistics have been gathered the next step will be to identify course content for the most frequent users, and to study effective ways of dissemination and presentation of that content.

6   Conclusions and Future Work

The advance of new technologies including powerful, small devices, improved connectivity and has affected the nature of the way we as a society communicate, access information, and connect with friends, colleagues, staff and institutions. Provided the increasing use for smartphones and the critical financial situation globally higher education is facing a growing anticipation to make use of and to deliver services and content to students' own mobile devices. Smartphone technology is powerful and affordable offering considerable potential to improve how higher education institutions channel relevant information and services to students especially when combined with back-end University technology. Students demand and expect better m-learning tools to enhance their learning experience, and given the raising fees in UK in particular this issue will be even more eminent. Smartphones technology presents an opportunity for higher education to reach its members in new and compelling ways, in addition creating the anytime, anywhere benefits of these ubiquitous devices.

This paper justified the educational value of such m-learning tools and demonstrated such tools requirements, like information and services provision to support learning and teaching and enhance student experience and satisfaction. It demonstrated how partially those requirements can be met with the development of the WMIN-MOBILE application that provides general information about ECS, at UoW and services like announcements, timetable and lab facilities and availability.

In order to test if the provision of such services can enhance student experience and satisfaction the application needs to be developed a bit further and get populated with real data, which is currently under development. Once the prototype is completed the application will be offered to new students at ECS, UoW in September 2011. A short period of time after the application will be offered to the students a usability testing study will be conducted to evaluate the effectiveness and efficiency of the application and test if it aids the learning experience and increases satisfaction. It will also gather directions that the application should develop in terms of services and information to be provided via the application, technical aspects of the application, as well as platforms for which such applications should develop in order to be flexible and scalable.

Acknowledgement. The authors are grateful to John Cronin for providing the statistics results from the UoW included in Section 2 of this paper.

References

[1]   Stahl, G., Koschmann, T., Suthers, D.: Computer-supported collaborative learning: An historical perspective. In: Sawyer, R.K. (ed.) Cambridge Handbook of the Learning Sciences, pp. 409–426. Cambridge University Press (2006)

[2]   Tavangarian, D., Leypold, M., Nölting, K., Röser, M.: Is e-learning the Solution for Individual Learning? Journal of e-Learning (2004)

[3]   Traxler, J.: Current State of Mobile Learning. In: Ally, M. (ed.) Mobile Learning: Transforming the Delivery of Education and Training. Athabasca Press (2009).

[4]   INTEL – white paper, The Positive Impact of eLearning (2010),
      http://download.intel.com/pressroom/archive/
      reference/Positive_Benefits_of_eLearning_whitepaper.pdf

[5]   JISC. Exploring Tangible Benefits of e-Learning: Does investment Yield Interest? (2008), http://www.jiscinfonet.ac.uk

[6]   Cook, J.: Unlocking Potential: harnessing the pedagogical benefits of e-learning. Investigations in University Teaching and Learning 5(1), 57–61 (2008)

[7]   Basogain, X., Izkara, J.L., Borro, D.: Educational Mobile Environment with Augmented Reality Technology. In: Proc. International Technology, Education and Development Conference (INTED 2007), Valencia, Spain, March 7-9, p. 369 (2007)

[8]   IS Survey Results: Mobile Services 2010, University of Edinburgh (2010),
      http://www.projects.ed.ac.uk/areas/itservices/integrated/
      ITS045/Other_documents/MobileSurvey2010.shtml

[9]   Pachler, N., Bachmair, B., Cook, J.: Mobile Learning: Structures, Agency, Practices. Springer, New York (2010)

[10] Bradley, C., Holley, D.: An analysis of first-year business students' mobile phones and their use for learning. In: Creanor, L., Hawkridge, D., Ng, K., Rennie, F. (eds.) Proc. 17th Association for Learning Technology Conference (ALT-C 2010), Intosomething Rich and Strange – Making Sense of the Seachange, pp. 89–98 (2010),
      http://repository.alt.ac.uk/797

[11] Bradley, C., Weiss, M., Davies, C., Holley, D.: A little less conversation, a little more texting please - A blended learning model of using mobiles in the classroom. In: Proc. Fifth International Blended Learning Conference "Developing Blended Learning Communities", University of Hertfordshire, Hatfield, UK, June 16-17, pp. 1–11 (2010)

[12] Adkins, S.S.: Ambient Insight Comprehensive Report: The US Market for Mobile Learning Products and Services: 2009-2014 Forecast and Analysis (2010)

[13] http://www.blackboard.com/

[14] http://www.blackboard.com/Platforms/Mobile/Overview.aspx

[15] http://www.ombiel.com/campusm.html

[16] Patterson, D., Glynn, J., Broadhead, G., Renate, H.: The UK e-learning market 2010 (2010), http://www.e-learningcentre.co.uk

Extending the Power of Mobile Phone
Using Service Oriented Computing*

Muthoni Masinde[1], Nyikal Zeba[2], and Antoine Bagula[3]

[1] Hasso Plattner ICT4D Research School, University of Cape Town, South Africa
emasinde@cs.uct.ac.za, muthonimasinde@yahoo.com
[2] School of Computing and Informatics, University of Nairobi, Kenya
zanyikal@gmail.com
[3] Department of Computer Science, University of Cape Town, South Africa
bagula@cs.uct.ac.za

Abstract. In 2009, only 3.6% of Kenya's households owned at least one computer; conversely, 63.2% of households owned at least one mobile phone; this is true for many developing countries of Africa. This implies that computing solutions that target mobile phone environments are bound to have greater impact in these countries. However, the inherent constraints of mobile phones present a challenge in implementing viable applications. One solution to this would be to adopt Service Oriented and/or Grid Computing on mobile phones. In this paper, we present results that demonstrate how Service Oriented Computing can enable computation on mobile phones. A java-based questionnaire was implemented as a set of services aimed at overcoming phones' storage limitation. This was achieved via a middleware that was implemented to manage the services; communication among the services running on different phones was via Bluetooth.

Keywords: Service Oriented Computing, Mobile Phone Grid, middleware, Developing Countries of Africa.

1 Introduction

1.1 Background

The developing countries of Africa continue to experience various forms of 'digital divides' [1] one of them being the inability to offer information systems in basic sectors such as health and education. Although still experiencing a mobile phone penetration lag[1] of close to 10 years, Africa has achieved an average penetration level of 41% [2] which is much higher than that of computers. For instance, according to Kenya's 2009 population sensors [3], only 3.6% of households owned at least one computer in comparison with 63.2% of households that owned at least one mobile

---

* This project is partially supported by Hasso Plattner ICT4D Research School, UCT
[1] The time gap between mobile phone penetration level in Africa, and the year that same level of penetration was achieved globally.

N. Venkatasubramanian et al. (Eds.): Mobilware 2011, LNICST 93, pp. 34–44, 2012.

phone. With well-designed solutions, the use of these phones can be extended from the traditional use (as mare communication devices) to computing devices on which the much needed e-applications can be executed. However, most phones in use in Africa are low-end and hence presenting a further challenge of using them as computing devices. Due to their versatility, mobile phones offer a fast, cost-effective and accurate way of collecting data at the survey location; they can be used in place of paper questionnaires. Phones also support reliable ways and formats of transferring data for processing and may as well be used for automated pre-processing of the data. There are products and case studies utilizing this ability such the Nokia Data Gathering (NDG) initiative (https://projects.forum.nokia.com/ndg/).   NDG is gathering momentum with some success stories reported in projects in agriculture, health, census and child welfare. In Africa, mobile phones have been used to collect data in projects such as [8], [9], [10], and [11].

1.2   Related Work

Service Oriented Computing (SOC) may address many of the issues raised by the use of mobile phones in Africa. This can be achieved by allowing phone users to access certain functionalities that are absent in their phones, as services from other phones. For instance, a user of a *black-and-write* phone may therefore have neither the ability to access a General Packet Radio Service (GPRS) service from which a map can be obtained, nor display a map, but may be able to get that service as directions in text format from a more sophisticated phone. In this case, the latter device can first, get the map from an appropriate source, and then translate this to text directions, assuming the *black-and-white* phone sent it some known relative position(s).

Full and/or partial implementation of the elements of the SOA framework described above can be found in the following service discovery protocols: Universal Description, Discovery and Integration (UDDI) (http://www.uddi.org), Jini (http://www.jini.org/wiki), Service Location Protocol (SLP) (http://www.ietf.org/rfc/rfc2608.txt), Salutation by the Salutation Consortium (http://www.salutation.org), Microsoft's Universal Plug and Play (UPnP) by an industry consortium (http://www.upnp.org) and the Bluetooth Service Discovery Protocol (SDP) (http://www.bluetooth.com). Among these protocols, SLP and UDDI have promising results [6] and [7] for mobile computing environments similar to the one targeted in this paper.

1.3   Contribution and Outline

The Kenya Medical Research Institute (KEMRI) is an organization involved in disease-related research, focusing on malaria. For this, they require constant demographic data, which until recently was collected manually. Mobile phone based applications were developed for KEMRI (www.kemri.org), to address issues of recording clarity/accuracy and delays experienced in the manual data entry. Using mobile phones, data can now be collected faster, recorded more clearly and accurately. Loading of the data into their computer systems is automated and no longer requires data entry personnel. This system is ideal when all the data collected is textual – even the limited storage space of mobile devices will suffice. However, in cases where a researcher wishes to include photos in the collected data, storage space may become a concern.

Building upon a simulation of this scenario to solve the limited storage capacity problem, this paper demonstrates how the use of service-based software applications in mobile phones can be utilized to overcome some of the common problems in mobile devices.   The elements of SOC implemented are service description, advertisement, discovery and invocation; service composition is not included in the implementation. Our application converts, by way of example, a part of the Steadman Group's (*www.steadman-group.com*) quantitative survey process into an application that is based on SOC paradigm. The system attempts to replace the paper questionnaires with software forms to be run on mobile phones. The implementation concentrated on closed questionnaires, that is, questionnaires with questions for which there are predefined sets of possible answers. Data collected using the phone is saved locally, or for lack of sufficient storage, in a remote phone. This remote storage is presented and accessed as a service.

The rest of the paper is structured as follows; section 2 describes our SOC system; it describes relevant details on the methodology used for its design. A detailed discussion of its implementation is presented in section 3 while section 4 presents our discussion and further work. A list of references is presented in section 5.

2   The Service Oriented Computing System

The main strength of Service Oriented Computing (SOC) is the concept of 'services'; the design principles behind these services being autonomy, platform-independence, loose coupling, discoverability, reusability, and statelessness. SOC is built over Service Oriented Architecture (SOA), which is defined as *"A paradigm for organizing and utilizing distributed capabilities that may be under the control of different ownership domains. It provides a uniform means to offer, discover, interact with and use capabilities to produce desired effects consistent with measurable preconditions and expectations"*[4]. As such, SOA links Service Providers, Service Discovery Agency and Service Requester (Client) with each other through publish, find and bind operations[5].

2.1   Service Oriented Architecture (SOA)

From SOA's view, each of services is a complete piece of software (interface and the actual implementation) that implements meaningful business functionality. The key elements of the SOA Framework are:

(a) *Service Description* – description of the function(s) and capabilities of the services in unambiguous syntax and semantics
(b) *Service Advertisement* – 'announcement' of the presence of a given service description; this is usually done via the service registry or/and directly to service clients

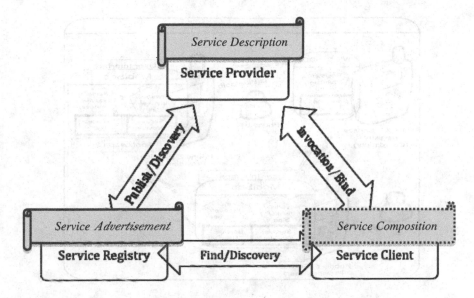

Fig. 1. Basic SOA (Adopted from [5])

(c) **Service Discovery** – Formulates the requests for service, matches these requests to specific service description(s) and then initiates communication with the service providers.

(d) **Service Invocation** – Transmits requests/results between the service provider and the service user.

(e) **Service Composition** – is an optional element responsible for formation of composite services by automatically merging the functionalities of more than one service.

2.2   System Development

2.2.1 System Analysis

This involved carrying out interviews with employees of Steadman Group, to find out the specifics of the organization's research process. The collected responses formed the basis of the case study of the organization. Steadman is a research company that carries out research in the in areas of Market Research, Social Research, Media Monitoring and Management Training. Among other things, Steadman is best known in Kenya for presidential candidate opinion polls. Their research process largely depends on the kind of research project in question, whether qualitative or quantitative. For all projects, the following steps are followed: Field Work → Coding → Scanning → Data Processing →Analysis and Reporting.

2.2.2 System Design

Using the analysis above a mobile phone application based on the Service Oriented Computing paradigm (as described in section 2.1) was proposed. The application was to be installed on all the phones that the researchers carried to the field and worked as per the architecture shown below:

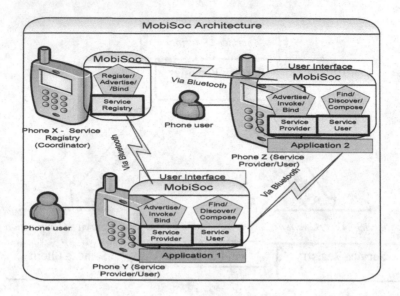

Fig. 2. System Architecture for implementing SOC on mobile phones

As shown in figure 2, main component of the system is MobiSoc; the middleware that handles the SOC functions. MobiSoc is made up of:

(a) ***Service Provider*** – for each installed application, the Service Provider advertises the application, e.g. application 1 (with the Service Registry) as a 'service' that can be invoked. Once a client requests to use the service, it is the work of the Service Provider to invoke and bind the request to the application.

(b) ***Service User*** – this is the interface between the client application (e.g. Application 2 running on Phone Z) and the service application (e.g. Application 1 running on Phone Y). It is responsible for looking up appropriate (through the help of the Service Registry) service(s) on behalf of the client application. In cases where a request for service is satisfied by more than one service, Service User handles 'service composition'.

3   System Implementation

3.1   Overview

Java2ME was used to implement the design described in section 3.4 as follows. A prototype consisting of only one application; a software questionnaire for data collection was implemented. This was implemented in form a java class; ***storageService.java***. In order to support the various SOC routines, three other classes (***sProvider.java***, ***sUser.java*** and ***qnMIDlet.java***) were also implemented. All phones were then treated as peers with each of them being installed with all the four classes.

Research assistants then took out the phones to the field to collect data. The hypothesis was that during the data collection process, some phones would run out of storage space; in this case, such phones would then transparently seek space advertised on other phones in their vicinity. Once all the required data was collected, the phones were then taken back to the office for data extraction and subsequent processing.

When a phone runs out storage, it seeks extra space as a service from a remote device. A layer of middleware (MobiSoc) that utilizes Bluetooth for communication abstracts the communication between the client and the service provider. The middleware comprised of: *Service_Provider*, which advertises and acts as a proxy for the service, and the *Service_ User*, which seeks advertisement for services required by a requesting application on the same phone, and also acts as a proxy for the requesting phone (client) in the communication.

Below is a description of each of the 4 classes

(a) *sProvider.java* - is responsible for service advertisement and revoking of adverts. It abstracts the underlying communication details, so that a service asking to be advertised need not know of the Bluetooth connection details facilitating this advertisement. A service will create an new instance of the class as follows, to advertise itself

```
sProvider myservice = new sProvider(String UniversallyUniqueID, String ServiceName);
To revoke an advert, the following method is invoked: myservice.sRemove();
```

(b) *sUser.java* - is responsible for service discovery and invocation, which it does on behalf of a client who wishes to find and use a given service. It hides the Bluetooth communication details from the client. The use of sUser for discovery and invocation is as follows:

```
sUser wantservice = new sUser(String data_to_be_stored, String UniversallyUniqueID);
```

(c) *storageService.java* - is the actual service. It advertises itself by creating a new sProvider(), and stores whatever string data is passed as an argument by a remote instance of sUser() to the new instance of sProvider(). It uses the Record Management System, a set of classes that facilitate usage of a simple database for persistent storage in mobile devices. storageService.java is the service used for demonstration 'services' concept of SOC. It is representative of any loosely coupled, remotely accessible service that might be run in a mobile device.

(d) *qnMIDlet.java* - is an application used for collecting field data. When it specifies that data should be saved, it may either be saved locally or remotely. When saves are remote, the application sending the record to be saved is a client to the server and it is facilitated by the SOC middleware. The application creates a new instance of sUser(), as described above, to access a service. This class is the application used for demonstration of the working of the SOC middleware. It is representative of any mobile device application that would access a remote service in a remote storage service; the communication between client and another mobile device.

The classes interact as shown in the following sequence diagram:

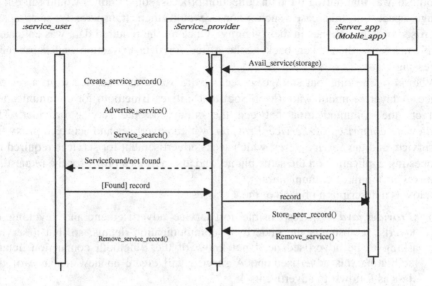

Fig. 3. Service Provider Advertising and Servicing Requests

3.2   Extent to Which SOC Imperatives Are Implemented

The four main aspects of SOA described in section 2.1 were implemented as follows:

(a) *Service Description*
    The storage service profile is comprised of the UUID and the service name. It
    has no details on host mobility. As for resource availability, as long as a host is
    advertising the storage service, it means there is at least one space available for
    remote storage No other details on resource availability are included in the
    service profile.

(b) *Advertisement*
    The advertisement consists of UUID, and a short service name. When a host
    device within Bluetooth range of a requesting client advertises storage
    availability, it is seen by a client no differently from an advert by another host in
    range, their differences in host address notwithstanding. This advert will also be
    seen by all requesting clients in range, as will all other advertised services. When
    a device is out of Bluetooth range, its advertisement will not be seen by clients,
    meaning a client cannot find an advert for a non-existent or unreachable service.

(c) *Discovery*
    A client discovers an advertised service by using the service's UUID. It need
    not know the address of the service host, or how the middleware finds the
    service – it simply makes a request and waits for a response.

(d) *Invocation*
    When a list of similar services is returned to the requesting client, it selects the
    first one only. The client does not know what the middleware does to avail this
    service for its use; neither does the service know the identity of the client

application. No motion profile was implemented to address the issue of unannounced disconnections, neither is there rebinding to a different service if unannounced disconnection occurs.

3.3   System Testing and Evaluation

3.3.1 System Start up

On start-up, the system displays the index screen, which contains two options: to *Run the Questionnaire* application, and *Display Saved Records*.

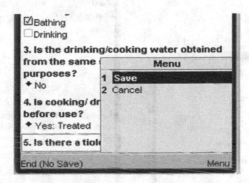

3.3.2 Run Questionnaire

On selection of the *Run Questionnaire* option, the questionnaire application opens. Navigation of this is done using the phone's *up* and *down* buttons. Selection is done using the phones *select* button. The only other commands possible are the ones on the soft-buttons at the bottom right and bottom left of the screen. The Menu has two options – *Save* or *Cancel* any entries made on this screen so far. The other alternative is to *End* the data-entry altogether without saving. The screen capture below show two screens of *Run Questionnaire* operation.

3.3.3 Alerts

Alerts are used to notify the user of *Local Save* (when the data is saved locally), *Remote Save* (when a device is running low on storage, and gets storage service from a peer device) and *Local-Save-and-Exit* (when no device offering service can be found). Alerts are used to notify the user of *Local Save* (when the data is saved locally), *Remote Save* (when a device is running low on storage, and gets storage service from a peer device) and *Local-Save-and-Exit* (when no device offering service can be found).

Below are three examples of alerts

4   Conclusion and Further Work

This paper is a demonstration of the application of service-oriented computing on mobile devices. It provides a roadmap towards realization of *software-for-all* developing countries of Africa. The latter has unique technological challenge/ opportunity where there are more phones than any other form of ICTs. It demonstrates how the concept of designing and implementing systems as a set of services can be used to aid in creating a platform for running applications on mobile phones, their low processing capability not withstanding. SOC was in this case used to help overcome storage limitation. Though storage in mobile phones has today become less of a problem (many phones now have expansion slots for additional memory), this work is aimed at demonstrating that SOC is an option for expanding the computing capability of a mobile phone. The concept of applications being a set of services can be used to provide phones that have low processing power, the capability to seamlessly gain access to computing facilities on another phone. Applications that offer this capability can then be accessible to the client device as services. This way, applications such as health information system and e-learning can be realized in the remotest villages of Africa.

This is an ongoing project and plans are underway to incorporate SOC within a mobile phone grid described in[12]. This will further extend the phone computation power to handle more complex scientific and business applications such as drought prediction. In its current form, the implementation did not take care of security issues and this need to be addressed before the system can be deployed in a real application. In the current application, there is no 'professional' way of select among similar services running different devices. To solve this, an algorithm for selecting the 'best' service provider is being implemented using the bully algorithm approach. Further research towards improving the system efficiency given the resource-constraint and mobility nature of mobile phones would provide an interesting extension to this work. Finally, Steadman, the organisation for which the application was developed, was acquired by another organisation (Synonvate) making system usage evaluation difficult.

References

[1] ICT4D Blog, 09/02/2011-last update, Global ICT Statistics on Internet Usage, Mobile, Broadband: 1998-2009 (2011),
http://ict4dblog.wordpress.com/2010/09/16/
global-ict-statistics-on-internet-usage-mobile-broadband-
1998-2009/ (February 10, 2010)

[2] ITU 2010. The World in 2010: ICT Facts and Figures (2010),
http://www.itu.int/ITU-D/ict/material/FactsFigures2010.pdf

[3] KNBS 2009. The Kenya Census 2009: Population and Housing Census Highlights (2009),
http://www.knbs.or.ke/Census%20Results/KNBS%20Brochure.pdf

[4] Wei, Y., Blake, M.B.: Service-Oriented Computing and Cloud Computing: Challenges and Opportunities. IEEE Internet Computing 1089(7801), 72–75 (2010)

[5] Pravin, P., van Aart, H., Kamran, S.: Enabling Context-Aware Computing for the Nomadic Mobile User: A Service Oriented and Quality Driven Approach. In: IEEE Communications Society Subject Matter Experts for Publication in the WCNC 2007 Proceedings, p. 2351. IEEE (2007)

[6] Hard, C., Michael, S.: File Location Management in Federated Computing Environments. International Journal of Recent Trends in Engineering 1(1), 512–517 (2009)

[7] Geihs, K., et al.: Service-Oriented Adaptation in Ubiquitous Computing Environments. In: International Conference on Computational Science and Engineering, p. 458. IEEE, IEEE/Computer Society (2009)

[8] Diero, L., Rotich, J., Bii, J., Mamlin, B., Einterz, R., Kalamai, I., Tierney, W.: A computer-based medical record system and personal digital assistants to assess and follow patients with respiratory tract infections visiting a rural Kenyan health centre. BMC Medical Informatics and Decision Making 6(1), 21 (2006)

[9] Shirima, K., Mukasa, O., Schellenberg, J., Manzi, F., John, D., Mushi, A., Mrisho, M., Tanner, M., Mshinda, H., Schellenberg, D.: The use of personal digital assistants for data entry at the point of collection in a large household survey in southern Tanzania. Emerging Themes in Epidemiology 4(1), 5 (2007)

[10] Fynn, R.: Remote HIV/AIDS patient monitoring tool using 3G/GPRS packet-switched mobile technology. In: Appropriate Healthcare Technologies for Developing Countries, pp. 129–138 (2006)

[11] Missinou, M.A., Olola, C.H.O., Issifou, S., Matsiegui, P.-B., Adegnika, A.A., Borrmann, S., Wypij, D., Taylor, T.E., Kremsner, P.G.: Short report: Piloting paperless data entry for clinical research in Africa. Amer. Journ. of Trop. Medicine and Hygiene 72(3), 301–303 (2005)

[12] Masinde, M., Bagula, A., Murage, V.: Middleware for Distributed Computing on Mobile Phones. In: Canessa, E., Zennaro, M. (eds.) m-Science: Sensing, Computing and Dissemination, 1st edn. ICTP - The Abdus Salam International Centre for Theoretical Physics, Trieste (2010)

Web of X Service Environment
for Ubiquitous Computing

Zhenyu Wu, Chunhong Zhang, and Yang Ji

Mobile Life and New Media Lab,
Key Lab of Universal Wireless Communications, Ministry of Education,
Beijing University of Posts and Telecommunications,
Xitucheng Road 10, 100876 Beijing, China
{shower0512,zhangch,jiyang}@bupt.edu.cn

Abstract. A central concern in the area of ubiquitous computing has been the integration of digital resources including devices and heterogeneous networks with the physical world and people. However, current systems are independent to each other, which means that resources for ubiquitous computing are separated and applications could not be created on cross-platform. The openness, simplicity, flexible and standardization of Web have given insights of building up a more uniform, open and scalable service environment for ubiquitous computing. Therefore, we propose the concept of Web of X (WoX) Service Environment for ubiquitous computing in this paper. In this article, we analyze the requirements of building a service environment for ubiquitous computing, and then the conceptual architecture of WoX Service Environment and some key technical solutions are proposed as well.

Keywords: Ubiquitous Computing, Web, REST, API, Mashup.

1   Introduction

A central concern in the area of ubiquitous computing has been the integration of digital resources including devices and heterogeneous networks with the physical world and people. In particular, the "Internet of Things (IoT)" has essentially explored the development of applications built upon various networked physical objects [1]. However, current related researches mainly focus on building applications and vertical systems based on specific scenarios and industries, or considering how to leverage current broadband wired or wireless access technologies to interconnect everyday object, which means that the applications are usually built upon independent systems, resources could not be shared and efficiently utilized among different infrastructures and even the development of pervasive applications becomes tedious for common users for the reason that most of interfaces in a system are defined proprietarily and there is a lack of clear, standardized, and interoperable communication protocols that can be understood by fridge, TV set, sensors and networks, so a uniform service environment which is cross-industry, cross-network, cross-terminal and opened to users to create personalized applications is necessary.

N. Venkatasubramanian et al. (Eds.): Mobilware 2011, LNICST 93, pp. 45–56, 2012.

With Web 2.0 applications the focus is on the user and user-generated content on the one hand, and on the other hand on a set of technologies (e.g., AJAX, RSS) that support the development of highly interactive interfaces that offer a rich user experience, similar to common desktop applications. As shown by the unparalleled scalability of the Internet, simple technologies (e.g. HTTP) can give birth to very efficient and flexible systems, where a large variety of hardware and software platforms coexist and interact smoothly. Open access to data through services on the Web has enabled information to be reused across independent system, therefore has lowered the access barrier that allows people to develop their own applications. Furthermore, the development of composite applications on top of the open and simple standards that made the Web so successful (REST, XML, HTTP, or Atom) to interconnect physical devices which called "Web of Things (WoT)" has now become another trend in the era of IoT and ubiquitous computing, which has given a vision for building a more uniform, open and scalable service environment for ubiquitous computing.

Based on these observations, we propose to leverage the existing and ubiquitous World Wide Web (WWW) as common ground where everyday devices and networks could interact with each other, and a user-centric Web of X (WoX) Service Environment for ubiquitous computing is also proposed in this paper. The X in WoX means heterogeneous resources surrounding persons for ubiquitous computing, such as devices, network resources, as well as current Web resources in Internet, and WoX Service Environment aims to facilitate efficient prototyping ubiquitous computing application and enable users to generate service by themselves according to their requirements and preferences by integrating the capabilities of heterogeneous network and distributed devices (mobile phone, sensors, appliances and etc.) via Web technologies.

The remainder of this paper is organized as follows: Section 2 summarizes related work. Section 3 describes the paradigms and requirements of designing a uniform service environment for ubiquitous computing. Section 4 proposes the conceptual architecture of the WoX Service Environment. Section 5 discusses the key technical issues related to constructing the service environment. Finally some challenges for future study are presented in the last section.

2   Related Work

A lot of work has proposed ideas to construct a cross-platform environment to eliminate the barriers between heterogeneous network infrastructures and different terminal platforms.

MUSE is proposed by Ji Yang et.al in [2] as a vision for future service and architecture for ubiquitous networking and computing. MUSE brings in the concept that enabling Always Best Experience (ABE) to users in terms of context awareness, flexibility and ubiquitous intelligence, through cooperation among various heterogeneous wire or wireless networks and devices. The essence of MUSE is to abstract the capabilities of both networks and terminal devices and specific services could seamlessly compose suitable capabilities to deliver to end users according to the requirements. Though the concept of MUSE brings in a vision of the trend of future ubiquitous computing, however, what exact technologies could be utilized in this concept is not discussed yet.

With the development of Web technology, accessing non-web-enabled to the WWW is not a new idea yet, while more and more researches have focus on aggregating heterogeneous resources into the Web and letting Web act as a ubiquitous hub to interconnect devices, network infrastructures and applications, which gives a technical option for MUSE. For example, webinos [3] project defines and delivers an Open Source Platform and software components for the Future Internet in the form of web runtime extensions, to enable Web applications and services to be used and shared consistently and securely over a broad spectrum of converged and connected devices, including not only mobile phones, but also PC, home media (TV) and in-car units, as well as to offer a common set of APIs to allow applications easy access to cross-device functionality. Nevertheless, the motivation of webinos is to enable web application to run on different kinds of devices and access the underlying resources in uniform standardized interfaces, however, the resources of devices could still not be linked, shared and reused through Web into Internet.

Thus, some researches are considering linking the Web and physical objects. For example, [4] put forward the concept of "Web of Things": propose to reuse and adapt patterns commonly used for the Web, and introduce architecture for the Web of Things [5]. Their research is focused on the development of composite applications on top of the open and simple standards that made the Web so successful (REST, XML, HTTP, or Atom) to interconnect physical devices. They embed Web servers [6], [7], [8] on smart things and apply the REST architectural style [9], [10] to the physical world, so the resource on the smart things could be opened and shared into Internet.

Furthermore, a number of implemented systems have already shown some features that integrating diversities of resources and being opened to the public as open APIs via web standard. For example, Pachube [11] is a global centralized website which could store, share/discover real-time sensor, energy and environment data from objects, devices & buildings around the world. It defines a uniform REST web API to gather third party resources and open to the public to implement applications, and also it defines an open data exchange format protocol which is called EEML[12] to guarantee that heterogeneous datum are packaged and exchanged in a uniform pattern. SenseWeb [13] is another unified system developed by Microsoft which could collect, share, process, and query sensory data from the globally shared sensor network. It aims to provide an open architecture such that third parties can easily register sensors or repositories of sensory data to contribute as part of SenseWeb by providing Sensor Gateways that provide a uniform interface to all components above it to get all sensors connected, and other components of SenseWeb access the gateway to obtain sensor data streams, to submit data collection demands, or access sensor characteristics through a standardized web service API. The gateway implements sensor specific methods to communicate with the sensor. Meanwhile, SenseWeb also enables third parties to easily develop sensing applications that use the shared sensing resources provided by SenseWeb. These approaches are based on a centralized repository and devices need to be registered before they can publish data, thus are not sufficiently scalable and are more concerned with data storage and retrieval.

3   Paradigms Required and Requirements Analysis

To design a user-centric uniform service environment for ubiquitous computing, it is necessary to analyze the requirements from both the user's and service's points of view.

What users concern about is how to access to a target service with the best user experience which could meet their requirements with the dynamic variance of the context and scenario. In a further stage, users are even not only the consumer of the service, but they could also act as a creator and manager of the service, which means that users could efficiently prototype new services within their preferences in different scenarios, and conveniently deploy them with as few configurations as possible.

While from the perspective of service, with the evolution of network technologies, such as 3G/4G and the increase of diversities of terminal platforms, all services are required to be delivered via a uniform platform which need not care about the details of heterogeneous terminals and networks and services could acquire the terminal capabilities and network capabilities through standardized open interfaces provided by the platform, so services provider or end users can develop and deploy more high quality services more flexibly, and service could be customized more dynamically.

Therefore, to feed the requirements above, several paradigms are required:

Paradigm 1: (the most important) the user-centric service environment for ubiquitous computing should be based on Web. The development of Web has shown the success of it, and previous researches have proven that Web is simple, open, standardized and flexible. Moreover, the interaction style of Web is accepted by more and more common users, and the development of web application becomes more and more convenient for developers than other desktop and mobile platforms, which means users could rapidly prototype personalized applications and build up a healthy ecosystem. So Web should be a first option to integrate heterogeneous platforms and different current technologies, and all the terminal, network and other computing resources should be abstracted as web resources.

Paradigm 2: User could share, manage and even deploy resources/services in the service environment. Web 2.0 and social network service has reveals the power of the involvement of end users into the sharing and innovating activities. More high-quality data and fascinating application appears. In pervasive computing, the more context data about specific user could share with others and the fewer configurations for users, the more customized applications could be created and the more possible the user's requirements could be met.

Paradigm 3: The architecture should be as flexible and scalable as possible. It is not only serving local area or specific scenario but also should support wide-area services and scenarios.

Paradigm 4: Security and privacy must be guaranteed. In ubiquitous computing, there must some personal and private information, so to prevent this information being stolen and opened to public must be guaranteed.

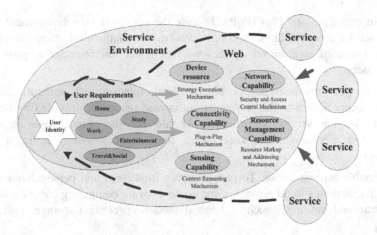

Fig. 1. Requirements analysis of user-centric uniform service environment for ubiquitous computing from both user's and service's points of view

According to the design paradigms, several specific technical requirements should also be met:

Req 1: Follow RESTful-stlye architecture design principle. The essence of REST is to focus on creating loosely coupled services on the Web so that they can be easily reused [14]. REST is actually core to the Web and uses URIs for encapsulating and identifying services on the Web. Resources should be available through a uniform interface with well-defined interaction semantics, as is *Hypertext Transfer Protocol (HTTP)*. For data exchange and resource description, On the Web, media type support in HTTP and the *Hypertext Markup Language (HTML)* allow peers to cooperate without individual agreements. For machine-oriented services, media types such as the *Extensible Markup* Language *(XML)* and *JavaScript Object Notation (JSON)* have gained widespread support across services and client platforms. Moreover, the interaction should be kept stateless which requires requests from clients to be self-contained, in the sense that all information to serve the request must be part of the request. HTTP implements this constraint because it has no concept beyond the request/response interaction pattern; there is no concept of HTTP sessions or transactions.

Req 2: Device and networks should access to Web. To make sure that the service environment is based on the Web and the capabilities provided by the service environment could be invoked in Web protocols, the devices and networks which are not support Web must be extended to support accessing to Web.

Req 3: The resource of every object could be identified, named and addressed in a standard way. All the capabilities of objects such as terminal and network components are abstracted as web resources, so the service environment should name all the resources with unique URI and provide a mechanism to address them.

Req 4: There should be a uniform resource or service model. A model/framework to describe resources and their relationships between them is necessary.

Req 5: Support Plug-and-Play (PnP). To ease the cost of device deployment for end user, the service environment should provide some mechanism for automatic resource discovery and configuration on devices with as fewer interferences as possible for common users.

Req 6: Support resource access control, authorization and authentication. To guarantee secure access to the private or authorized resources provided by terminals and networks, the service environment should provide some authorization and authentication mechanisms to make sure that every resource is in a secure environment.

Req 7: Enable context-aware. To provide more intelligent and personalized service, service environment should provide some context-aware computing capabilities based on semantic and ontology, such as context modeling, context storage, lookup and reasoning.

Req 8: Provide a uniform user interface and engine for service mashup. To facilitate the quick prototype of customized application for non-tech users, service environment should provide an intuitive interface for user to create their own composite service in a drag-and-pull way, and a mashup engine is also necessary to support service orchestration based on the Web Service capabilities provided by terminals and networks.

4   Web of X Service Environment Architecture

In this section, we have proposed a conceptual architecture for Web of X Service Environment for ubiquitous computing according to the requirements analyzed in the previous section.

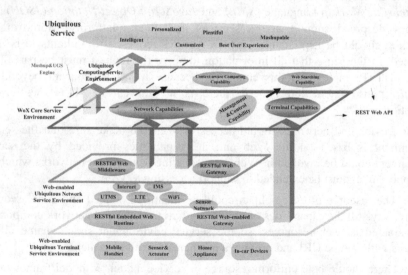

Fig. 2. Web of X Service Environment Architecture

The **WoX Service Environment** consists of four main components as Figure 2 shows: web-enabled Ubiquitous Terminal Service Environment (wUTSE), web-enabled Ubiquitous Network Service Environment (wUNSE), Web of X Core Service Environment (WoXSE) and Ubiquitous Computing Service Environment (UCSE).

wUTSE is a service environment surrounding terminals with web access which may include web-enabled devices (mobile handsets) with an embedded web runtime and non-IP devices (sensors, home appliance or in-car devices) brokered by web-enabled gateways. It may be offered by single terminal equipment or a set of networking distributed components.

wUNSE is a service environment based on heterogeneous networks which cover from wired network to wireless network, from IP network to non-IP network, from access network to core network, from telecom domain to Internet domain such as Internet, IMS, UMTS, LTE, WiFi and even sensor network. wUNSE bridges the components of networks into the WWW by web middleware or web proxy, so the capabilities of different networks could be exposed as Web Service in uniform Web standard.

The wUTSE and wUNSE shield the details of internal architecture of terminals and networks, and the connectivity between them. Moreover, the wUTSE and wUNSE also both offer services the information about terminal and network capabilities in a REST way, which means that the capabilities of terminals and network will uniformly be abstracted as Web resources with unique identities (URI) and could be accessed via HTTP in a stateless client-server way with uniform method (GET, PUT, POST and DELETE).

WoCSE is a service environment which acts as a control components for all the exposed REST web service resources. The capabilities of networks and terminals are all opened as a REST web API and abstracted as web resources, so WoCSE should be responsible for managing these web resources, such as web service resource registration, update and discovery within global area, and data storage and management, as well as scheduling of service and authorization/authentication. The same as wUTSE and wUNSE, the capabilities of WoCSE are opened a REST Web APIs and could be invoked by applications as well.

UCSE is a service environment for context-aware computing and Web searching to support intelligent and personalized services. Resources exposed from wUTSE and wUNSE are all service context information surrounding end users, so UCSE is responsible for context data modeling, storage and reasoning by invoking web services provided by wUTSE and wUNSE to retrieve raw date of context information from devices and networks. There may exist diversities of context-aware computing engines and semantic web searching engines which are built upon cloud computing infrastructures according to different scenarios. Also these computing capabilities are opened as REST Web APIs and could be invoked by services.

Furthermore, as a user centric service environment, WoX Service Environment also provides some kind of User Generated Service (UGS)/Mashup engine for both tech-savvy users and non-tech users to create composite services by their own need and preference based on the Web API provide by the devices and networks. The UGS/Mashup engine could provide an intuitive interface for user to drag-and-pull components to generate target services at front end and process dynamic service orchestration at back end, so that users only need only concern about the logic of the service.

5   Key Technical Issues Discussion

For WoX Service Environment, there remain some key technical issues that should be discussed, such as how to access resources on non-web devices into Web and how to discovery resources based on WoX Service Environment, and some solutions should be proposed as a reference to implement and deploy the WoX Service Environment.

5.1   Resource Access

To build up a Web-oriented service environment, it is necessary that the non-web resources, especially the resources on the non-web devices, such as mobile phones, sensors, actuators, and home appliance could be accessed via Web interface. In Fig 3, two ways to get non-web devices' resources accessed via RESTful Web interface are proposed as follows:

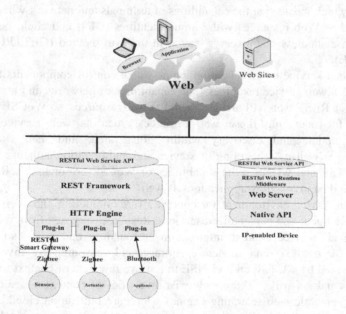

Fig. 3. Two ways to get heterogeneous resource accessed via Web

Most embedded devices do not always have an IP (Internet Protocol) address and are thus not directly addressable on the Internet. However, it is very likely that more and more real-world devices will become IP-enabled and have embedded HTTP servers (in particular with 6LowPAN), making them able to understand the Web languages and protocols [15] [16]. Such Web-enabled devices can be directly integrated and make their RESTful APIs directly accessible on the Web. This integration process is shown on Fig 3: each device has an IP address and runs a Web Server on top of which it offers a RESTful API to the mashup developer, and we call it **RESTful Web Runtime Middleware**.

While such Web-enabled devices are likely to be widely spread in the near future, direct integration of real-world devices into the Web is still a rather cumbersome task. In particular, when devices do not support IP or HTTP as is usually the case with wireless sensor networks (WSN), a different integration pattern is needed. So we propose to use the concept of **RESTful Smart Gateways** as intermediate element that bridges the Web with devices that do not talk IP. The RESTful Smart Gateway is composed of three main components. The Plug-ins acts as drivers to discover the devices on a regular basis by scanning the environment in other communication protocols, and for each kind of communication there is a plug-in, such as plug-in for Bluetooth API and plug-in for Zigbee APIs, so the Smart Gateway could directly access data via native requests of different proprietary communication protocols. The HTTP engine acts as an embedded web server which handles HTTP requests and responses. The RESTful Environment acts as a REST framework to support REST operations, and it could map the URLs to the resources the devices possess and provide uniform interfaces (HTTP Method: GET, PUT, DELETE, POST) to interact with the resources.

5.2   Resource Discovery

To lower the cost of deployment and management for end user, the WoX Service Environment should be as free as possible from explicit human administration. This is especially challenging in ubiquitous computing, where devices can dynamically enter and leave the network. If all the devices require explicit configuration to work together, the burden of administration quickly overwhelms any potential benefit, so some kind of PnP mechanism is required to eliminate the burden of administration.

In the vision of WoX Service Environment, the capabilities of global networks and devices are abstracted as RESTful web resources which are identified by HTTP URI, so a large-scale, multi-domain service infrastructure requires a resource discovery system that is open, scalable, robust and efficient to a greater extent than a single-domain system. For existing discovery system, two common models are usually adopted. One is non-directory based way; the other is directory-based way. For globally resource discovery, the directory-based way is the most suitable model [17].

Therefore, in the WoX Service Environment, a directory-based resource discovery model is proposed. It is assumed that the resources are distributed into different domains according to specific features, such as location, type of device, etc. and there is unique directory in each domain which is responsible for registration, update and discovery of resource in the domain. Furthermore, every identified resource should be described in a uniform *descriptive record* to describe its address (URL) and its attributes, such as its location, type, owner and the method to invoke it. In the proposed model, the whole framework is divided into three logic entities:

Resource Agent (RA) is a logical entity that possesses web resources on smart objects, such as web-enabled devices and smart gateway. In each RA, its resources will be identified with URLs as a RESTful web service interface.

WoX Proxy/Directory Agent (WP/DA) is a logical entity that maintains resource descriptive information and processes queries and announcements from RAs and clients, and each WP/DA will be responsible for managing all the RAs in its local domain. The topology of the WP/DA could be hierarchical or Peer-to-Peer structure, and the descriptive information of registered resources will be maintained and synchronized among these WP/DAs in certain mechanism.

Bootstrap Agent (BA) is a logical entity where clients and services attempt to initiate the discovery process via establishing the first point of contact within the system. With initial configuration, the BA will manage lists of all WP/DAs' information including the address and the domain information in its charge.

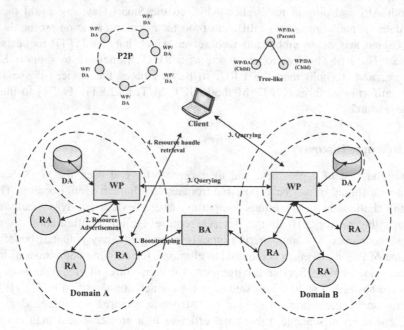

Fig. 4. Directory-based resource discovery model in WoX Service Environment

Specifically, the process of the resource discovery could be viewed in four steps as Figure 4 shows:

•**Bootstrapping:** the RA will query BA to find the local or the nearest WP/DA and BA will return the address of target WP/DA that is responsible for its registration.

•**Resource Advertisement:** the RA advertises itself by registering with the target WP/DA a *description file*. This record follows the XML schema and represents a description of the attributes of the resource and contains series of operations to that resources as well as the URL of the resource.

•**Querying:** the client will look for a desired resources. The querying process is handled by the WP/DA with which a RA is associated; the client may first ask any

WP/DA to find out which WP/DAs provide a desired resource, i.e. the resource that matches the *description file* provided by the client, and finally select one and ask its related WP/DA to retrieve the *description file* from it. The lookup process among WP/DAs could be based on a tree-like hierarchical structure or P2P structure [18]. If the attributes of the resource is refreshed, the WP/DA can periodically check the availability of the resource and update its *description file*.

•**Resource Handle Retrieval:** the client receives the *description record* of desired resource and access to the target URL via RESTful web service API provided by the RA.

6   Challenges for Future Study

As a design for future service and architecture, there are still lots of open issues in the WoX Service Environment design for further investigations.

In WoX Service Environment, the capabilities of devices and networks are abstracted as Web resources in REST way; however, a uniform resource representation framework is still needed to describe heterogeneous resources. A semantic-based or ontology-based method might be adopted that not only human could understand the language but also could machine understand to support automatic and intelligent resource discovery and configuration.

Security is always a critical factor in system design. Without the guarantee by an all around and powerful security mechanism, any system will become far from practical services and applications. Since existing security mechanisms are designed for certain kinds of applications, networks and terminals, although fulfilling the tasks well in their fields, they are definitely insufficient when dealing with the complicated heterogeneous network environments, varied services and terminal environment in the future, where the access control of resources on different devices and networks, delegated authentication mechanism for third party mashup should be considered much. Therefore, a customized, complete and effective security architecture is very important and absolutely necessary for this open, cross-platform, heterogeneous and multi-serviced environment of WoX.

Moreover, since WoX Service Environment introduces more decentralized and self-organized paradigms in resource discovery, allocation and management, the peer-to-peer mode service provisioning should be supported in the whole architecture, not only in connectivity aspects, but also in operational and business aspects. There is some peer-to-peer solution available already. Therefore, how to utilize these peer-to-peer solutions into the WoX Service Environment needs to be well studied in the future.

7   Conclusion

In this paper, we propose that Web technologies are — contrary to popular belief — a suitable protocol for constructing a uniform service environment for ubiquitous computing and building applications on top of services offered by different devices and heterogeneous networks. After summarizing the core design paradigms and requirements of the future ubiquitous computing service environment, we have proposed a conceptual architecture for the WoX Service Environment based on RESTful architectural principles. Then several key technical issues in constructing the WoX Service Environment, such as resource access framework and resource discovery mechanism, are discussed and relative solutions are also proposed. Finally, some challenges, such as the resource representation model, security mechanism, as well as peer-to-peer solution are also discussed for future study.

Acknowledgments. The work is supported by the International Science and Technology Cooperation Plan Project (No. 2010GR0002) and National Science and Technology Major Project (No. 2011ZX03005-004-04) and Fundamental Research Funds for the Central Universities (No. 2010PT17).

References

1. Fleisch, E., Mattern, F.: Das Internet der Dinge, 1st edn. Springer (July 2005)
2. Yang, J.I., Ping, Z., Zheng, H., Xu, W., Yinong, L., Xiaosheng, T.: Towards mobile ubiquitous service environment. Wireless Personal Communications 38(1), 67–78 (2006)
3. webinos, http://webinos.org
4. Guinard, D., Trifa, V.: Towards the Web of Things: Web Mashups for Embedded Devices. In: 2nd Workshop on Mashups, Enterprise Mashups and Lightweight Composition on the Web (MEM 2009), Madrid, Spain (April 2009)
5. Guinard, D., Trifa, V., Wilde, E.: A resource oriented architecture for the web of things. In: Proc. of IoT 2010 (IEEE International Conference on the Internet of Things) (November 2010)
6. Hui, J.W., Culler, D.E.: IP is dead, long live IP for wireless sensor networks. In: SenSys 2008: Proceedings of the 6th ACM Conference on Embedded Network Sensor Systems, pp. 15–28. ACM, New York (2008)
7. Duquennoy, S., Grimaud, G., Vandewalle, J.-J.: The Web of Things: interconnecting devices with high usability and performance. In: 6th International Conference on Embedded Software and Systems (ICESS 2009), Hangzhou, Zhejiang, China (May 2009)
8. Guinard, D., Trifa, V., Pham, T., Liechti, O.: Towards Physical Mashups in the Web of Things. In: Proceedings of the 6th International Conference on Networked Sensing Systems, INSS 2009 (2009)
9. Fielding, R.T., Taylor, R.N.: Principled design of the modern web architecture. ACM Transactions on Internet Technology 2(2), 115–150 (2002)
10. Richardson, L., Ruby, S.: RESTful Web Services. O'Reilly (2007)
11. Pachube, http://www.pachube.com
12. Extended Environments Markup Language (EEML), http://www.eeml.org
13. Kansal, A., Nath, S., Liu, J., Zhao, F.: SenseWeb: an infrastructure for shared sensing. IEEE Multimedia 14(4), 8–13 (2007)
14. Pautasso, C., Wilde, E.: Why is the Web Loosely Coupled? A Multi-Faceted Metric for Service Design. In: Proc. of the 18th International World Wide Web Conference (WWW 2009), Madrid, Spain, pp. 911–920 (2009)
15. Dunkels, A., Vasseur, J.: Ip for smart objects alliance. Internet Protocol for Smart Objects (IPSO) Alliance White paper No.2 (September 2008)
16. Hui, J., Culler, D.: Extending IP to Low-Power, wireless personal area networks. IEEE Internet Computing 12(4), 37–45 (2008)
17. Zhu, F., Mutka, M., Ni, L.: Service Discovery in Pervasive Computing Environments. IEEE Pervasive Computing 4, 81–90 (2005)
18. Stoica, I., et al.: Chord: A Scalable Peer-to-Peer Lookup Protocol for Internet Applications. IEEE/ACM Trans. Net. 11(1), 17–32 (2003)

An Autonomous Middleware Model for Essential Services in Distributed Mobile Applications

Marcio E.F. Maia, Lincoln S. Rocha,
Paulo Henrique M. Maia, and Rossana M.C. Andrade

Group of Computer Networks, Software Engineering and Systems
Federal University of Ceara. Av. Mister Hull, s/n - Campus do Pici, Bloco 942-A,
CEP: 60455-760, Fortaleza, CE, Brasil
{marcio,lincoln,paulomaia,rossana}@great.ufc.br

Abstract. The evolution and popularization of mobile devices and wireless networks give rise to the creation of a new interaction paradigm, where the devices cooperate to execute short tasks. In this scenario, the problem of how to handle environment changes, which may increase the complexity of distributed mobile applications management and maintenance, needs to be addressed. This paper presents an autonomous and evolutionary model to permit a prompt adaptation of essential services (i.e. message exchange, service description service discovery, service coordination, mobility support and security) to context changes. To validate it, a mathematical model describing the time complexity to diffuse an efficient implementation of an essential service (strategy) taking into account the number of devices is proposed. Finally, the diffusion approach is implemented in a simulator to reason about its impact on the overall efficiency of the essential services and, consequently, the performance of the application.

Keywords: Mobile Middleware, SOA, Autonomic Computing.

1 Introduction

The popularization of mobile devices and wireless communication technologies has influenced the architectural design of networks and applications. Networks evolved from centralized, static and cable-based to mobile and wireless [1]. In addition, the communication between mobile applications that use different network interfaces simultaneously has become common.

Although it increases flexibility and robustness, it can make the development and management of these applications more complicated. The core of this problem is that application-level protocols are designed considering a limited subset of information from the executing environment. While protocols designed to architectures like Wi-Fi and cellular networks may use centralized approaches, protocols developed to ad-hoc networks are fundamentally decentralized [3].

Throughout this paper, application-level protocols will be called *essential services*. They are key services used to create service-oriented mobile applications,

N. Venkatasubramanian et al. (Eds.): Mobilware 2011, LNICST 93, pp. 57–70, 2012.

such as message exchange, mobility support, service description, service discovery, service coordination and security. For instance, a chat application may require that message exchange, service description and discovery are available and a museum guide running on a PDA might also need service coordination.

To implement essential services, application developers can rely on abstractions provided by middlewares [2]. Here, these implementations are called *strategies*. For example, remote method invocation and tuple-based are two strategies for implementing message exchange. The strategy to be used in the application is defined at design time and coded using middleware libraries. Although it may reduce development time and complexity, it may also produce a rigid design that is unable to cope efficiently with changes in the execution environment.

Changes in the execution environment occur in two levels: network and application. An example of the former is the use of a different network interface or variation in the communication latency. Changes in the latter may be the unavailability of a centralized server or the use of a different language to describe services. The consequences of binding the application and middleware at design-time may vary from loss in performance to application crashing.

This paper presents *AMESMA*, an autonomous and evolutionary middleware model for essential services in distributed mobile applications. It promptly selects the best strategy (most efficient) for an essential service according to changes in the environment. Here, efficiency is described by a quality of service (QoS) descriptor, which depends on the application and essential service. For instance, service discovery efficiency can be measured by the number of services discovered or the average time to discover one service. Thus, by autonomously choosing the most efficient strategies, the model tries to improve the overall performance of the essential services. It also permits new strategies to be incorporated on-the-fly, with a minimum effort to maintain the essential services.

The benefits of this approach are threefold: firstly, strategies for an essential service can be replaced more easily, according to their efficiency. Secondly, an autonomous layer, placed between the applications and the strategies, rapidly defines which strategy should be used when changes in the environment are detected. Thirdly, instances of the model running on different devices cooperate to define efficient strategies. As devices interact and the efficient strategies are identified, these strategies are diffused throughout the network. After a short period of time, the strategies being used should converge to one or a small set of efficient strategies, increasing the overall performance of the essential services.

AMESMA was evaluated according to an analytical model that described the time to diffuse one strategy to all devices. That time is affected by the probability of diffusing an strategy (fanout factor). A higher fanout factor means a faster diffusion, but at a higher cost. The analytical model described how to adapt this factor, minimizing the cost on the network with an acceptable diffusion time. The second evaluation investigated in a simulator how the overall performance of the essential services varied as efficient strategies are diffused.

The rest of this paper is organized as follows. Section 2 gives a brief overview on the background of essential services. Section 3 details the AMESMA model and an analytical model used to describe the strategy diffusion, while section 4 presents some simulation results. Section 5 compares our approach to some related work and, finally, section 6 presents the conclusions and future work.

2 Essential Services for Mobile Applications

Service orientation (SOA) permits applications to be decomposed in atomic parts called services [6], facilitating their deployment and management. SOA-based applications require mechanisms to describe, find, access and compose these parts in a secure, fault-tolerant and context-aware manner. Here, these mechanisms are called essential services. Due to space restrictions, this paper only describes service discovery strategies, since this is the essential service implemented to validate the proposed model.

2.1 Service Discovery

Service discovery allows services to be discovered and accessed when available, permitting the creation of loosely-coupled and robust applications, since service information is accessed at runtime. Service discovery strategies can be divided according to how service information is published and how it is stored [3].

There are two strategies to publish a service: push-based, where information is published when the service becomes available, and pull-based, which publish information when requested. The former has a lower discovery latency and a higher cost on the network. The latter has a higher latency and a lower cost.

How service information is stored refers to the number and location of service registries and can be implemented by three strategies: centralized, totally distributed and hybrid. Centralized strategies publishes information in a single registry. It is easy to implement and less resilient to failures. In totally distributed strategies, every device is a registry, which increase failure resilience. In hybrid strategies, few devices act as service registries. This strategy is harder to implement than the other two strategies, but has a lower cost on the network than the distributed strategy and is more resilient to failures than the centralized strategy.

3 AMESMA

AMESMA is an autonomous and evolutionary middleware model to increase the performance of mobile applications by autonomously monitoring and searching for more efficient strategies. The main characteristic of the model is try-and-error, from evolutionary computing, in which new solutions are generated and tried in the environment and efficient solutions out live inefficient ones. The goal is to allow a rapid adaptation of the essential services to momentary conditions of the execution environment, along with minimizing coupling between application and middleware, facilitating the maintenance of the essential services.

Different strategies for an essential service are monitored at runtime and dynamically chosen based on information collected from the application layer. To use an essential service, an application informs its *quality of service (QoS) descriptor*, a particular metric relevant to that application. In a service discovery essential service, the QoS descriptor may be the number of services discovered or the average number of sent messages necessary to discover one service.

When new strategies are discovered in a nearby device, the efficiency level of the remote strategies is compared to the efficiency level of the equivalent local strategies. More efficient remote strategies are deployed locally. Strategy monitoring and substitution is performed transparently to the applications. When an application requires the execution of an essential service, it invokes an interface associated to that service. The actual strategy used is defined by the model using the QoS descriptor informed by the application and the efficiency values of the strategies. The most efficiency strategy is used to invoke this essential service.

3.1   Middleware Architecture

Figure 1 divides the architecture of the middleware model into essential service interfaces, which are packed with the application at compile-time, and middleware core, responsible for managing the essential services, i.e., the strategy selection and evolution. The middleware core is deployed in each device and is divided into QoS and context management and Middleware management. We discuss theses modules of the architecture in more details below.

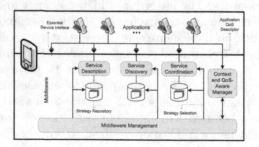

Fig. 1. Middleware architecture

Essential Services Interfaces. Applications invoke the essential services using an interface for each service, compiled with the application. Strategy selection is performed by the middleware management module based on QoS descriptor and context information received from the QoS and context module.

This separation between interface and execution is possible if different strategies are accessed equally. Considering the service discovery essential service, regardless whether the strategies and centralized, distributed or hybrid, they have similar service discovery messages. The fields in this message can be summurized in 1) ID, that uniquely identifies a device/application; 2) available or required resources; 3) service description, that contains information about a service (*Pull* model) or search parameters (*Push* model); 4) Time to Live, number of times a message can be retransmitted and 5) amount of time message remains valid.

Different strategies from devices distributed in the network communicate using the service discovery message. Amongst its fields, the service description is application-dependent. Instead of standardizing service description to guarantee interoperability, it should be defined by each application to promote flexibility.

QoS and Context Manager Module. This module manages QoS requirements from the application. When an application invokes an essential service, it informs its QoS descriptor for that service. That descriptor helps to define which strategy should be picked from a local strategy repository and to compare two strategies to define the most efficient.

This module stores information about strategy efficiency in different contexts. Upon context change, it informs the middleware management module of this new context. Based on context information received from the QoS and context manager, the middleware management module decides whether or not to change the strategy being used.

Context information may be acquired by different sources. It can be accessed using sensors presented in the device itself or from context provision services present in the environment.

Middleware Management Module. Autonomy and evolution are implemented in the middleware management module. It autonomously monitors, detects and diffuses efficient strategies and receives essential service invocation. Upon receiving an invocation, the middleware management module access the QoS and context management module to define which strategy is the most efficient at that specific moment. Applications only invoke an interface for an essential service and are unaware of which strategy will be used. Additionally, evolution is accomplished by diffusing efficient strategies and minimizing the presence of inefficient ones.

3.2   Middleware Internals

The mechanisms executed by the middleware are: essential service invocation and strategy diffusion. To invoke an essential service, an application informs its QoS descriptor, its ID and the parameters of the required essential service. Since this invocation is unblocking, the application can continue its execution and access the *result* later, using an object returned to the application. That invocation triggers an event to the middleware management module, which defines the correct strategy to be executed using the QoS descriptor and context information, accesses the strategy repository and executes the selected strategy.

The QoS descriptor is also important in a distributed execution of a strategy. For instance, a service discovery based on a distributed strategy is executed by numerous devices throughout the network. The service discovery message carries the QoS descriptor, which is used to select the correct strategy. This approach allows all devices to struggle to provide a higher efficiency according to the required QoS metric.

Simultaneously to the essential service invocation, the middleware management module periodically contacts a subset of its neighbors searching for more efficient strategies. If efficient strategies are found, a compatibility test is performed to define whether that remote strategy can be deployed locally.

The number of neighbors chosen to compare the strategies is called *fanout factor*. A lower fanout factor means that strategies will be diffused slower, with a lower cost on the network. On the contrary, a higher fanout factor means faster diffusion and higher cost on the network. Therefore, it is relevant to understand how the fanout factor impacts on the strategy diffusion time and cost on the network.

3.3   Strategy Diffusion Analytical Model

The dynamic nature of mobile networks requests quick adaptation of essential services to network conditions. Hence, it is important to understand how long diffusing one strategy takes and how it impacts on the overall efficiency of the essential service. This analytical model is based on a paper published by Groenevelt [13], which analyzes the mean time to diffuse a message to an specific node. However, our goal is to understand when all nodes receive the message. Furthermore, our model allows nodes to leave the network, creating a birth-death model.

Suppose there are N nodes in the network, moving independently according to the random way point mobility model [26], with a limited connection range. Each node has its own strategy $s_i, i \in E$, where E is the set of strategies. Moreover, initially only one node has the most efficient strategy, called s_e. Whenever that node contacts another node, that strategy is diffused. This approach is called *contact-and-infect* or *epidemic* diffusion [25].

Strategy Diffusion Delay. Assume that the system is in state k whenever there are k nodes using strategy s_e. The system starts at state 1 and reaches an absorbing state N. Figure 2 shows a Markov Chain for the states the system can enter. Once the system enters state i, it never returns to state $i - 1$, since there is no strategy more efficient than s_e and this model assumes that all nodes do not leave the network during the diffusion process.

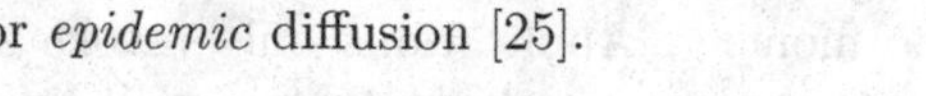

Fig. 2. Strategy diffusion Markov chain

Instead of diffusing the strategies to all nodes it meets, one node chooses a subset of these neighbors to compare their strategies. The fanout factor v represents the percentage of neighbors chosen to compare their strategies.

That approach tries to minimize the number of messages being exchanged without compromising the diffusion time.

Suppose there are i nodes with strategy s_e, then it leaves state i to $i+1$ at a rate $\lambda i(N-i)v$ (I), where λ represents the meeting rate and dependends on the average node speed, mobility pattern, area and antenna range. That meeting rate follows an exponential probability distribution [13]. If S_i represents the total time the process spends in state i, then $S_i = \frac{1}{\lambda i(N-i)v}$.

Let T_S be the time the process reaches state N (diffusion time) , then

$$E[T_S] = \sum_{i=1}^{N-1} S_i = \sum_{i=1}^{N-1} \frac{1}{\lambda i(N-i)v} = \frac{2}{\lambda v N}[\log(N-1)+\gamma+o(\frac{1}{N-1})], \text{ where}$$

γ is the Euller constant.

Birth and Death Model. The previous model assumed that nodes do not leave or arrive in the network. This restriction is now relaxed by considering that one node leaves the network at a rate μ and another node enters the network at the same rate. It keeps the number of nodes constant but varies the number of nodes using the efficient strategy.

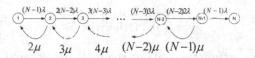

Fig. 3. Strategy diffusion Markov chain with departure

Figure 3 shows the strategy diffusion Markov chain with node departure. The process leaves state i to $i+1$ when an efficient strategy is diffused at a rate $i(N-i)\lambda v$ and from state $i+1$ to i when an node with an efficient strategy leaves the network at a rate $i\mu$. It is important to highlight that this analysis assumes that $\lambda v > \mu$, or otherwise the strategies would not be diffused. From that, the diffusion time expectation is $E[T_J] = \frac{2}{\lambda v N-\mu}[\log(N-1)+\gamma+o(\frac{1}{N-1})]$.

Graphics. The main objective is to understand how the number of neighbors chosen to compare the strategies impact on the strategy diffusion time. Figure 4 shows the strategy diffusion delay for both scenarios, without departure on Figure 4a, and with departure on Figure 4b.

In the graphic without departure, when the number of nodes is less than 20 nodes, a fanout factor of 0.5 has a similar delay as if all neighbors were chosen. When the number of nodes increases, even a fanout of 0.3 behaves similarly as the fanout factor 1.

In Figure 4b, the node departure was considered, and the fanout factor chosen was 0.3. This value was chosen to analyze the impact of the node departure rate, and it presents a good trade-off between diffusion time and cost. When the number of nodes is smaller than 20 nodes, the diffusion time increases considerably and the fanout factor must be increased. However, as the number of nodes raises, the departure rate gradually loses its influence.

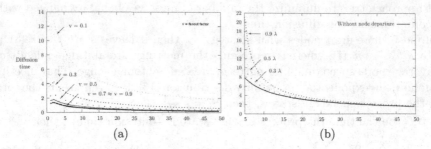

Fig. 4. (a) Strategy delay without departure varying the number of nodes. (b) With departure varying the number of nodes.

The fanout factor may be adapted based on the number of neighbors known at a given moment. According to [15], if d_{avg} is an estimate for the average number of neighbors and n the total number of nodes, then $d_{avg} = \pi \ln n$. Thus, using this estimate and the number of 20 nodes from Figure 4b as an adaptation parameter, the fanout factor can be adapted as follows:

$$v = \begin{cases} 0.5 \text{ If } d_{avg} < 9, \\ 0.3 \text{ Otherwise} \end{cases}$$

This estimate makes assumptions about the node density and mobility pattern. Since the goal is to obtain an approximation to guide the adaptation process instead of knowing the exact number of nodes, and the maximum and minimum number of neighbors is of the same magnitude as the average number of neighbors [15], this estimate gives an acceptable adaptation guide.

4   Simulation Results

AESPmob was implemented in the Jist/Swans [16] network simulator to verify how the strategy diffusion mechanism impacts on the overall performance and cost on the network. Simulation parameters are shown in Tables 1 and 2.

Table 1. Simulation parameters

Parameter	Value
Area	1000m x 1000m
Simulation time	400s
Transmission radius	100m
Mobility pattern	Random Way Point
Minimum velocity	3 km/h
Maximum velocity	5 km/h
Pause time	0s

Table 2. Model parameters

Parameter	Value
Number of devices	20 - 100
Fanout factor	0.2 - 0.8
Strategy verification period	10s
Density of services	10%
Service requisition rate	10 every 15s
Number of simulation	500

The simulation aims to analyze how the overall performance behaves as the strategies are diffused, varying the number of devices and the fanout factor. The number of nodes ranged between 20 and 100, and the fanout factor from 0.2 to 0.8. Each scenario was simulated 500 times, with the average values shown.

Three important concepts about the simulation must be understood. The first one is the service discovery strategies that were implemented. In this work, four strategies have been implemented: a Flooding-based, a probabilistic gossip-based [18], a reliable push-based, called RAPID [19], and a hybrid strategy [3].

The second one is the QoS metric used to evaluate the efficiency of the strategies: 1) *number of services discovered*, where strategies that find more services are diffused, 2) *ratio between number of services discovered and number of messages sent*, where a higher ratio defines the strategies that are diffused and 3) *average latency time*, where a lower latency means a higher efficiency.

The third one is how the efficiency information is collected. The more precise this information is, the higher the probability that more efficient strategies are diffused. The first approach called *local view* decides which strategy is more efficient based only on information locally collected. The second approach is the *cooperation view* and uses a combination of information locally collected with information obtained from devices nearby. While the third approach is called *global view* and the decision about which strategies are more efficient is based on information shared by all devices.

4.1 Overall Efficiency

The overall efficiency of an essential service is the sum of the efficiencies of all strategies. For instance, the overall efficiency of a service discovery essential service is the total number of services discovered in a period of time by all devices. The individual efficiency is the number of services discovered by one strategy in the same period.

The Y-axis in Figure 5 shows how the overall efficiency of the service discovery essential service varies during the execution as the strategies are diffused. The X-axis represents the simulation time.

The global view has a higher chance of making correct decisions. This was confirmed by simulation, since the global view was the most efficient in all scenarios simulated. However, distributed global information is hard to collect and update. Moreover, it usually introduces an overhead that very often prohibits its use. The cooperation view is not as efficient as the global view, but has a considerable lower impact. Decisions based on local information are less reliable, but it has the lowest cost.

Figure 5a and 5b shows the overall efficiency varying as the strategies are diffused according to the QoS metric called number of services found. The overall efficiency of the global view approach increases until the execution time of approximately 160 seconds, when the most efficient strategy is totally diffused and all devices are using the same strategy. After that, the overall efficiency is constant.

The cooperation and local view increase the efficiency at a lower rate. It happened because they are not as reliable as the global view, and inefficient strategies were diffused. However, despite inefficient strategies may eventually be diffused, the strategies that performed better are diffused after all. These two approaches presented a better performance that the scenario without diffusion.

Figure 6 shows how the ratio between the number of services discovered and messages sent varies as strategies are diffused. All approaches with diffusion presented an efficiency gain. The difference between the Global View and Cooperation View is smaller. This happened because strategies based on flooding and gossiping send more messages than the other two strategies. It makes the value of the ratio to decrease and facilitates the identification of the efficient strategies, which are the other two.

Figure 7 shows the QoS metric that considers the average time to discover one service. As the simulation happens, services requests sent at the beginning of the simulation arrive, which makes the average time to discover one service to increase. The no diffusion approach initially behaves more efficiently, but as time passes, the other three approaches with strategy diffusion behave more efficiently. This happened because initially, even using the global View approach, inefficient strategies were diffused. After a while, the average time started to become constant, or decrease in the case of the global view. This means that the time to discover one service is actually decreasing, since services requests sent at the beginning are still arriving (higher discover time), but the average time is being kept constant, or decreasing a little, which shows again that the overall efficiency is indeed increasing (smaller time to discover one service).

4.2 Diffusion of Efficient Strategies

Initially, the four strategies were randomly assigned to the nodes according to an uniform probability distribution. During simulation, the number of strategies used may increase or decrease according to their efficiency. The goal is to maximize the number of efficient strategies and to minimize inefficient ones.

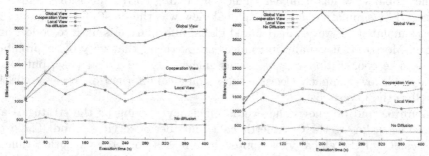

(a) 20 nodes and a fanout factor of 0.4 (b) 60 nodes and a fanout factor of 0.2

Fig. 5. Number of services discovered during the simulation

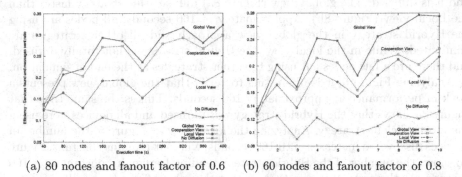

(a) 80 nodes and fanout factor of 0.6   (b) 60 nodes and fanout factor of 0.8

Fig. 6. Ratio between the number of services discovered and messages sent

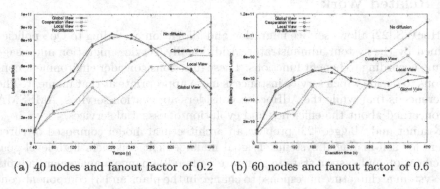

(a) 40 nodes and fanout factor of 0.2   (b) 60 nodes and fanout factor of 0.6

Fig. 7. Average discovery time

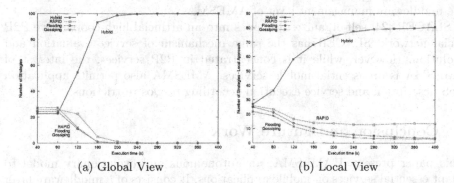

(a) Global View   (b) Local View

Fig. 8. Number of each strategy for 100 nodes and a fanout factor of 0.4

Figure 8 shows the number of each strategy during simulation, using the number of services found to guide the diffusion. Figure 8a shows how the number of each strategy varies using the global view and Figure 8b presents the local view. The Hybrid strategy has a better performance than the other strategies, and it is diffused. The global view (Figure 8a) diffuses this strategy faster than the Local view (Figure 8b). Approximately at 160 seconds, all nodes are using the Hybrid strategy in the global view approach and all other strategies are eliminated. While in the local view, the Hybrid strategy is not totally diffused, and there are a few nodes left using the other strategies at the end of simulation.

Analyzing Figure 5, it is interesting to verify that the global view presents a peak in performance at approximately 160 seconds. This is the same time that Figure 8a shows that the Hybrid strategy was diffused and all devices were using the most efficient strategy. Analyzing the local view in Figure 5, the number of services discovered increases until 160 seconds, where it remains constant. Figure 8b shows the number of the Hybrid strategy tending to remain constant after 160 seconds. At the end, strategies that are not the most efficient are still present.

5   Related Work

AdHocWS [22] allows service migration and allocation according to QoS policies defined by the system administrator. Additionally, service migration and usage occurs according to benefit functions. These functions consider environment conditions to decide which service instance is more appropriate at that moment. The difference is that while the AdHocWS considers application services, AMESMA is concerned about the efficiency and evolution of essential services.

Kramer and Maggee [23] propose an architectural model composed of three layers for self-managed systems: 1) goal management considers high-level goal specification and system state to generate a plan; 2) change management adapts the system architecture in response to change in the plans and 3) component control, formed by the system components providing state information to the higher layers. This model proposed by Kramer and Maggee can be used to implement the middleware management layer of AMESMA.

SLACER [24] self-organizes its nodes into an artificial high-cooperative P2P social network. SLACER has the same mechanism of service evaluation and evolution. However, while it is concentrated in P2P services, the interest of AMESMA is on essential mobile services. AMESMA also permits application QoS description and service execution according to Qos restrictions.

6   Conclusion and Future Work

This paper presented AMESMA, an autonomous and evolutionary model to adapt essential services on mobile applications. It consists of a middleware layer where different strategies are selected according to their efficiency, increasing the probability that the most efficient strategies are used by the applications. Our major contribution is the improvement in the overall performance of mobile applications. In addition, our model eases the maintenance and evolution of the essential services, since new strategies can be automatically found and deployed.

A mathematical model investigated the time it takes to diffuse one strategy. That model showed how to minimize the cost on the network inserted by

AMESMA without compromising the diffusion time, by adapting the fanout factor based solely on information collected locally by the devices.

Simulation results indicated that decisions based on global view would lead to an efficiency gain when compared to cooperation and local view. It also showed that any form of diffusion improves the efficiency when compared to the no diffusion approach. Although global view proved to be more efficient, it is impractical, or at least inefficient, in dynamic mobile applications due to the cost associated to gathering and updating information. The goal is to investigate more efficient forms of collecting information locally and regionally.

The problem addressed here is complex and needs to be thoroughly investigated. Validation is performed by means of simulations, where results showed that the general efficiency of the essential services has been improved, giving us confidence that similar results will be obtained when the model is implemented in real devices. We have started the development process to produce a concrete solution of our model. Moreover, we envisage other essential services being analyzed and how to improve the local and cooperation view, while keeping the cost at an acceptable level. Furthermore, we intend to scrutinize existing QoS description models to decide how these models can be used in our approach.

References

1. Chiani, M.: Wireless technologies. In: Bellavista, P., Conradi, A. (eds.) The Handbook of Mobile Middleware, ch. 3, pp. 52–73. Prentice Hall (2006)
2. Jaroucheh, Z., Liu, X., Smith, S.: A perspective on middleware-oriented context-aware pervasive systems. In: Ahamed, S.I., Bertino, E., Chang, C.K., Getov, V., Liu, L., Ming, H., Subramanyan, R. (eds.) COMPSAC (2), pp. 249–254. IEEE Computer Society (2009)
3. Engelstad, P.E., Zheng, Y., Koodli, R., Perkins, C.E.: Service discovery architectures for on-demand ad hoc networks. International Journal of Ad Hoc and Sensor Wireless Networks 2(1), 27–58 (2006)
4. Viana, W., Andrade, R.M.C.: Xmobile: A mb-uid environment for semi-automatic generation of adaptive applications for mobile devices. J. Syst. Softw. 81(3), 382–394 (2008)
5. Maia, M.E., Rocha, L.S., Andrade, R.M.: Requirements and challenges for building service-oriented pervasive middleware. In: ICPS 2009: Proceedings of the 2009 International Conference on Pervasive Services, pp. 93–102. ACM, New York (2009)
6. Erl, T.: Service-Oriented Architecture : Concepts, Technology, and Design. Prentice Hall PTR (August 2005),
   http://www.amazon.ca/exec/obidos/
   redirect?tag=citeulike09-20&path=ASIN/0131858580
7. Coulouris, G.F., Dollimore, J.: Distributed systems: concepts and design, 4th edn. Addison-Wesley Longman Publishing Co., Inc., Boston (2005)
8. Schade, S., Sahlmann, A., Lutz, M., Probst, F., Kuhn, W.: Comparing Approaches for Semantic Service Description and Matchmaking. In: Meersman, R. (ed.) OTM 2004, Part II. LNCS, vol. 3291, pp. 1062–1079. Springer, Heidelberg (2004)
9. Andrade, R.M.C., Logrippo, L.: Morar: A pattern language for mobility and radio resource management. In: Dragos Manusecu, J.N., Volter, M. (eds.) Pattern Language of Program Design 5, ch. 10, pp. 213–256. Addison-Wesley (2006)

10. Liu, C., Peng, Y., Chen, J.: Web services description ontology-based service discovery model. In: WI 2006: Proceedings of the 2006 IEEE/WIC/ACM International Conference on Web Intelligence, pp. 633–636. IEEE Computer Society, Washington, DC (2006)
11. IBM, An architectural blueprint for autonomic computing (2005)
12. Eiben, A.E., Smith, J.E.: Introduction to Evolutionary Computing, ch. Introduction, pp. 1–14. Springer (2003)
13. Groenevelt, R., Nain, P., Koole, G.: The message delay in mobile ad hoc networks. Perform. Eval. 62, 210–228 (2005)
14. Feller, W.: An Introduction to Probability Theory and Its Applications, vol. 1. Wiley (January 1968)
15. Bar-Yossef, Z., Friedman, R., Kliot, G.: Rawms - random walk based lightweight membership service for wireless ad hoc networks. ACM Trans. Comput. Syst. 26(2), 1–66 (2008)
16. Cornell, U.: Jist/swans java in simulation time/scalable wireless ad hoc network simulator (2008), http://jist.ece.cornell.edu/
17. De Meyer, K., Bishop, J.M., Nasuto, S.J.: Small-World Effects in Lattice Stochastic Diffusion Search. In: Dorronsoro, J.R. (ed.) ICANN 2002. LNCS, vol. 2415, pp. 147–152. Springer, Heidelberg (2002)
18. Khelil, A., Marrón, P.J., Becker, C., Rothermel, K.: Hypergossiping: A generalized broadcast strategy for mobile ad hoc networks. Ad Hoc Netw. 5(5), 531–546 (2007)
19. Drabkin, V., Friedman, R., Kliot, G., Segal, M.: Rapid: Reliable probabilistic dissemination in wireless ad-hoc networks. In: 26th IEEE International Symposium on Reliable Distributed Systems, SRDS 2007, pp. 13–22 (October 2007)
20. Liu, J., Issarny, V.: Qos-aware service location in mobile ad hoc networks. In: Proceedings of 2004 IEEE International Conference on Mobile Data Management, pp. 224–235 (2004)
21. Rellermeyer, J.S., Alonso, G.: Concierge: a service platform for resource-constrained devices. SIGOPS Oper. Syst. Rev. 41(3), 245–258 (2007)
22. Liu, J., Issarny, V.: Qos-aware service location in mobile ad hoc networks. In: Proceedings of 2004 IEEE International Conference on Mobile Data Management, pp. 224–235 (2004)
23. Kramer, J., Magee, J.: A rigorous architectural approach to adaptive software engineering. Journal of Computer Science and Technology 24, 183–188 (2009)
24. Hales, D., Arteconi, S.: Slacer: A self-organizing protocol for coordination in peer-to-peer networks. IEEE Intelligent Systems 21(2), 29–35 (2006)
25. Bailey, N.: The Mathematical Theory of Infectious Diseases and its Applications. Griffin, London (1975)
26. Tracy Camp, V.D., Boleng, J.: A survey of mobility models for ad hoc network research. Wireless Communications and Mobile Computing 2(5), 483–502 (2002)

Designing Smart Adaptive Flooding in MANET Using Evolutionary Algorithm

Wahabou Abdou, Christelle Bloch, Damien Charlet,
Dominique Dhoutaut, and François Spies*

Computer Science Laboratory of the University of Franche-Comté,
1, Cours Leprince-Ringuet 25201 Montbéliard - France
firstname.lastname@univ-fcomte.fr

Abstract. This paper deals with broadcasting warning / emergency messages in mobile ad hoc networks. Traditional broadcasting schemes tend to focus on usually high and homogeneous neighborhood densities environments. This paper presents a broadcasting protocol that locally and dynamically adapts its strategy to the neighborhood densities. The behavior of the protocol is tuned using various internal parameters. Multiple combinations of those parameters have been pre-computed as optimal solutions for a range of neighborhood densities, and the most relevant one is dynamically chosen depending on the locally perceived environment. The combinations were determined by coupling an evolutionary algorithm and a network simulator, using a statistically realistic radio-propagation model (Shadowing Pattern). This approach is compared with other probabilistic methods while broadcasting an emergency message in vehicular ad hoc networks with variable and heterogeneous vehicle densities. In such a context, it is expected from the network to enable each node to receive the warning message. The results show that our protocol covers the whole network, whereas other methods only have a probability of 0.57 to 0.9 to cover the entire network.

Keywords: MANET, VANET, Flooding, Broadcast Storm Problem, Evolutionary Algorithm.

1 Introduction

The broadcast is a regularly used mode of communication in Mobile Ad hoc Networks (MANETs). It is used by routing protocols for route discovery and maintenance. In such networks, a wide spread of packets is possible only if they are relayed by some nodes. However, nodes share the wireless channel and an inappropriate relay strategy can lead to a channel saturation or packets losses

* Authors wish to aknowledge "Pays de Montbeliard Agglomeration", Franche-Comte Council, "Vehicule du Futur" French competitive cluster, French ANR National Programme and French Research Council for their financial support on this research topic. They also thank Samuel Buendia for his work on the Vanet Data Representation (VDR) project.

N. Venkatasubramanian et al. (Eds.): Mobilware 2011, LNICST 93, pp. 71–84, 2012.
© Institute for Computer Sciences, Social Informatics and Telecommunications Engineering 2012

and prevent a wide dissemination. The diffusion scheme depends on the network density. Several broadcasting methods have been proposed for MANETs to optimize the channel use. Notably, probabilistic methods determine the probability P to retransmit a packet for every node, and each packet is retransmitted at most once per node. This solution reduces the number of redundant packets.

In general, existing solutions have not been designed for very low densities networks. This paper proposes to add new parameters to probabilistic broadcasting methods to adapt the diffusion strategy to various network densities. Accordingly, it expands the search space and the complexity of the problem. Therefore an evolutionary algorithm is used to determine the parameter combinations that best fit to various levels of the network density. A network simulator (ns-2) is used to assess the dissemination of packets using each parameter combination. The proposed broadcast protocol is then compared to three other probabilistic methods on a problem of sending an emergency message in a vehicular ad hoc network, e.g. to indicate the presence of ice on road or an ambulance approaching a traffic jam. This is an example, it does not restrict the areas of application of the proposed protocol which is more general. Initially, comparisons are made for networks with homogeneous densities, then for a heterogeneous network.

The remainder of this paper is organized as follows. Section 2 presents an overview of MANETs broadcasting methods. Section 3 describes the proposed adaptive broadcast protocol. The experiments for both homogeneous and heterogeneous networks are outlined in Section 4. Section 5 presents concluding remarks and outlines future work.

2   Broadcasting Methods in Ad Hoc Networks

Message broadcasting, in MANETs, involves sending a packet from one node to every node within its transmission range. This kind of communication is a recurring task which is specially used by routing protocols for route discovery. To reduce the risk of interference and thus optimize the use of the radio channel, several broadcasting methods have been proposed for MANETs. They could be classified with respect to the nature of the algorithms: deterministic or stochastic. Some methods are dedicated to delay tolerant networks.

2.1   Deterministic Methods

They are methods whose behaviors are (quasi-)predictable, and whose decisions are not based on random variables[1]. This group, gathers simple flooding, neighbor-knowledge approaches and multi-point relay methods.

Simple Flooding: Is the simplest broadcasting strategy. Each node relays received packets exactly once. Duplicate messages are discarded. This method does not

---

[1] This notion of determinism concerns only the decisions of the broadcast but not the channel access (layer 2) which may be based on random methods.

take into account the neighborhood density of nodes. In high density networks, the simple flooding wastes the bandwidth and may leads to network contention.

Neighbor Knowledge-Based Methods: Using "Hello" packets, nodes build a 1-hop or 2-hop neighbors lists. These lists are suffixed to the broadcast packets so that the receiver (r) can compare the sender's list to its own list.This comparison determines the additional nodes that will receive the message if r forwards it. For static or low mobility networks, it is a fair method. But when the node's velocity is high, the information about the neighbors become quickly inaccurate. Alba et al. [1] have proposed an improvement of the knowledge-based methods using a cellular multi-objective genetic algorithm.

Multi-Point Relay (MPR): It is a variation of knowledge-based techniques. To reduce the number of redundant broadcasts of a packet in the network, each node chooses several nodes among its neighbors that will relay its communications. The selected nodes are called MPRs [2]. When a node sends a packet on the radio channel, all its neighbors will receive it, but only the MPRs of the source node will relay the message. That means each node will have a list of all nodes that have chosen it as their "repeater" (MPRs selectors list). The MPRs are selected among the 1-hop neighbors so that they enable the node that has chosen them to reach all its 2-hop neighbors. The goal is to have the smallest list of MPRs in the network. The MPRs require a bidirectional link.

2.2 Stochastic Methods

Probabilistic Methods: They aim to improve the simple flooding method. Upon the reception of a packet, the node forwards or discards it depending on a given probability P [3] [4] [5]. A challenge is to set the value of P. Although Li et al. [6] suggest that values between 0.6 and 0.8 are optimal, it is obvious that they are not optimal for all network densities. If $P = 1$, this method is equivalent to simple flooding.

Counter-Based Schemes: They require nodes to count the number of the redundant copies of a single message over a short period of time called Random Access Delay (RAD) [7]. When the RAD expires, if the number of copies is less than a given threshold (c_t), the message is forwarded. Otherwise, it is dropped. This method involves additional latency.

Location-Based Methods: Before relaying a message, the node evaluates the additional coverage area that will result from this retransmission. This technique does not consider whether nodes exist within that additional area or not. To evaluate the extra coverage area, the node can use the distance between itself and each node that has previously relayed the message (distance-based scheme) or the geographical coordinates (location-based scheme). In both distance-based and location-based schemes, a RAD is assigned before the message is relayed (if the additional coverage area is higher than a fixed threshold) or dropped.

2.3   Diffusion Methods Dedicated to Delay Tolerant Networks

In a sparse environment, communications in Vehicular Ad hoc Networks (VANETs) behave like those studied by the Delay/Disruption Tolerant Network (DTN) community. Thus, flooding protocols developed for DTN might be used in VANETs. The epidemic routing [8] scheme proposes that a node relays the message to all the nodes it crosses, which did not know about it. This is a monotone relay strategy. The PRoPHET protocol [9] (Probabilistic Routing Protocol using History of Encounters and Transitivity) applies probabilistic routing instead of doing blind epidemic replication of bundles through the network. it uses a metric called *delivery predictability* established at every node A for each known destination B.

Because of the low reception rate found in such environments, most of these protocols schedule multiple transfers of the same message. The number of replica may range from one copy (e.g., direct transmission protocol [10]) to an infinite as in epidemic routing. As it has a direct impact on the network load, much effort has been undertaken to leverage the cost of forwarding by finding the most valuable tradeoff between cost and reliability [11]. It should be noted that most of the advanced schemes are tuned for sparse environments, and do not scale to be used in medium or high density environments.

3   A New Neighborhood Density-Aware Method

3.1   Challenges

One major challenge of broadcasting problems in wireless ad hoc networks is to reach the maximum number of nodes while avoiding useless repeats. Recent work in this field shows the need to reduce the number of relay nodes in high-density networks. However, as mentioned in Section 2, a part of those improvements is to the detriment of the delay, especially because a waiting time (RAD) is added. Another weakness of existing methods is the impracticability of their proposals in very sparse networks (i.e. the probability that a node has a neighbor is very low) and environments where the broadcast packets may be lost. Indeed, according to the WiFi standard, broadcast packets are not acknowledged. Thus, the source node cannot be sure that the packets are received. To solve this problem, it is necessary to retransmit packets more than once in certain cases. In our proposal, we suggest to improve the existing probabilistic methods by adding new parameters. We use the following four parameters to regulate broadcast in MANETs:

- The probability (P) to relay a packet. Upon the reception of a packet, each node decides to forward or to drop it depending on the value of P. This is the main parameter of the probabilistic methods.
- The total number of times each packet will be repeated (Nr). In the case of low-density mobile networks, a node may not have a neighbor in its coverage area when it forwards a packet. By repeating the packets more than once, this node increases its chance of being heard by another mobile node. This parameter can also be useful when the initial transmission is lost due to collisions or other phenomena related to radio propagation conditions.

- The delay (Dr) between two successive repeats. Indeed, if a node has to repeat the packets several times, one must determine the frequency at which the redundant copies should be sent. Note that in a dense network, low values of Dr could lead to the increase of the number of collisions.
- The TTL (Time To Live). This parameter permits to confine the spread of messages in a given geographic area. It specifies the number of hops allowed to the packets.

The variation range of these parameters is given in Table 1. Using these four parameters, the solutions are simulated thanks to the Network Simulator 2 (ns-2) [12]. As the simulations are stochastic processes, each solution is evaluated by the simulator 500 times[2] to obtain statistically reliable results. ns-2 assesses the solutions using the four following criteria:

Table 1. Variation ranges of decision variables

Parameter	P	Nr	Dr (in seconds)	TTL
Lower bound	0	1	0	10
Upper bound	1	30	2	40

- NC: the average number of collisions;
- PT: the average propagation time (the time spent until all the nodes in the considered area receive the message);
- R: the average number of retransmissions during the simulation.
- FR: the full reception ratio. It is the ratio between the number of successful simulations[3] and the total number of simulations (500 in our experiments).

Relying on these parameters and criteria, our method is based on three steps:

- simulating ad hoc networks with different neighborhood densities to determine the appropriate values of P, Nr, Dr and TTL in every context;
- enabling the nodes to determine their neighborhood density (without sending "Hello" packets, or adding a waiting time);
- making the nodes able to automatically change their broadcasting strategy by choosing the one that best suits the environment of each node.

The following subsections detail these three steps.

---

[2] This value is determined empirically. It represents a good compromise between the result confidence interval and the simulation time.

[3] For each of the 500 simulations, if the channel is saturated, the number of collisions may prevent the message from being normally transmitted to all the nodes. In very low density networks, communications between nodes may also break or deteriorate gradually and prevent a complete reception by the nodes. In these cases, the simulation is stored as a failed simulation.

3.2   Setting Broadcasting Parameters for Various Densities

The variation ranges given in Table 1 result in a search space that contains 9.10^{16} possible combinations. Running each combination requires from a dozen seconds up to a few minutes according to the considered neighborhood density. Simulating all possible cases with ns-2 would take a long time. That is why an evolutionary algorithm (EA), inspired by the theory of natural evolution, is used to assess a subset of interesting solutions. Figure 1 illustrates the three main modules of the proposed approach and their interaction.

Firstly, the EA randomly generates a set of n possible solutions called initial population. Each solution, i.e. a set of possible parameters, must be evaluated and fitness is assigned to it. In our case, the evaluation process is done in two steps: the first is performed by the "Network simulator" and "Log analyzer" modules; the second is assessed by the EA. First, each set of parameters is transmitted to the network simulator. The latter integrates the received parameters into the simulation scripts. Thereafter, the simulations are run and some log files are built. These files describe the network behavior. The log files are passed on to the log analyzer that extracts the values of the objective functions. The calculated objective values are then conveyed to the optimization engine that ranks the solutions according to these values, using the concept of Pareto dominance. Pareto solutions are those for which improvement in one objective involves the worsening of at least one other objective. Four Pareto ranks (also called fronts) are built (R_1, R_2, R_3 and R_4. R_4 represents the dominated solution list). Thereafter two individuals (called parents) are selected for recombination.Each parent is chosen by two random selections. The Pareto front is first selected according to a computed probability. The probability to select each list both takes into account a priority level associated to each list's and the list length. This favours the best solutions while preventing the dominated solutions from having very low values of fitness, in order to preserve the diversity of the successive populations. Then an individual is randomly selected among the individuals belonging to this front, using equal probabilities for all these individuals. Each pair of selected parents is recombined using a simulated binary 10-point crossover (variables are first converted into binary strings). The k-point crossover operator was chosen because it is a classical method of recombination. The value of k was empirically tuned. Finally, a uniform mutation is applied: a gene is randomly chosen and the EA generates a new value for this variable with respect to its variation range. These operators permit to generate a list of offspring, whose fitness is again computed using ns-2 simulations. Each offspring replaces the first parent it dominates in the population list. If the offspring does not dominate any parent, it is not added to the list of individuals of the next generation. All these steps (evaluation, selection, crossover, mutation, replacement) are repeated until a given stop criterion is met. The EA finally returns an archive of R_1 built over generations. In Figure 1 the "P_0 ?" condition is used to check if the current population is the initial one.

The evolutionary algorithm used is detailed in [13] where we presented our first results in smaller homogeneous networks with a narrow search space.

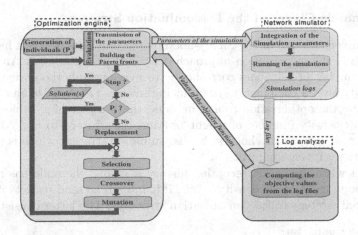

Fig. 1. Flow chart of the optimization tool

3.3   Detection of the Neighborhood Density

When it is assumed that nodes have identical and uniform transmission range (d), the number of nodes (N_i) at a distance less than d from i can be used as an indicator of neighborhood density of each node i. This is particularly the case when using a deterministic propagation model. However, when using a model that spreads the packet losses depending on the distance, this definition becomes inapplicable. Therefore, we consider for each node the number of active neighbors it has detected. As an indicator of density, we used this number of neighbors, weighted by the reception ratio.

Through communications in the network, each node builds a local view of its neighborhood. This view is mainly based on the number of different neighbors repeating the same packet. To this end, each node keeps a history of the number of neighbors it overhear repeating each packet. Whenever a node receives a packet for the first time, it saves the packet's identifier and set the number of sources for this packet to 1. This number is incremented each time a copy of this packet is received for the first time from a neighbor. This allows to observe the evolution of communications over time. It should be noted that multiple repetitions by a single source do not increment the number of sources. In order to both save the mobile nodes memory and keep information up-to-date, the packets sources history has limited size and older information are discarded.

The current number of neighbors, denoted $\overline{ngh}$ is an average computed from the number of neighbors that sent the packets received in the recent history.

In this paper each node uses a simple and passive algorithm to evaluate the actual number of neighbors. As we focus on applications in which information messages are generated regularly, we can manage without active "Hello" packets.

3.4   Dynamic Choice of the Dissemination Strategy

For the implementation of the Smart-flooding, several density levels have been studied using the optimization approach described in Section 3.2. An average weighted number of neighbors corresponds to every neighborhood density. For each density level a combination of input parameters (P, Nr, Dr and TTL) is proposed by the optimization tool. The nodes have a matching table between the network density (number of neighbors) and the strategy to use. After each update of $\overline{ngh}$, every node chooses the dissemination strategy which is the most appropriate for its environment.

However when the packet reception history is empty, the node has no information about the network density. Thus, if it intends to send packets it should use a special strategy called "initialization strategy". The latter consists of:

1. sending the packet;
2. waiting for a time period t and then controlling $\overline{ngh}$;
3. adjusting the communication strategy based on $\overline{ngh}$;
4. waiting for a time period t then refining the dissemination strategy depending on the new value of $\overline{ngh}$.

4   Experiments

4.1   Validation of the EA

The Elitist Simulated Binary Evolutionary Algorithm (ESBEA) [14] is used for the following experiments. ESBEA is first compared with three EAs found in literature: two well-known EAs (NSGA-II [15] and SPEA2 [16]) and a more recent one (DECMOSA-SQP [17]).

The four algorithms are compared using the CEC 2009 competition procedure on two constrained multi-objective problems proposed in this competition (constrained problems 1 & 2) [18]. As shown by the results presented in [14], ESBEA provides positive gains for the comparison when using the Inverted Generational Distance (IGD) metrics recommended in CEC 2009 competition.

4.2   Experimental Procedure

The proposed broadcasting protocol is compared with Simple Flooding (which is known as the reference method for broadcasting problems in MANETs) and two probabilistic methods with probability values respectively equal to 0.6 and 0.8. These four broadcasting methods are initially evaluated in homogeneous density networks. The simulated networks are Vehicular Ad hoc Networks (VANETs).

VANETs can enhance safety on the roads by communicating traffic information, accidents, bypass, etc. In the remainder of this section, we evaluate the behavior of the broadcasting methods when a vehicle sends a warning message. It is obvious that, under such circumstances, it is essential to spread the message as quickly as possible and most importantly, the message must reach as many vehicles as possible in the vicinity of the transmitter. The experiments were carried out using network simulator 2 (ns-2.34). We had to be careful concerning the simulation models because the radio environment has a very strong impact on communications, especially in the very hostile VANET condition. We chose to use the Shadowing Pattern [19] propagation model which is a realistic and probabilistic model based on outside monitored communications and it is well suited for our needs. It can produce particularly realistic statistical errors distributions, such as slow and fast fading, but it is still computationally easy enough to be carried out on medium to large simulations. Radio communications can be impacted among others by the topography, the buildings, the cars and vehicles passing by, the presence of trees, other radio communications, antenna design and even the weather. Shadowing Pattern does not aim at exhaustively simulating all the complex occurring phenomena. Instead it makes use of experimental calibration to exhibit a global statistical behavior much closer to reality than that of a more realistic but partial model.

We conducted experiments and made use of Vanet Data Representation (VDR), a software we developed in order to make the analysis of the massive amount of real data collected easier. As shown on Figure 2, VDR displays on a single window various configurable metrics along with the context presented as a dynamic map and even video when available.

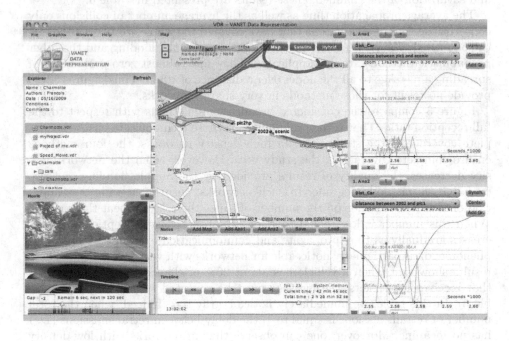

Fig. 2. Vanet Data Representation (VDR) - a tool to analyse real world experiments and to calibrate the Shadowing Pattern radio propagation model

4.3   Tests in Homogeneous Networks

For experiments in a homogeneous context, we considered four levels of neighborhood densities. For each network, we built a chain topology that illustrates cars lined up on 10 km. We varied the distance between two consecutive vehicles to regulate the density as mentioned in Table 2. In medium density context, each message may be received by about twenty of nodes. Low density topology is similar to a highway network.

The Very low-density network represents a collection of vehicles in a rural area where traffic generally flows steadily. A vehicle might have no neighbor in its coverage area. To simulate such a sparse vehicule distribution, we built a network topology that mimics the very intermittent presence of neighbors. Thus a given vehicle can communicate only periodically. For this density level the total of communicating periods is about 20% of the simulation time for each vehicle (during the remaining time, the vehicle is considered to be without any neighbor). This scenario is simulated using an average distance of 1000 m between vehicles.

For these various density levels, the evolutionary algorithm returned a set of solutions (those in the first Pareto front) [13]. We then sorted the best solutions in order to select the one that offered the best balance between the reachability and saturation of the channel. These results are presented in Table 3.

The average propagation time as well as the average number of collisions only concerns the runs of simulations that have covered the whole study area (among the 500 runs). For very low density networks, the simple flooding and the other probabilistic methods are not applicable. They have almost zero probability of spreading a message to all the nodes over a distance of 10km. Thus, figures 3 to 5 provide no result for those methods in very sparse networks.

Figure 3 compares the considered broadcasting methods with respect to the full reception ratio. That is the probability for those techniques to ensure a complete coverage of the study area. In high density networks, the four methods ensure complete coverage of the study area. However, when the network density decreases, the quality of results provided by the Simple flooding and two probabilistic methods degrade. In such networks, ensuring a wide dissemination of messages depends on the number of times the relays repeat the packets. When this number is low (equal to 1 for example), packet reception ratio decreases gradually as they propagate and communication eventually stops. This phenomenon is particularly noticeable for networks with very low density. These results show that when a vehicle has about 20% of chance to have a neighbor that receives its packets, the message must be repeated twenty times (see Table 3). In this table, we immediately notice a gray box. Indeed, when the total number of retransmissions is equal to 1, the delay between retransmissions (Dr) has no meaning. Moreover, one can observe that in networks with low-density neighborhood, it is necessary to retransmit the packets twice, with a probability of about 0.9. If the packets are retransmited only once (probability equals to 1) in sparse networks, the chance of being received by all the nodes (FR) is about 95% (see Figure 3).

For full coverage in very low-density networks, Smart-flooding advocates to resend packets several times. The protocol assumes that collisions or distance between the source and the destination may cause an interruption of the broadcast. The message will reach all nodes after a new issue. The histogram in Figure 4 illustrates this by the relatively high propagation delay of the Smart-flooding in the low density levels. We conclude that the total coverage of the network is at the expense of dissemination speed. In dense or very dense environments, the propagation time of the different broadcasting methods are equivalent. This reflects the fact that in such cases, the first front of broadcast ($Nr = 1$) enables the dissemination of the emergency message throughout the study area. As expected, the number of collisions decreases with network density (Figure 5). The difference between the four broadcasting methods is slight. Even when Smart-flooding repeats packets more than once, it regulates the broadcast using good P and Dr values.

Table 2. Network densities

Density level	Inter-vehicle distance	Number of nodes	Weighted average neighbors
Very low	1000 m	10	0.468
Low	200 m	50	7.07
Medium	75 m	134	20.496
High	25 m	400	63.888

Table 3. Smart-flooding solutions

Density level	P	Nr	Dr (in seconds)	TTL
Very low	0.999	21	0.559	20
Low	0.916	2	0.729	28
Medium	0.776	1		26
High	0.359	2	0.076	18

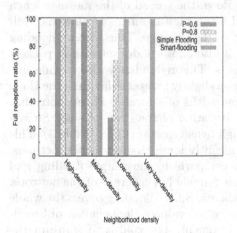

Fig. 3. Full Reception Ratio

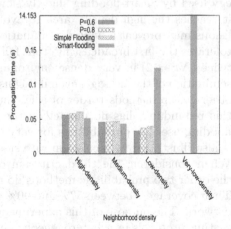

Fig. 4. Average propagation time

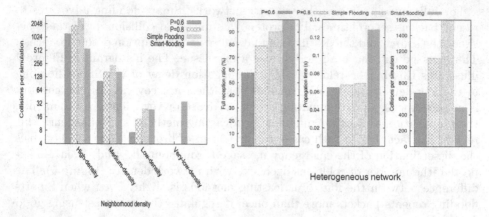

Fig. 5. Average number of collisions   **Fig. 6.** Heterogeneous network results

4.4   Tests in a Heterogeneous Network

The density of VANETs is not generally homogeneous. In a urban environment for example, the density is not the same at a downtown and on the outskirts of the city. The network topology depicted in Figure 7 is used to compare the four broadcasting methods. This network is composed of three main levels of density: low-density, medium-density and high density.

The results of experiments in the heterogeneous network are shown in Figure 6. The warning message is sent by the rightmost node of Figure 7. The strategy used by Smart-flooding slightly slow down the spread of the message when it reaches the high density area to avoid a too high number of collisions. Collisions may prevent a wide dissemination of the message. Thus, Smart-flooding tolerates the first broadcasting front fail. It also allows nodes retransmit packets twice ($Nr = 2$) in very dense environments. This redundancy allows wide dissemination of the message, even if it causes a slightly greater delay than the three other gossip methods (order of a few hundredths of seconds). Please note that this redundancy has no impact on the saturation of the channel since Smart-flooding uses low probabilities for very high density network (see Table 3). This is also illustrated by a collision rate significantly lower than for other methods. When considering the third criterion of comparison, the simple flooding and the other two probabilistic methods do not provide full coverage of the network. Their coverage is between 57% and 90% whereas Smart-flooding covers the whole network. The purpose of this experiment was to evaluate the behavior of broadcasting protocols in a heterogeneous environment. The goal is to transmit the message quickly and to make it reach all nodes in the studied area. The slight difference of propagation time does not diminish the Smart-flooding results. The difference with the results of other protocols is only a few hundredths of seconds.

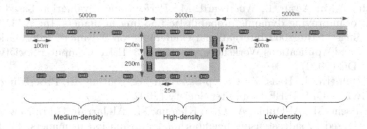

Fig. 7. Heterogeneous network topology

5   Conclusion

A new broadcasting protocol for MANETs (Smart-flooding) is proposed in this paper. Its parameters are determined by an evolutionary algorithm. Smart-flooding is compared to three other probabilistic methods on a sending emergency message problem in a VANET with low, medium and high densities. This comparative study shows that Smart-flooding covers the whole network while other methods have a lower coverage probability (from 57% to 90% coverage) for the same network. The average number of collisions and the average time of propagation remain almost equivalent for the four methods, except that the propagation time increases to about 14 seconds in very low-density. But in this case, Smart-flooding manages to spread the warning message to all nodes, while other methods fail. The two main prospects of this work are to extend this protocol to dynamic multi-radio networks, and integrate a criterion of minimizing energy consumption in order to define the best compromise between performance and longevity of the network.

References

1. Alba, E., Dorronsoro, B., Luna, F., Nebro, A.J., Bouvry, P.: A cellular multi-objective genetic algorithm for optimal broadcasting strategy in metropolitan manets. In: IPDPS 2005: Proceedings of the 19th IEEE International Parallel and Distributed Processing Symposium (IPDPS 2005) - Workshop 6, p. 192.1. IEEE Computer Society, Washington, DC (2005)
2. Nguyen, D., Minet, P.: Analysis of mpr selection in the olsr protocol. In: AINAW 2007: Proceedings of the 21st International Conference on Advanced Information Networking and Applications Workshops, pp. 887–892. IEEE Computer Society, Washington, DC (2007)
3. Karthikeyan, N., Palanisamy, V., Duraiswamy, K.: Optimum density based model for probabilistic flooding protocol in mobile ad hoc network. European Journal of Scientific Research 39(4), 577–588 (2010)
4. Hanashi, A.M., Siddique, A., Awan, I., Woodward, M.: Dynamic probabilistic flooding performance evaluation of on-demand routing protocols in manets. In: CISIS 2008: Proceedings of the 2008 International Conference on Complex, Intelligent and Software Intensive Systems, pp. 200–204. IEEE Computer Society, Washington, DC (2008)

5. Hanashi, A.M., Awan, I., Woodward, M.: Performance evaluation based on simulation of improving dynamic probabilistic flooding in manets. In: WAINA 2009: Proceedings of the 2009 International Conference on Advanced Information Networking and Applications Workshops, pp. 458–463. IEEE Computer Society, Washington, DC (2009)
6. Li, L., Halpern, J., Haas, Z.: Gossip-based ad hoc routing. In: Proceedings of the IEEE INFOCOM. IEEE Computer Society (2002)
7. Bani Yassein, M., Al-Dubai, A., Ould Khaoua, M., Al-Jarrah, O.M.: New adaptive counter based broadcast using neighborhood information in manets. In: International Parallel and Distributed Processing Symposium, pp. 1–7 (2009)
8. Vahdat, A., Becker, D.: Epidemic routing for partially-connected ad hoc networks. Technical report (2000)
9. Lindgren, A., Doria, A.: Probabilistic routing protocol for intermittently connected networks, internet draft. Technical Report draft-irtf-dtnrg-prophet, Internet Engineering Task Force (February 2010), http://tools.ietf.org/html/draft-irtf-dtnrg-prophet
10. Spyropoulos, T., Psounis, K., Raghavendra, C.S.: Single-copy routing in intermittently connected mobile networks. In: IEEE Communications Society Conference on Sensor and Ad Hoc Communications and Networks, pp. 235–244 (2004)
11. Fall, K., Farrell, S.: DTN: an architectural retrospective. IEEE Journal on Selected Areas in Communications 26(5), 828–836 (2008)
12. The Network Simulator Project - ns-2, http://www.isi.edu/nsnam/ns
13. Abdou, W., Henriet, A., Dhoutaut, D., Spies, F., Bloch, C.: Optimizing communications in vehicular ad hoc networks using evolutionary computation and simulation. In: Int. Conf. on Soft Computing as Transdisciplinary Science and Technology, CSTST 2008, pp. 158–165. ACM, Cergy-Pontoise (2008)
14. Abdou, W., Henriet, A., Bloch, C., Dhoutaut, D., Charlet, D., Spies, F.: Using an evolutionary algorithm to optimize the broadcasting methods in mobile ad hoc networks. Journal of Network and Computer Applications (2011)
15. Deb, K., Agrawal, S., Pratap, A., Meyarivan, T.: A fast and elitist multiobjective genetic algorithm: Nsga-ii. IEEE Trans. Evolutionary Computation 6(2), 182–197 (2002)
16. Zitzler, E., Laumanns, M., Thiele, L.: Spea2: Improving the strength pareto evolutionary algorithm. Technical report, Computer Engineering and Networks Laboratory (TIK), Swiss Federal Institute of Technology (ETH) Zurich (2001)
17. Zamuda, A., Brest, J., Boškovic, B., Žumer, V.: Differential evolution with self-adaptation and local search for constrained multiobjective optimization. In: CEC 2009: Proceedings of the Eleventh Conference on Congress on Evolutionary Computation, pp. 195–202. IEEE Press, Piscataway (2009)
18. Zhang, Q., Zhou, A., Zhao, S., Suganthan, P.N., Liu, W., Tiwari, S.: Multiobjective optimization test instances for the cec 2009 special session and competition. Technical report, The School of Computer Science and Electronic Engieering (2009)
19. Dhoutaut, D., Regis, A., Spies, F.: Impact of radio propagation models in vehicular ad hoc networks simulations. In: VANET 2006: Procs. of the 3rd Int. Workshop on Vehicular Ad Hoc Networks, pp. 40–49. ACM Press, Los Angeles (2006)

Peer-to-Peer Cooperative Networking for Cellular Mobile Devices

Niranjan Suri[1], Giacomo Benincasa[1], Mauro Tortonesi[2],
Enrico Casini[1], and Andrea Rossi[1,2]

[1] Florida Institute for Human and Machine Cognition,
Pensacola, FL USA
{nsuri,gbenincasa,ecasini,arossi}@ihmc.us
[2] University of Ferrara,
Ferrara, Italy
mtortonesi@ing.unife.it

Abstract. Cellular mobile devices, and in particular smartphones, have become ubiquitous. While bandwidth has steadily increased from 2G devices with Edge to 3G and now 3G LTE (4G), so has the demand for bandwidth intensive applications and streaming of multimedia content. Supporting high densities of such users in urban environments has become a challenge. In this paper, we describe an approach to peer-to-peer cooperative networking that exploits the WiFi interface in peer-to-peer mode in order to reduce the demand on the cellular network while at the same time increasing the reliability of data delivery. We describe multiple scenarios that benefit from such middleware and present some experimental results.

Keywords: Cooperative Networking, Peer-to-peer Networks, Multimedia Streaming, Information Dissemination, Opportunistic Communications.

1   Introduction

Mobile phones have evolved from simple devices that supported voice calling and text messaging into powerful and sophisticated multimedia devices with audio and video streaming. While the design capacities of the cellular networks have increased steadily from 2G devices with Edge to 3G and now 3G LTE (labeled 4G by some vendors), so has the user appetite for bandwidth intensive applications. Given that the cellular bandwidth is shared across multiple users, the available bandwidth quickly diminishes with an increase in user density. For example, the 3G LTE specification calls for a minimum of 100 Mbps downlink, but also a minimum support for 200 users in one cell. With large numbers of users, that reduces the bandwidth per user to 500 Kbps. Given the unreliability of wireless communications, the actual bandwidth realized is significantly lower, especially with users in indoor environments and with users on the move. Therefore, there is a requirement to alleviate the congestion on cellular networks and to increase the reliability of data delivery.

N. Venkatasubramanian et al. (Eds.): Mobilware 2011, LNICST 93, pp. 85–97, 2012.

One approach to solving this problem lies in exploiting with WiFi interface in order to offset the load on the cellular interface. Most mobile phones provide support for WiFi, which typically provides a shorter-range, higher-bandwidth communications link. Mobile phones are able to automatically switch their data access to the WiFi interface when an access point is available, in order to offload the cellular network. With Unlicensed Mobile Access (UMA), mobile phones are able to automatically switch their voice calls to the WiFi interface as well. This feature is often used with access points at home in order to compensate for poor cellular coverage in remote areas. While such an approach reduces the load on the cellular network, we propose an alternate approach that does not require WiFi access points.

This paper describes an approach to peer-to-peer cooperative networking among mobile phones in order to reduce cellular network load as well as increase reliability of data delivery. In particular, we propose to allow mobile phones to communicate via their WiFi interfaces, but in ad-hoc mode, with their peers. This peer-to-peer communication can be used to compensate for data loss on the cellular network by allowing one mobile phone that has received the data successfully to provide the data to another mobile phone that failed to receive the original data. We describe an abstract method to realize this capability, as well as a concrete implementation based on our DisService peer-to-peer information dissemination service. We begin by describing some scenarios.

2   Scenarios

2.1   Live Multicast Streaming

We begin with the simplest scenario – streaming live audio or video via a multicast transmission. This scenario involves multiple mobile phone users receiving a multimedia stream from a provider via their cellular network. Examples include watching live events such as a newscast, a show, or a sporting event. In this scenario, the multimedia stream being provided to each user is the same, regardless of when they subscribe to the stream. Therefore, the stream can be multicast over the cellular network and requires only the bandwidth for a single copy of the stream. We contrast this to a later scenario, where users can begin a stream from an arbitrary point on demand, which requires that the stream be potentially unicast to each user.

Cooperative networking in this scenario involves mobile devices using their peer-to-peer network to request and exchange packets that they did not receive successfully over the cellular network. In the absence of cooperative networking, a device that has missing packets would either have a break in the rendered media, or would have to request missing packets over the cellular network, requiring further bandwidth.

2.2   Live Multicast Relaying

This scenario is a variation of the simple streaming scenario above. In this situation, some of the mobile devices have either a poor or non-existent cellular link and hence cannot receive the multicast stream directly. For example, consider multiple users in an office environment, where some users may be in interior rooms (with poor connectivity) whereas others may be in exterior rooms with good connectivity. Cooperative networking in this scenario involves one or more mobile devices that have a good quality connection relaying the stream that they are receiving to the disconnected (or poorly connected) mobile devices via the peer-to-peer WiFi link.

2.3   On Demand Streaming

This scenario differs from the previous two scenarios in that each mobile phone has an independent multimedia stream that is transmitted on demand. This scenario arises when users select viewing an archived multimedia stream from a website[1]. Given that the multimedia stream is not synchronized across users, it would not be possible to multicast the stream to multiple users. However, we make the observation that multiple users may watch a subset of popular videos at any given moment in time[2]. Consider a crowd of users gathered at an urban area, city center, or at a sporting event. Cooperative networking in this scenario involves one or more mobile devices caching their multimedia content for a period of time after it has been rendered in order to provide it to other peers on demand, over the peer-to-peer WiFi link. The duration of the cache may depend on a variety of factors, including recency of use and storage space available.

2.4   Generic Web and Data Caching

This final scenario is a generalization of the on-demand streaming and turns mobile phones into dynamic web and data caches. In this scenario, when a mobile phone decides to download content via the cellular network, it first queries other mobile devices via the WiFi link in order to determine if any of the peer devices already have the desired data in their cache. When a device retrieves an object (either via the cellular or WiFi link), the device caches the object in case it can provide the object to other peers at a later point in time. As in the above scenario, the duration of the cache may depend on a variety of factors.

The following section discusses related work that provides capabilities relevant to the above scenarios.

3   Related Work

Many research studies have focused on data replication in ad hoc networks. Padmanabhan et al. [1] and Derhab and Badache [2] provide a comprehensive survey of the topic. However, most of the proposals focus on the realization of medium to long term availability of data that gets rarely updated [3], and try to address related

---

[1]   YouTube® is a popular worldwide example, along with Netflix® and Hulu® in the United States.
[2]   This phenomenon is sometimes referred to as Cyber Rubbernecking.

issues such as network partition-aware [4] or energy consumption-aware [5] replication solutions. Other solutions leverage on federated tuple-spaces and configurable replication profiles [6]. Instead, we are interested in short term, time limited, and localized dissemination of data.

Among the existing proposals that seem to address a similar scenario to the ones presented in Section I, the most interesting one seems to be REDMAN [7]. However, REDMAN focuses on replica placement and does not address the problem of replica updates.

Researchers have also addressed the problem of reliable group communications in ad hoc networks. Several reliable multicast protocols designed to operate on top of an IP multicast infrastructure, such as NORM [8] and PGM [9], have also been proposed on mobile ad hoc networks. In addition, researchers recently started studying opportunistic communications, paying a particular attention to social networking concepts [10] [11] [12] [13] [14].

4   DisService

4.1   Overview

DisService is a peer-to-peer dissemination service that realizes cooperative networking for mobile devices. DisService is middleware that sits between the application and transport layer and offers an information dissemination service that provides a message-oriented, publish-subscribe paradigm.

DisService was designed to perform in mobile ad-hoc networks, and relies on the assumption that in this context, the cost of unicasting and broadcasting are equivalent and therefore the latter is always preferred to the former. The use of broadcast has the important feature of allowing all the neighboring peers to receive and opportunistically cache data that are not directed to them at no additional cost. We call this capability "opportunistic listening." Opportunistic listening allows a higher degree of availability and survivability of the data and ultimately allows greater overall dissemination performances.

Note that while we use the term broadcast in this paper to describe the exchange of data between DisService instances, DisService can also be configured to use multicast instead. The only requirement would be a mechanism to select a specific multicast address to be used by nodes. For example, all the devices that are receiving a specific live stream may subscribe to a single multicast group, which could be specified as part of the broadcast from the cell tower.

DisService implements several dissemination protocols, such as probabilistic (epidemic) protocols, reliable flooding, and heuristic protocols; the choice of which algorithm better suits the particular scenario is left up to the user. Furthermore, DisService lets the applications choose, for each of their subscriptions, whether they want the data to be delivered in a reliable and/or sequenced fashion.

Unlike most protocols, when reliable transmission is chosen, the receiver will be in charge of requesting the missing messages. This approach has the advantage of leaving the decision to request the missing fragments up to the receiver; it is possible that different applications that subscribed to the same group have different reliability requirements. Moreover, this approach allows the receiver to autonomously retrieve the missing messages from different subsets of peers.

The guaranteed decoupling between sender and receiver as a result of the publish/subscribe architecture, the extensive use of broadcasting, and the use of "reliable reception" instead of "reliable transmission" all make DisService an effective architecture to deal with unreliable networks by means of cooperative caching. A more detailed architectural view of DisService is presented later, following an example of using DisService for the scenarios presented above.

4.2   Live Multicast Streaming Scenario

Consider the live multicast streaming scenario presented in section 2.1. Figure 1 below shows a snapshot of two users receiving a live feed from a cell tower and using cooperative networking in order to improve their reception. Each mobile device has a FIFO buffer that is used to hold packets that have been received via the cellular interface but have not yet been consumed and rendered by the device. Such a buffer is normally used to offset any jitter that might occur in the reception of data. In this scenario, this same buffer is also used to fill in missing packets by requesting that data from neighboring peers, over the WiFi interface. For example, User 1 did not happen to receive packet n+4 and n+6 and User 2 did not receive packet n+3 and n+6. Each of them requests the packets they are missing from other users, with the result that User 1 receives packet n+4 and User 2 received packet n+3. Neither of them received packet n+6, so that would result in some degradation in the received stream despite the cooperative networking capability.

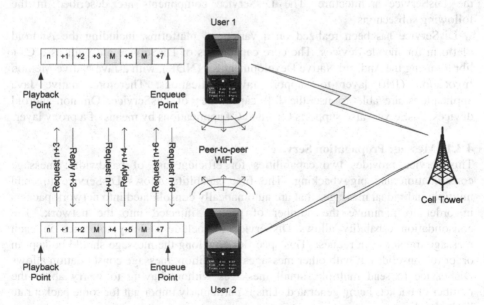

Fig. 1. Live Multicast Streaming Scenario with DisService

While the example above demonstrates a two user scenario, this is easily extensible to multiple users, in which case a user's device may receive the missing packets from any of the other devices. In the DisService architecture, the request for a missing packet is broadcast to all the other devices within reach, and any of them that have the desired data may respond.

Also note that the stream being transmitted over the cellular network will likely use Forward Error Correction, which embeds some redundant information in each of the packets in order to support recovery of missing packets. The DisService approach to cooperative networking is fully compatible with such streams of data. In the example above, the decoder for the multimedia stream may still be able to recover the data missing in packet n+6, which was not received by either user. Using DisService decreases the number of missing packets, which increases the quality of the rendered stream as well. Cooperative networking will also reduce the quantity of redundant error correction information that is selected to be included in the stream, which reduces the bandwidth required.

We are currently working on also realizing variations of DisService to support the other three scenarios described in sections 2.2, 2.3, and 2.4 respectively. In the following section, we describe the overall architecture of DisService.

4.3   DisService Architecture

DisService provides efficient and peer-to-peer dissemination of data without any reliance on centralized components. There are no assumptions made about the presence of stable network connectivity. Instead, DisService dynamically adapts itself to network changes and disseminates information as best as possible. Figure 2 shows the DisService architecture. The DisService components are described in the following subsections.

DisService has been realized on a variety of platforms, including the Android platform for mobile devices. The core capabilities of DisService are built as a C++ library using the Android Native Development Kit (NDK), with a Java Native Method Invocation (JNI) layer to support Java applications. Therefore, native Java applications are able to use the full capabilities of DisService. On non-android devices, DisService also supports C++ and C# applications by means of a proxy layer.

4.3.1 Message Propagation Service

This service provides two capabilities for efficient use of bandwidth: message consolidation and piggybacking. The first capability allows DisService to send multiple individual messages that are automatically consolidated into network packets in order to minimize the number of packets injected into the network. The consolidation capability allows DisService to include a delay tolerance in each message transmission request. This specifies how long the message should be kept in order to consolidate it with other messages. In addition, message consolidation allows DisService to send multiple, small messages without having to worry about the number of packets being generated. This is particularly important for some packet rate limited radios.

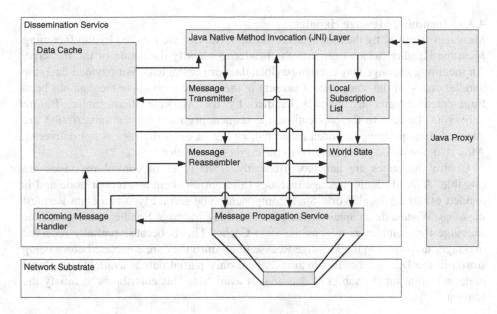

Fig. 2. Architecture of DisService

4.3.2 Data Cache

The design choice for DisService is to aggressively cache data on every node, limited only by the local storage capacity. Therefore, any data that has been previously pushed or received by a node is held in the Data Cache. This allows the node to readily provide the data both to local applications as well as any peer nodes that need the data. The current implementation of the Data Cache uses the SQLite library [15], a public domain embeddable SQL database library. The Data Cache can be configured to suit application requirements. For example, for the live multicast streaming scenario described in section 2.1, the Data Cache only needs to hold as many packets as the overall streaming buffer size. However, each of the subsequent scenarios described require more and more caching of data.

Expiration of data is controlled via an Expiration Controller that can take into account different policies for expiration, based on the group, sender, last request time, and potentially other parameters for selecting data to expire.

4.3.3 Message Transmitter

The Message Transmitter handles fragmentation of large messages and controls the bandwidth utilization of outgoing traffic. Messages that are larger than the Maximum Transmission Unit (MTU) are automatically fragmented. Each message contains a header that identifies the portion of the data contained in the message. Messages that are transmitted may be rate-limited in order to not overload the network. When multiple messages are awaiting transmission, the message priority is used to determine the transmission order.

4.3.4 Incoming Message Handler

Messages received by the Message Propagation Service are handled by the Incoming Message Handler, which examines the header to identify the nature of the message. An incoming message may contain payload data or control data. For payload data, the handler checks if the whole data is present in the current message or the data has been fragmented. Fragmented data is handled by the Message Reassembler. Before delivering the data to the application, the sequencing rules for the subscription are checked. If sequencing has been requested, an out of order message is not delivered. After that, the message is delivered to the correct applications.

Control messages are handled differently. Two types of control messages are possible. A World State message includes information about a neighbor node and is handed off to the local World State component. The second type is a Data Request message. When a data request arrives, the Incoming Message Handler checks both the Message Reassembler as well as the Data Cache. This is because partially received messages are stored in the Message Reassembler until they are complete before being stored in the Data Cache. In situations where only partial data is available, the local node will transmit the subset of data that is available. This contributes to satisfy the request.

4.3.5 Message Reassembler

This component takes incoming data fragments and reassembles them in the correct order. If reliable delivery has been requested by the subscribing application, the Message Reassembler identifies missing fragments, requests them from other nodes, and performs the reassembly procedure when all the missing fragments have been received. If an application has subscribed to the group with a request for sequenced delivery, two possibilities exist. If reliability is requested too, messages received out of order are buffered until the missing messages are received and then delivered in order to the application. If no reliability is requested, old messages that are received later are simply dropped. That is, delivery of a message with sequence number n ensures that no message prior to sequence number n will ever be delivered. The Message Reassembler periodically checks for missing messages or messages that have missing fragments and sends out a request to the peers for retransmission of the missing fragments.

4.3.6 World State

The World State maintains the best known information about the state of other nodes in the network, including the messages that they contain. Given the distributed nature of the system, this information might not be accurate and up to date. Each node maintains its own view of the world in the local World State component. As part of the World State, each node maintains information about local neighbors and their subscriptions, as well as all known remote nodes. The information held for a remote node includes the distance to the remote node (in terms of the number of network hops), the path to the remote node, and the lowest link capacity, which limits the overall bandwidth available to that node. A sequence number is attached to each World State, which is incremented at every change to the World State. Periodically each node will broadcast its presence and the sequence number of its World State. This broadcast is received by all the peer nodes, which may request the complete World State if the node is new or if the sequence number has been updated. This reduces unnecessary transmissions of the World State.

4.4   Unique Features of DisService

The DisService design and implementation incorporate four unique features that are described in this section.

4.4.1 Self-describing and Self-contained Packets

DisService includes sufficient metadata in each packet transmitted on the network in order to allow any node receiving an individual packet to be able to interpret the packet correctly. In particular, each packet contains the identity of the sender, the group context for the message, the unique message sequence number for the message (unique from the perspective of a sender in a group), as well as the offset and length of the packet payload in the context of the message. This metadata allows any peer node in the network to receive and cache packets, and be able to respond to missing fragment requests from other peers.

4.4.2 Aggressive Broadcasting and Caching of Data

As described earlier, DisService always transmits data by broadcasting (or multicasting) the data, and aggressively caching the data on any node that happens to receive it. Combining this capability with the above notion of self-describing packets allows DisService to realize the notion of cooperative networking as described in this paper. Data that is cached is stored in the SQLite database, which is used to realize the data cache inside of DisService.

4.4.3 Neighbor Dependent Probabilistic Response Model

An important aspect of DisService is that a request for data may be received by multiple peers, which act independently from each other. In such cases, the receiver may get multiple responses for the same data request, wasting network capacity. In order to reduce this duplicated traffic, the probability of a node responding to a request is computed based on the number of neighbors of the requesting node. Each node maintains the number of its neighbors. When a node transmits a request for data, the request is received by all the neighbors. All of them potentially reply and transmit duplicate copies of the data. To avoid this, the requesting node includes its neighbor number, in the data request. Each node will then transmit with a probability that is the inverse of the number of neighbors. It is also possible that some nodes don't have the data sought. For instance, if just one neighbor has the data, the requesting node may not receive the data sought, due to the nature of the probabilistic response model. To alleviate this situation, when a node sees a repeated request for data, the probability measure is ignored and the requested data is always transmitted.

4.4.4 Reliable Reception Instead of Reliable Transmission

When reliable data transmission is desired, traditional network protocols such as TCP rely on the sender to ensure that the data being transmitted is received by the recipient. The DisService model differs significantly from the point-to-point model assumed by TCP. The first difference is that communication in DisService is point-to-multipoint: several peer nodes may be recipients of some data transmitted by one node. The second difference is that each recipient may independently request or not request reliable reception of data. The third difference is that the set of nodes that are reachable may change continuously. For instance, if a node is pushing information to another, and the second node moves away and loses network connectivity with the pusher, the TCP model would result in having the pusher node continuously attempting to retransmit data to the receiver. In the DisService model, when the receiver moves away, the pusher node does not care. Eventually, if the receiving node comes in contact again with the original pusher or some other node which has the messages, then the receiver will request and receive the missing messages at that time. Another difference is that the recipient node does not need to go back to the original transmitting node to get the missing information. This is because it may be obtained from any other peer node that has the desired information. This is an effective strategy for reliable delivery, especially when coupled with the design choice to aggressively cache as much data as possible at each node.

5   Experimental Results

The following experimental results show the benefits of cooperative networking with mobile cellular devices. We use a scenario consisting of 10 mobile devices that are receiving data from one transmitter via a cell tower. We use different settings for the reliability of the network link, and report on the number of packets that are received with or without the use of cooperative networking via DisService. Figure 3 below shows the scenario for the experiment.

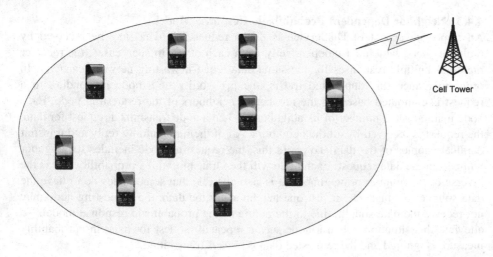

Fig. 3. Cooperative Networking Experiment Scenario

The experiment has been setup on the NOMADS Testbed, which emulates mobile ad-hoc networks and wireless links. The testbed allows control of the capacity, reliability, and latency of each individual network link in the network being emulated.

We set the capacity of the link between the cell tower and the mobile nodes to 256 Kbps, while the mobile nodes are connected in a full topology with links of 1 Mbps of capacity. The reliability of the cellular link varies from 70% to 80% in the first case, and from 30% to 50% in the second case. The results, in Table 1, show how the capacity to retrieve messages from cooperating peers benefits the performances in terms of number of delivered messages. Furthermore, as expected, the results show that the improvement is higher when the reliability of the cellular link is lower.

It is important to note that when a link reliability is set to a certain value (e.g., 70%), the implication is that the independent probability of a packet being delivered correctly to each node is 70%. Hence, when a specific packet is sent to the set of six nodes, the probability of at least one of the nodes receiving the packet and sharing it with the other nodes over the peer-to-peer link is high.

Table 1. Performance Improvement of Packets Received with DisService

Cellular Link Reliability	P2P Network Reliability	Packets Sent	Packets Rcvd		Success Rate	
			Multicast	DisService	Multicast	DisService
70% to 80%	80%	1293	976.0	1293.0	75.48%	100.00%
30% to 50%	80%	1305	546.6	1297.1	41.89%	99.39%

As described earlier, one of the benefits of cooperative networking is to save bandwidth by transmitting less Forward Error Correction (FEC) data. Using NORM [8], we sent a data stream of 800 KB in total to each of the 10 mobile nodes. We set the cellular link quality to 70%, and measured the number of nodes that successfully received the complete stream intact, with varying amounts of FEC data. Note that in the case of DisService above, all 10 nodes successfully received the complete stream.

The results, shown in Table 2, indicate that in order for all 10 nodes to receive the complete stream, NORM must be configured to use 48 FEC blocks per 64 blocks of real data (i.e., an FEC overhead of 75% and a total measured overhead of 94%). This extra bandwidth could be used for transmitting other useful data, or be used to improve the quality of the stream, such as increased resolution. As the results indicate, using cooperative networking significantly reduces the bandwidth requirements on the cellular network while at the same time improving the reliability of the data delivered.

Table 2. Forward Error Correction Performance in NORM

FEC Blocs per 64 Data Blocks	Stream Size (Bytes)	Total Bytes Transmitted	Nodes Successfully Receiving Stream	FEC Overhead	Total Overhead
16	811008	1102640	0	25.00%	35.96%
32	811008	1339760	4	50.00%	65.20%
36	811008	1399040	8	56.25%	72.51%
40	811008	1458254	9	62.50%	79.81%
48	811008	1576484	10	75.00%	94.39%

6   Challenges for Cooperative Networking

Security is one of the primary challenges raised by cooperative networking as suggested in this paper. In particular, a user may be concerned with a peer user maliciously modifying the content of a packet that is being forwarded through another peer. To some extent, such a problem occurs with other peer-to-peer protocols such as BitTorrent [16] as well. BitTorrent addresses the tampering problem by using checksums. Each block of data has an independent checksum that is included in the original meta information that is downloaded by each peer. DisService can also implement a checksum scheme. Since the data is being continuously streamed from a central location, an effective approach is to using a rolling checksum, which computes a checksum over the last x packets. For example, if x is set to 6, packet n would contain cumulative checksums for packets n-5, n-4, n-3, n-2, n-1, and n. Such a checksum mechanism would allow a peer to receive and validate missing packets from other peers. As long as the rolling checksum did not exceed the buffer window size, each node can validate the packets prior to attempting to consume them (e.g., by trying to decode the multimedia stream).

A second challenge raised by cooperative networking is resource utilization of the peers. For example, mobile devices would have to activate their WiFi interfaces in addition to their cellular interfaces, which could consume additional power. This is a tradeoff between improved reliability, lower bandwidth utilization over the cellular link, and increased battery utilization of the mobile devices.

A third challenge is being able to setup the mobile devices to use WiFi networks in Ad-hoc mode. For example, a current limitation in the Android operating system prevents many handsets from creating ad-hoc peer-to-peer networks between themselves. A workaround is to have another node (e.g., a PC) create the ad-hoc network, and have the mobile nodes join the ad-hoc network. Another possibility is to use base stations to create the WiFi networks.

7   Future Work

Much work remains to be done to further explore and exploit the notion of cooperative networking for mobile devices. We are currently enhancing the DisService-based solution to also address the other three scenarios mentioned in this paper. We are also integration DisService into an Android-based application to show video, either streaming, or archived (e.g., from YouTube®). Finally, we are conducting additional experiments to measure the advantages of cooperating networks under different network conditions.

Acknowledgements. This research was sponsored in part by the U.S. Army Research Laboratory under Cooperative Agreement W911NF-04-2-0013.

References

1. Padmanabhan, P., Gruenwald, L., Vallur, A., Atiquzzaman, M.: A survey of data replication techniques for mobile ad hoc network databases. VLDB Journal 17(5), 1143–1164 (2008)
2. Derhab, A., Badache, N.: Data Replication Protocols for Mobile Ad-Hoc Networks: A Survey and Taxonomy. IEEE Communications Surveys & Tutorial 11(2) (Second Quarter, 2009)
3. Hara, T.: Data Replication for Improving Data Accessibility in Ad Hoc Networks. IEEE Transaction on Mobile Computing 5(11) (November 2006)
4. Wang, K., Li, B.: Efficient and guaranteed service coverage in partitionable mobile ad hoc networks. In: 21st Annual Joint Conference of the IEEE Computer and Communications Societies (INFOCOM 2002), vol. 2, pp. 1089–1098 (2002)
5. Thanedar, V., Almeroth, K.C., Belding-Royer, E.M.: A Lightweight Content Replication Scheme for Mobile Ad Hoc Environments. In: Mitrou, N.M., Kontovasilis, K., Rouskas, G.N., Iliadis, I., Merakos, L. (eds.) NETWORKING 2004. LNCS, vol. 3042, pp. 125–136. Springer, Heidelberg (2004)
6. Murphy, A.L., Picco, G.P.: Using LIME to Support Replication for Availability in Mobile Ad Hoc Networks. In: Ciancarini, P., Wiklicky, H. (eds.) COORDINATION 2006. LNCS, vol. 4038, pp. 194–211. Springer, Heidelberg (2006)
7. Bellavista, P., Corradi, A., Magistretti, E.: REDMAN: An optimistic replication middleware for read-only resources in dense MANETs. Pervasive and Mobile Computing 1(3), 279–310 (2005)
8. Adamson, B., Bormann, C., Handley, M., Macker, J.: NACK-Oriented Reliable Multicast (NORM) Transport Protocol. IETF Request For Comments 5740 (November 2009)
9. Speakman, T., Crowcroft, J., Gemmell, J., Farinacci, D., Lin, S., Leshchiner, D., Luby, M., Montgomery, T., Rizzo, L., Tweedly, A., Bhaskar, N., Edmonstone, R., Sumanasekera, R., Vicisano, L.: PGM Reliable Transport Protocol Specification. IETF Request For Comments 3208 (December 2001)
10. Zyba, G., Voelker, G., Ioannidis, S., Diot, C.: Dissemination in Opportunistic Mobile Ad-hoc Networks: the Power of the Crowd
11. Hui, P., Crowcroft, J., Yoneki, E.: BUBBLE Rap: Social-based Forwarding in Delay Tolerant Networks. In: MobiHoc (2008)
12. Mtibaa, A., May, M., Diot, C., Ammar, M.: PeopleRank: Social Opportunistic Forwarding. In: INFOCOM Mini Conference (2010)
13. Hossmann, T., Spyropoulos, T., Legendre, F.: Know Thy Neighbor: Towards Optimal Mapping of Contacts to Social Graphs for DTN Routing. In: INFOCOM (2010)
14. Daly, E.M., Haahr, M.: Social Network Analysis for Routing in Disconnected Delay-Tolerant MANETs. In: MobiHoc (2007)
15. SQLite Relational Database Library. Online Reference, http://sqlite.org/
16. BitTorrent Protocol Specification. Online Reference, http://www.bittorrent.org/beps/bep_003.html

PSD: One-to-Many Routing Protocol for Publish/Subscribe Applications in DTN

Feng Hong, Chunlei Guo, Xiqing Zhang, Zhongwen Guo, and Yuan Feng

Department of Computer Science and Technology, Ocean University of China
{hongfeng,guozhw,fengyuan}@ouc.edu.cn,
{guochunlei.ouc,xiqingzhang.ouc}@gmail.com

Abstract. More and more applications appear in delay tolerant networks (DTN) with the popularity of mobile devices such as smart phones and PDAs. The one-to-many routing nature of Publish/Subscribe applications brings new challenges to DTN routing design. This paper proposes a one-to-many routing protocol (PSD) for Publish/Subscribe applications in DTN, which combines two one-to-one routing protocols of Spray&Wait and epidemic routing. Simulations confirm that PSD can achieve high delivery rate, low latency and low cost.

Keywords: DTN, publish, subscribe, routing, one-to-many.

1 Introduction

With Bluetooth and WiFi technology widely exploited today, mobile devices such as smart phones and PDAs can easily form networks to exchange information or share data [1]. Such kind of networks are feature of that there may not exist a complete message routing path between source and destination, for the links between nodes aren't always connected, which is called delay tolerate network (DTN) [2].

DTN brings more and more new applications to our daily lives. For example, shopping centers, fast food restaurants and cinemas, etc. want to advertise their product information to the public. People who are interested in such news may hope to receive them periodically by their mobile devices. However, such kind of publish/subscribe (Pub/Sub) applications bring new challenges in DTN environment.

Pub/Sub problems in DTN need to consider performance metrics of delivery rate, delay, and cost. Firstly, users always need to receive the subscribed news in certain time interval, so the message delivery rate should be high and the delivery latency should be limited by the timeliness of the news. And communication power consumption is one major concern for handheld devices, which requires the news dissemination to limit the number of rely times.

Most previous researches in Pub/Sub system are implemented under the assumption that there is a complete path between source and destination. Relay node forwards the message to next hop without storing the message. In DTN, the node may carry the

N. Venkatasubramanian et al. (Eds.): Mobilware 2011, LNICST 93, pp. 98–106, 2012.
© Institute for Computer Sciences, Social Informatics and Telecommunications Engineering 2012

message when no links around itself can be used to transmit it. As a result, traditional Pub/Sub routing algorithm cannot completely meet the requirement in DTN environment.

DTN routing strategy based on replication usually injects a number of copies into the network, where any copy reaching the destination represents a successful delivery. The core of such a mechanism is to determine an optimum number of injected copies. The easiest way is direct transmission [3], where the source node keeps the message until it encounters the destination node, which will not add additional overhead, but the delivery latency is high and the delivery rate is low. Conversely, epidemic routing [8] increases the number of copies to ensure delivery rate and latency, in which the message will be copied to all its neighbors when the message holding node encounters other nodes without that message. Redundant messages will be largely increased in epidemic routing. It is important to limit the times of transitions or the number of copies in performance optimization. Spray&Wait routing [5] injects a fixed predefined number of copies into the network. In each encounter, the node holding messages will assign half of the tasks to the meeting node. In such routing, fundamental metrics like message delivery ratio, goodput, and end-to-end delay are greater than routings introduced above, which causes wide attention of scholars. However, all the DTN routing protocol only focus on one to one message delivery problem. Previous DTN routing protocols [6-7] cannot fully comply with Pub/Sub application demand, which is one-to-many routing as its nature. We propose a routing strategy called PSD for Pub/Sub problem in DTN, which aims to achieve the tradeoff between deliver rate, latency and cost. The core of PSD is to combine Spray&Wait routing and epidemic routing together to fulfill the target of one to many message dissemination in DTN.

In PSD, publication sources will inject certain number of copies of current news into the network according to the number of subscribers. The routing process of such messages is mostly conducted under the protocol of Spray&Wait. However, subscribers and helpers (non-subscribers satisfying some condition) will operate in limited epidemic transmission style for its last copy of current news. By integration of Spay&Wait and epidemic transmission, PSD achieves flexibility in solving one to many routing problem of Pub/Sub in DTN.

The contributions of this paper are: (1) we propose a new routing protocol of PSD, which solves one to many routing problem for Pub/Sub applications in DTN; (2) Extensive simulations confirms performance of PSD on delivery, rate latency and cost.

The rest of the paper is organized as follows. Section 2 presents the design of PSD. Section 3 discusses the simulation results in details. Section 4 concludes this paper.

2   Design of PSD

In this section, we first review the design of Spray&Wait routing protocol in Section 2.1, which is the basis of PSD. Section 2.2 presents the core design of PSD, which focuses on illustration of difference between PSD and Spray&Wait. Section 2.3 gives an example of PSD routing scenario.

2.1   Introduction on Spray&Wait

In Spray&Wait routing [5], the number of message copies is determined by the source node. This protocol contains two components in message routing process: Spray stage and Wait stage. At Spray stage, when one node carrying news encounters another node that hasn't cached this news, it will relay this news to that node and gives it half of the copies. Then half number of copies will be further relayed by that node. When there is only one copy left, the node will go into Wait stage. The node in Wait stage will hold the news until the target node appears, and deliver the message to the target node, which finishes the delivery process of this news.

Spray&Wait routing can achieve the balance of delivery rate and cost in one-to-one routing. PSD scheme is to improve Spray&Wait routing to fulfill one-to-many routing nature of Pub/Sub applications, containing three major differences which will be discussed in details in next section.

2.2   Core Design of PSD

In Pub/Sub applications, there will be many nodes who subscribe to the same source. The number of the subscribers is dynamically changed over time. The target of Pub/Sub applications is to make sure that all subscribers can receive the news published from the source before such kind of news messages loses its effectiveness. Therefore, for Pub/Sub applications the success delivery contains a time limit in its nature, which shows delivery latency should also be taken into consideration.

As mentioned above, Spray&Wait routing protocol aims to deliver one copy of message from one source to one target. The source injects predefined number of copies into the network to ensure certain deliver rate of that message. The first difference between PSD and Spray&Wait routing is that the number of copies injected by the source is determined according to the number of subscribers in PSD, not like according to the target delivery rate in Spray&Wait routing. We will show that there is no need for the copy number of published message to be higher than the number of subscribers in the simulation section, which helps in limiting the delivery cost and still keeps certain delivery rate.

It may be questioned how every subscriber can get one copy of the news message, if the copy number of that message is lower than the subscriber injected by the source. The answer lies in the second difference between PSD and Spray&Wait. PSD changes the method of direct transmission of Spray&Wait routing in Wait phase, which exploits limited epidemic routing in that phase. The word "limited" is to illustrate that such kind of epidemic transmission does not happen between any nodes in Wait phase. Only when one subscriber holding one copy of published news meeting another subscriber without that message, the epidemic transmission happens, where the holding one will create one more copy and transfer that copy to another subscriber. So with this limited epidemic routing, the copy number can be increased in the transmission process.

However, there is still one more problem how PSD can keeps the delivery rate and latency requirement of Pub/Sub applications, if the number of subscribers is very low. The answer lies in the third change of PSD to Spray&Wait routing. PSD introduce a new role of "helper" for non-subscribers in Pub/Sub applications that some non-subscribers will operate in limited epidemic routing mode like the subscribers under two conditions. The first condition is that the non-subscriber only holds one copy of published news message; otherwise, it can directly transmit half number of its copies to the subscriber according to Spray&Wait routing rule. The second condition is the density of subscribers. Nonsubscribers record the recent T encounters to estimate the density of subscribers. If the proportion of subscribers in T encounters is less than a certain rate, the node changes its status to be a helper; on the contrary, if more than that rate, the node will change its helper role back to ordinary non-subscriber role. The appropriate rate plays an important role in keeping the delivery rate and latency, which will be carefully evaluated through simulations.

As a conclusion, PSD is a one-to-many routing protocol, which combines Spray&Wait and epidemic routing to fulfill Pub/Sub applications. Epidemic routing only happens on certain subscribers and helpers in order to increase the copy number in message delivery process. With such kind of epidemic routing, the source can inject certain number of copies only according to subscribers' number.

2.3   Example of PSD

In order to illustrate PSD clearly, we give an example in Fig. 1 to describe the operating scenario of PSD. Figure 1 shows a snapshot of a Pub/Sub application in a DTN system.

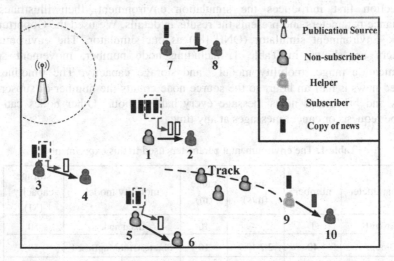

Fig. 1. Example of PSD operating process. Rectangles represent copies conducted by the publication, the black ones is original copies; the red ones represent the copies conducted by helpers or subscribers; while, the white is the original black ones being transferred.

In PSD, mobile nodes may send request message to subscribe interesting news at any time, which is labeled as blue person in Fig. 1. The subscribe message will be transferred through one-to-one routing protocol like Spray&Wait. After sending out the subscribe message, such node changes into a subscriber labeled as red person in Fig. 1. And subscribers can send quit message to cancel the current subscription at any time. When it sends out quit message, it will turn into nonsubscriber again.

The publication source creates new message periodically. Certain number of news copies will be injected into the network through Spray&Wait protocol when there are some nodes passing by. The initial number of news copies is determined according to the count subscriber number on publication source. Figure 1 shows the publication source still has 8 copies of the current news to be transferred through Spray&Wait protocol.

When some node holding more than one copy of the current news, it will transfer half of copies through Spray&Wait protocol. As shown in Fig. 1, the copies transferring between node 1 and node 2, node 3 and node 4, node5 and node 6 belong to Spray&Wait protocol.

Limited epidemic transmission happens when a subscriber carrying one copy or a helper meets another subscriber. The transferring between node 7 and node 8 in Fig. 1 shows the epidemic transmission between two subscribers. Node 9 is a nonsubscriber with the last copy of current news, which changes into helper (labeled in yellow) after meeting several nonsubscribers. Node 9 will conduct epidemic transmission when it meet node 10, which is another subscriber.

3   Simulations

This section first introduces the simulation environment, then illustrates the performance parameters and presents the results in details. We used the Opportunistic Network Environment simulator (ONE [8]) as our simulator. The environmental parameters are shown in Table 1, including node number, movement speed, communication range, mobility model, and storage capacity. The timeliness of published news is half an hour, so the source node counts the number of subscribing requests and broadcasts news message every half an hour. Other nodes can send subscribe requests or cancel messages at any time.

Table 1. The environmental parameters used in this experiment

parameter	number	speed (m/s)	range (m)	mobility model	storage capacity (M)
Group1	1	--	10	fixed node	50
Group2	40	2.7-13.9	10	ShortestPathMapBased	50
Group3	40	7.0-9.0	10	ShortestPathMapBased	50
Group4	41	7.0-10.0	10	MapRoute(tram3.wkt)	50
Group5	2	7.0-10.0	10	MapRoute(tram4.wkt)	50
Group6	2	7.0-10.0	10	MapRoute(tram10.wkt)	50
Group7	50	8.0-10.0	10	MapRoute(tram10.wkt)	50
Group8	75	6.0-8.0	10	ShortestPathMapBased	50

We introduce several labels in the simulations. S represents the number of subscribers which the source has counted in current time. L is the initial value of news copies that will be injected into the network by the source. T represents the encounter number of unsubscribe nodes in order to determine the density of subscribers in the network. Subscriber rate (SR) is the threshold for the unsubscribed node to change to helper. If one unsubscribed node holding only one copy of some news find that the proportion of subscribers met in T encounters is low than SR, it will make a conclusion that the density of subscribers on such news is too low and change itself into "helper" role. We repeat the simulations by using different values of above four parameters to evaluate the performance of PSD.

In our simulations, four metrics are evaluated and defined as following:

Delivery rate (DR): DR is defined as the proportion of subscribers that successfully received the news in current timeliness of that message.

Average Latency (LA): LA is defined as the average latency of all news messages successfully delivered. We count it in seconds.

Cost: Cost is defined as the ratio of the message relayed to the message successfully received by the subscribers.

DR/Cost (DRC): DRC is defined as the ratio of DR to Cost, which represents the tradeoff between delivery rate and cost.

For the first simulation scenario, we chose T=15 to statistic the proportion of subscribers. We set L/S= 20%, 25%, 33.3%, 50%, 100% and conduct five groups of experiments. In each group, we further chose different SR values as 0%, 10%, 20%, 30%, and 40%. We compare the performance results with original Spray&Wait protocol in Fig. 2, which shows all the results of PSD are better than Spray&Wait routing.

Figure 2(a) illustrates the results on delivery rate, which first shows that high threshold of subscriber rate leads to high delivery rate. Because more unsubscribed nodes will become helpers when the subscriber rate is high, the actions of limited epidemic routing between helpers and subscribers will increase. And the delivery rate has not clear increase when the subscriber rate is higher than 20%. For the same value of subscriber rate, larger L/S value, larger delivery rate. This is directly benefited from more copies injected into the network.

Figure 2(b) shows the results on cost. It shows that the cost gets larger when the subscriber rate gets larger. This conclusion is somehow not intuitive. The key is the action of limited epidemic transmission of helpers, which only happens when a helper meets a subscriber. All such limited epidemic transmissions are effective actions, which will help in decreasing cost. If the subscriber rate is very high, e.g. 100%, every unsubscribed node will become helpers, which will surely help decrease cost, but will cost the cache space of such nodes. And the cost has not clear decrease, when SR is over 20%, there is no need to further increase SR. Figure 1(b) also shows that large L/S leads to high cost.

Figure 2(c) shows the results on average delivery latency. It shows that the latency gets lower when the subscriber rate gets larger or L/S gets larger. As the timeliness of the news is of 30 minutes, all the average latency values are lower than that value. So in our simulations, every result keeps the timeliness. Moreover, SR=20%, it is still an inflection point for average latency.

In Fig. 2(c), we can calculate that the difference between maximum and minimum on average latency is about 300s, no more than 5 minutes; therefore, we focus on the ratio of delivery rate to cost in Fig. 2(d). It shows CDR of L/S=50% is higher than other L/S values, so L/S=50% achieves better tradeoff of delivery rate and cost. Moreover, CDR gets its maximum value for L/S =50%, when SR=20% in our simulation environment.

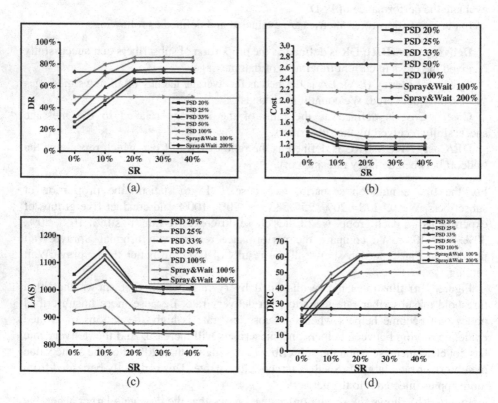

Fig. 2. Simulation results of five groups on different values of SR and L/S (a) delivery rate (b) cost (c) latency (d)delivery rate/cost (the percent number in legend presenting the value of L/S)

In another simulation, we evaluate the impact of parameter T. We compare two groups (T=15 and T=20) with Spray&Wait routing. In Spray&Wait routing, we let the initial value L of news copies to be one and two times of the subscriber number. The result is shown as in Fig. 3. No matter L/S=100% or 200%, the performance in Spray&Wait routing is far lower than PSD. And the result difference between two T values is not that clear, especially when subscriber rate is over 20%. So we can conclude that the encounter interval T has little impact on the performance of PSD.

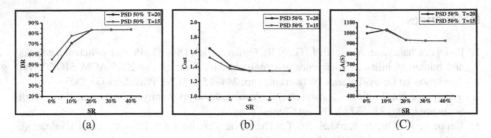

Fig. 3. Results of PSD on T=15 and T=20(L/S=50%) (a)delivery rate (b)cost(c)latency

We further evaluate the impact of subscriber quantity under the best configuration of L/S=50% and SR=20%. Fig. 4 depicts that the delivery rate, average latency and cost almost are the same under different proportions of subscribers. X axis presents the proportion of subscribers to all nodes in the system, labeled as SP (subscriber proportion).This kind of stability comes from the impact of limited epidemic transmission of helpers, which make up to the quantity of such routing only between subscribers. This confirms the feasibility of PSD: the performance stays stable, no matter how many subscribers there are.

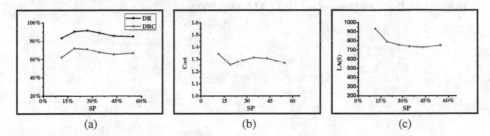

Fig. 4. Simulation results of CD, CDR, Cost and LA on different proportions of subscribers

4 Conclusion

Pub/Sub applications bring new challenges to DTN routing design. Traditional one-to-one routing protocol cannot solve Pub/Sub problem efficiently. This paper proposed the combination of Spray&Wait and Epidemic routing to solve one-to-many routing problem of Pub/Sub applications in DTN. The simulation results confirm that the proposed PSD protocol achieves better performance in delivery rate, cost and latency than Spray&Wait and can realize the tradeoff between delivery rate, cost and latency in Pub/Sub applications.

Acknowledgement. This research is partially supported by NSF program of China under granted number of 60933011, and Teaching and Research program of Ocean University of China under granted number of 2009JY10.

References

1. Pan, H., Chaintreau, A., Scott, J., Gass, R., Crowcroft, J., Diot, C.: Pocket switched networks and human mobility in conference environments. In: Proc. of the 2005 ACM SIGCOMM Workshop on Delay-Tolerant Networking, pp. 244–251. ACM, Philadelphia (2005)
2. Yongping, X., Limin, S., Jianwei, N., Yan, L.J.: Opportunity to network. Journal of Software (20), 124–137 (2009) (in Chinese)
3. Keranen, A., Ott, J., Karkkainen, T.: The ONE Simulator for DTN Protocol Evaluation, http://www.netlab.tkk.fi/tutkimus/dtn/theone/
4. Becker, V.D.: Epidemic routing for partially connected ad hoc networks. Technique Report, CS-2000-06, Department of Computer Science, Duke University, Durham, NC (2000)
5. Spyropoulos, T., Psounis, K., Raghavendra, C.S.: Spray and wait: An efficient routing scheme for intermittently connected mobile networks. In: Proc. of the 2005 ACM SIGCOMM Workshop on Delay-Tolerant Networking, pp. 252–259. ACM, Philadelphia (2005)
6. Nelson, S.C., Mehedi, B., Robin, K.: Encounter-Based Routing in DTNs. In: Proc. IEEE INFORM 2009 (April 2009)
7. Binbin, C., Munchoon, C.: MobTorrent: A Framework for Mobile Internet Access from Vehicles. In: Proc. IEEE INFOCOM 2009 (2009)
8. Grossglauser, M.: Tse DNC. Mobility increases the capacity of ad hoc wireless networks. IEEE/ACM Trans. on Networking 10(4), 477–486 (2002)

Satcom Access in the Evolved Packet Core

Mirko Cano, Toon Norp, and Mariya Popova

TNO (Netherlands Organization for Applied Scientific Research),
Brassersplein 2 2612 CT Delft, The Netherlands
{Mirko.Cano,Toon.Norp,Mariya.Popova}@tno.nl

Abstract. Satellite communications (Satcom) networks are increasingly integrating with terrestrial communications networks, namely Next Generation Networks (NGN). In the area of NGN the Evolved Packet Core (EPC) is a new network architecture that can support multiple access technologies. When Satcom is considered as another access technology, EPC can provide the multiple access features and to integrate Satcom and NGN services. The current paper outlines the opportunities for NGN and Satcom integration, focusing on the mobility issues between EPC and DVB-RCS standards (representing the Satcom network) under a common Mobile IP based EPC core network.

Keywords: Next Generation Networks, Evolved Packet Core, Satellite communications, DVB-RCS, Mobile IP.

1   Introduction

Satellite communications (Satcom) are emerging in the broadband access market. The development of standards like DVB-RCS [1], that were initially intended for broadcast applications, have expanded the satellite communications market towards more interactive applications such as the Internet access in remote areas or the back up network for disaster scenarios.

There is a general trend in satellite communication to move away from Satcom specific stove-pipe architectures (e.g. Satcom access combined with Satcom specific core network and service architectures) to an integration of Satcom access with Next Generation Networks architectures. Within the concept of a Next Generation Network, the Satcom access will become one of the available access technologies; next to fixed, cellular and wireless access network technologies.

In the area of Next Generation Mobile Networks there is a new network architecture that can support multiple access technologies: the Evolved Packet Core (EPC) network [2]. The EPC is developed by 3GPP as the core network for the new LTE radio interface, but it also supports other access technologies like WiMAX, WLAN, and CDMA.

There are two versions of the EPC. One version is based on GPRS mobility management and is geared to mobility between LTE, UMTS and GSM. The other version is based on Mobile IP [3] technology and is more suited for mobility between LTE/UMTS and access network technologies like WLAN and WiMAX. Integration of Satcom with EPC is a logical extension of the two above trends.

N. Venkatasubramanian et al. (Eds.): Mobilware 2011, LNICST 93, pp. 107–118, 2012.

This paper focuses on how mobility would be supported across a DVB-RCS Satcom and a terrestrial access network, through a common Mobile IP based EPC core network.

2   Scenario

Alfred, who is travelling with his mobile phone in a cruise in the Mediterranean, would like to use his mobile phone for both voice and data services during his trip. Luckily his mobile network operator has an integrated satellite network or has an agreement with a satellite network provider that ensures the continuity of their services.

The mobile phone can connect to both the 4G network (LTE) and WLAN networks, depending on the coverage. When the cellular network coverage is lost, the mobile phone has the capability to switch to WLAN automatically if this network is available.

Alfred embarks the ship and when the ship leaves the port, there is a point when there is no more terrestrial network coverage. Inside the ship there is a WLAN that has access to land based telephony networks and Internet, thanks to the satellite connection. Alfred can make and receive phone calls when connected to the WLAN of the ship. He can also browse the Internet; his user experience is not affected by the change of access technology.

When the ship reaches the cellular coverage again, the mobile phone switches back to the terrestrial cellular network.

Although current technologies allow the mobile phone to switch from/to WLAN under 3G coverage, it is still to be studied how to combine the new EPC network with the satellite network in scenarios like this.

In the remainder of this paper, the feasibility of an implementation of the above scenario will be examined.

3   Technical Overview

3.1   DVB-RCS/C2P/Satellite Networks

Satellite Networks are widely used for commercial and governmental applications. The currently deployed satellites generally do not have any on-board digital processing, and the ground terminal basically uses the satellite to reflect its transmission to the coverage area (beam). Traditionally, the beam covers both the destination and also the transmitting terminal (single beam).

In other words, these satellites are classified as *transparent satellites*; they are either a bent-pipe satellite or a satellite that is able to perform physical layer switching without demodulation of the signal. *Regenerative satellite* is the term for satellites that include an on board processor, involving demodulation and capability of processing the data stream.

Within this paper, the role of the satellite is only to transmit the signal (i.e. a transparent satellite), since on board processors are not yet widely deployed and it is still unclear to what extend it will be deployed in the future.

As a representative of Satcom communications in this paper we chose DVB-RCS [1]. DVB-RCS is currently in the scope of the main activities of the European Space Agency (ESA) and standardization bodies such as ETSI with regards to the integration of Satcom and NGN, including the work towards the next DVB-RCS2 version of the standard. Also the DVB-RCS standard, together with the C2P protocol [4], provide the functionalities that are needed to bring further the topic of the satellite and terrestrial interworking.

DVB-RCS was recently updated with the DVB-RCS+M version, which provides support for a variety of types of terminals including mobile and nomadic terminals. In addition to this, it provides enhanced support for direct terminal-to-terminal communication (mesh connectivity).

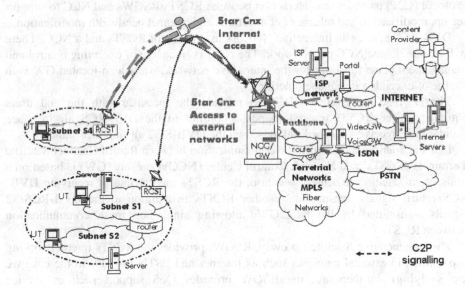

Fig. 1. Star Transparent Network Reference Scenario [4]

In DVB-RCS, any terminal can directly communicate with a specific hub (e.g. localised in the terrestrial network) and via the hub to the other terminals (e.g. with other ships, trains and so on). The management of the satellite connection is realized via (see Fig. 1):

- **The Network Control Center (NCC)** controls the satellite network, provides session control, routing and resource access to the subscriber RCSTs.
- **The Return Channel Satellite Terminal (RCST)** is the interface between the System and the external users. It can have different equipment attached to it, like a WLAN router.

– **The Regenerative Satellite Gateway (RSGW)** provides interconnection with terrestrial networks (e.g. Internet or in our case EPS). At the same time it manages all its subscribers, guaranteeing their Service Level Agreement. Since it is acting as the interface with the terrestrial sources, it supports Generic Routing Encapsulation[1].

In Fig. 1 we can see the generic view of an Interactive Network (formed by the RCSTs and the NCC), where a star configuration is represented. The NCC/GW can be located anywhere geographically as long as it is within the satellite beam. The RSGW would be located where the NCC is in the figure, acting as a bridge between the Satcom network and the terrestrial network.

The subscriber RCSTs work as routers in front of the final user terminals and provide IP connectivity, QoS, security and multicast facilities.

The connection control requires the usage of a signaling protocol between the satellite terminals and the Network Control Center (NCC). The Connection Control Protocol (C2P) provides this interaction between RCSTs/RSGWs and NCC to support set-up, modification and release of connections and channel bandwidth modification.

DVB-RCS defines an Interactive Network as a group of RCSTs and a NCC. There will be one unique NCC per Network. The NCC is in charge of executing control and management plane functions for the interactive network, while a co-located GW is in charge of executing user plane functions.

The DVB-RCS Terminals (RCSTs) provide the interface with the end users equipment. The RCSTs transmit bursts according to the DVB-RCS air interface standard and receive a forward link based on the DVB-S/S2 air interface standard.

In a star transparent network the communication between Return Channel Satellite Terminals (RCSTs) and Network Control Centre (NCC)/Gateway (GW) is based on a transparent satellite. In a mesh scenario, the RCSTs are capable of receiving DVB-RCS return signals transmitted by other RCSTs in addition to the DVB-RCS/S2 signals transmitted by the NCC/GW, allowing single-hop mesh communication between RCSTs.

The Regenerative Satellite Gateway, RSGW, provides the RCSTs internetworking capabilities to external networks such as Internet and PSTN (or EPS in the case we are studying). Furthermore, the RSGW provides QoS support such as service differentiation, QoS guarantees and traffic shaping.

3.2   The Evolved Packet System

EPS (Evolved Packet System) (see Fig. 2) is the evolution of the current mobile networks. It is formed by a new access radio network, LTE (Long Term Evolution)

---

[1] **Generic Routing Encapsulation** (GRE) is a protocol designed for performing tunneling of a network layer protocol over another network layer protocol (e.g. IP). It can encapsulate a wide variety of network layer protocol packet types inside IP tunnels, creating a virtual point-to-point link to various brands of routers at remote points over an Internet Protocol (IP) internetwork. It is used for example, in EPS mobility.

and a new core network, the EPC (Evolved Packet Core). A main characteristic of this system is that it is all based on IP protocols, removing the dependency on the previous circuit switched networks. The new all-IP network brings about a reduced number of nodes, better capacity and performance, and lower latency. Furthermore, it is backwards compatible, supporting previous mobile technologies (2G, 3G, HSPA).

Another important feature of the EPC is the capability to interwork with other access networks [5]: WiMax, WLAN, et cetera. EPC defines the mobility and connectivity with these systems (based on Mobile IP protocols).

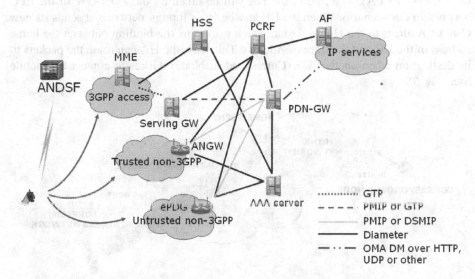

Fig. 2. Evolved Packet Core (EPC) general overview

The PDN-GW is the mobility anchor between 3GPP and non-3GPP accesses. It performs:

- User Equipment IP allocation
- Policy enforcement
- Per user packet filtering
- Charging support
- Lawful interception
- Packet screening.

The UE (User Equipment) can discover new access networks in the vicinity through the ANDSF (Access Network Discovery and Selection Function).

EPC is connected to various access networks through peripheral gateways, referred generically as Access Networks Gateways (ANGWs). They constitute the interface between the access networks and the Evolved Packet Core performing IP address allocation, mobility functions, QoS enforcement functions, et cetera.

4   IP Mobility and the Evolved Packet Core

The basic IP stack does not provide support for mobility. Problems arise when the UE moves and attaches to different networks acquiring different IP addresses, so packets destined to the UE's old IP address will not reach it and get discarded.

Mobile IP protocols [3] provide support for session mobility. With MIP the UE can change its point of attachment while maintaining its IP address for current transport sessions. The Home Agent (HA), in the Home Network, maintains the binding between both the local IP address and the IP address in a foreign network (called Care of Address or CoA). The role of the HA will be taken by the PDN GW of the EPC network in our scenario. When the UE attaches to a foreign network, it sends its new Care of Address to the Home Agent, which maintains the binding between the home address of the UE and the Care of Address. This way, the HA can route the packets to its destination when another UE (Correspondent Node) wishes to contact the mobile user (Fig. 3).

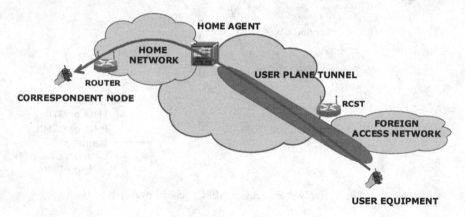

Fig. 3. Mobile IP concept

There are different variants of MIP, but we will focus on two of them: DSMIPv6 (Dual Stack MIP) [6] and PMIPv6 (Proxy MIP)[7], since both are supported by the EPC.

Dual Stack Mobile IP supports both IPv6 and IPv4. Although IPv6 will be introduced gradually, it is expected that IPv4 networks will still be present for some time. In EPC, the philosophy is that IPv6 is mandatory and IPv4 is optional, so it supports both IPv6 and IPv4. The foreign access network can be easily configured to support both IP versions as well. In case that the Satcom network between the home network and the foreign network supports only IPv4, the IPv6 packets from the UE are encapsulated in IPv4 packets. This does not mandate the RCST to support IPv4 since DSMIP can handle both versions of the IP protocol. The requirement that is imposed by DSMIP is that the UE must have an IPv6 Home Address in the EPC network. In case that IPv4 is used throughout all the access networks, EPC can support the use of MIPv4 as well [8]. In MIPv4, the Foreign Agent (FA) is the router that provides mobility services to the UE and where the UE is also registered (in the foreign access network).

Proxy MIPv6 (PMIP) shares a lot of things with MIPv6; the main difference is that it is a network-based mobility protocol, meaning that the UE is released from the mobility procedures and it doesn't need to have any mobility protocol implemented. Another entity, called the Mobility Access Gateway (MAG), acts on behalf of the UE as the Mobile IP client. In our scenario the RCST would perform this role. The Local Mobility Anchor (LMA) maintains the binding between the Home Address of the UE and its current point of attachment (the IP address of the MAG), see Fig. 4. The role of the LMA is very similar to the Home Agent in MIP, and it would also be performed by the PDN GW.

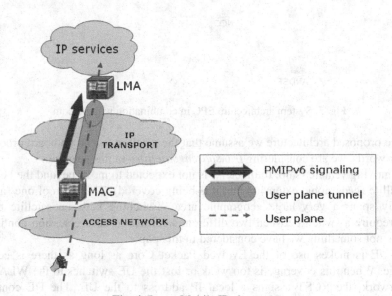

Fig. 4. Proxy Mobile IPv6 concept

The MAG makes sure that the UE gets the same IP address (Home Address) and other IP configuration so that the UE is not aware at IP level that it has changed the network. In order to do this, the LMA establishes a bidirectional user plane tunnel with the MAG. The MAG informs the LMA about its IP address (CoA) when the UE registers into the new network, and gets the information of the Home Address of the UE in response.

PMIPv6 supports dual-stack enhancements, so the foreign access network could be IPv4 only and IPv6 messages would be then encapsulated.

5   Mobility across DVB-RCS and EPC Networks

Fig. 5 depicts the architecture for mobility across the terrestrial network and the Satcom network. The architecture consists of three IP networks interworking with each other, detailed in the following sections.

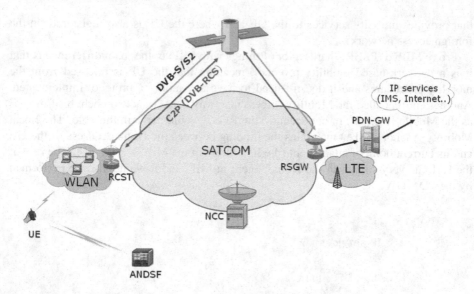

Fig. 5. System architecture EPC in combination with Satcom

In the proposed architecture we assume that the satellite has no on board processor. In other words, we are considering *transparent satellites* in this scenario.

The moving vehicle (ship, train, etc...) is not expected to move beyond the beam of the satellite (geographic extension that it is being covered). The beam of one satellite generally spans a very large geographic area. Switching between satellite beams would require a switch between two different satellites to ensure session continuity, which is not something we have considered in this paper.

The UE is makes use of the Evolved Packet Core as long as there is cellular coverage. When this coverage is too weak or lost the UE switches to the WLAN. In this network, the RCST assigns a local IP address to the UE. The UE continues sending and receiving IP packets, but these are now delivered through the RCST. The RCST encapsulates the packets and sends them through the satellite access network by making use of the DVB-RCS protocol. The DVB-RCS protocol has a return channel that can be used to receive the data destined to the UE.

There are two kinds of mobility to be considered here:

- The mobility of the RCST, which switches from the terrestrial network to the satellite network and back. This mobility is handled with the DSMIPv6 protocol. The PDN GW would keep track of the RCST mobility.
- The mobility of the UE, which switches between the LTE network and the WLAN. This mobility is handled with the PMIPv6 protocol. The RCST would act as a proxy on behalf of the UE, whereas the PDN GW would keep track of the mobility of the UE as well.

Once the packets reach the other end, the RSGW, they are de-capsulated and sent to the PDN-GW. In case that the UE in the WLAN is sending data to another UE in the terrestrial network (Correspondent Node), the PDN-GW makes sure that the packets reach their destination on both sides by keeping the binding between the home IP address and the WLAN IP address of the UE that is moving.

The RCST in the moving LAN acts both as a gateway and as a RCST (endpoint in the satellite network). The RCST receives broadcasts via DVB-S or DVB-S2, and it sends data by using the return channel and the C2P protocol specified in DVB-RCS.

The RSGW acts as the link between the satellite and the terrestrial network. It receives the IP packets from the moving network and forwards them after des-encapsulating, to the PDN GW via the standardized interface S2a (being either DSMIP or PMIP the protocol used). The RSGW works as the Access Gateway in 3GPP terms, serving as the link between both networks. The interface with the PDN GW has to support both DSMIP and PMIP, in order to serve the two kinds of mobility: the RCST mobility in DSMIP and the UE mobility in PMIP.

The interface between the RSGW and the PDN GW (S2a) is based on PMIP. There is also an interface between the UE and the PDN GW based on DSMIP (S2c). These messages have to be encapsulated and delivered through the Satcom network as well.

The PDN Gateway acts as a Home Agent (HA) as specified in MIP, or Local Mobility Agent (LMA) in terms of PMIP, storing the IP Home address of the RCST in the mobile network and its IP assigned by the satellite network (Care of Address). In this way it keeps track of the RCST wherever it is attached. It also stores the IP home address of the UE in order to forward the packets that are sent to the terminal when it is attached to the mobile network.

5.1   The Moving Network (LAN/WLAN)

The issue of a moving network has been widely studied [9], with some of the solutions leading already to the definition of the Mobile IP protocols. Nevertheless, in this case we need to make some new considerations since we have a moving element moving in and out of a moving network.

The means of transportation studied in this scenario, a ship, a train, a car, etc…has implemented a Local Area Network. The UE attaches to this network when the terrestrial network (LTE) is no longer available. This requires from the UE that it has a dual WLAN/LTE mode in order to switch between these networks. The UE switches according to the network conditions (e.g. coverage) or to the policies of the network operator (e.g. "switch from WLAN only when LTE is available" or "switch to WLAN only when no 2G/3G/LTE network is available").

The gateway of the network is the RCST, which acts both as a router and as an end point for the Satcom network. It also implements PMIP for the mobility of the UE, and DSMIP for its own mobility when it attaches/detaches to the terrestrial network. It also performs the switching according to some predefined policies that can be static.

The scenario of this moving network does not differ too much from what is described in the NEMO (Network Mobility) [9]. Mobile IP protocols (DSMIP and PMIP) are used in order to support the mobility of both the UE and the RCST. The

RCST stores the IP addresses of the terminals attached and it activates a flag on the IP header along with the IP prefix of the network to the PDN GW in order to communicate that it is a mobile router or proxy instead of a UE (as specified in NEMO [9]). It also distributes the IP packets destined to each of the terminals attached to the WLAN.

5.2   RCST Mobility

The RCST acts both as a router and as an end-point in the satellite network (see Fig. 6). When the RCST is connected to the terrestrial network (e.g. when the ship is in the port or the train is in the station), it behaves as an UE registered in the EPC network. It also behaves as a member of the WLAN, so it has multiple interfaces, for both WLAN and the satellite network.

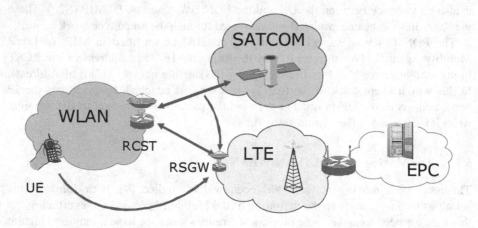

Fig. 6. RCST and UE mobility

When the RCST moves outside the coverage of the terrestrial network, it switches to the satellite network. The RCST in this case is connected to the RSGW that bridges the communication towards the PDN GW of the terrestrial network maintaining the IP connectivity. The mobility is handled by using DSMIP, a host-based protocol, so the RCST needs to have implemented the necessary software to support the protocol.

The RCST, as mobile equipment, sends its Care of Address (CoA) to the PDN GW, which keeps a table with the Care of Address and the original IP address of the RCST (Home Address). The PDN GW, or the Home Agent in MIP terms, sends the packets addressed to the RCST (via the RSGW) and/or the UE that is in the WLAN.

The PDN GW keeps track of the mobility of the moving WLAN, since every time the RCST attaches to a different network, it sends a BIND UPDATE message to the PDN-GW. Generic Routing Encapsulation encapsulates the packets that are sent through the Satcom network. They are later de-capsulated in the RSGW.

5.3   User Equipment Mobility

The UE is not aware of the mobility of the network. This means that it does not need to have implemented any mobility mechanisms. The procedures are simplified since a proxy, in this case the RCST, handles the work on behalf of the UE. The protocol that fits better here is PMIP.

The RCST acts as a proxy, it stores the original IP address of the UE and sends its own IP address to the PDN GW (LMA, or Local Mobility Agent in PMIP terms). The PDN GW knows about the RCST address and is aware of delivering the packets destined to the UE to that address.

The UE can switch back to a terrestrial network once it detects the coverage of a 3GPP network. It can also discover the available networks through the Access Network Discovery and Selection Function (ANDSF), as detailed in [5]. The Access Network Discovery and Selection Function can be used by the UE to understand the operator policies with regards to handover, for example whether to stay in the 3GPP network or switch to the WLAN in the ship or vice versa.

5.4   Quality of Service

With regards to the interworking between Satcom and EPS, the most important application is undoubtedly the Voice over IP (VoIP) service. DVB-RCS is mature enough and reliable to provide with VoIP transport. With the addition of QoS differentiation VoIP can have precedence to the available bandwidth when the up-link is congested. Dynamic resource allocation of bandwidth brings both satisfactory QoS for voice and maximizing bandwidth utilization.

However, there is still a lack of common design for the IP telephony features and applications over satellite, and for the Radio Resource Management and QoS that support VoIP. Standardisation activities should find optimized solutions for protocols, inter-working techniques and QoS mechanisms in this scenario.

Achieving end-to-end QoS is also a challenge, which would imply studying the mapping and interworking of the mobile terrestrial techniques (e.g. QCI in EPS) and satellite network techniques (dynamic bandwidth allocation). This is complicated by the fact that nowadays there is no standardized end-to-end QoS technique, since most satellite Bandwidth on Demand algorithms are proprietary.

It is also worth considering the inclusion of the Policy and Charging Control (PCC) framework [10], which is already an important part of the EPS and IMS systems, for a more dynamic QoS control of the sessions. For instance, one approach would be to implement the Bearer Binding and Event Reporting Function (BBREF) functionality in the RSGW, as specified in [5], to make the EPC system aware of session events (e.g. disconnection). Policies could be enforced in the RSGW, although this would need a standardized interface between the RSGW and the Policy and Charging Rules Function (PCRF). This possibility is being currently studied in ETSI SES (Satellite Earth Stations and Systems) BSM (Broadband Satellite Multimedia).

6   Conclusions

In this paper we have proposed a possible solution for the scenario of a Satcom network interworking with an EPS network in order to keep the IP connectivity when a mobile UE is switching between both.

Mobility between EPS and non-3GPP networks has been already specified in the standards, although the satellite network has not been considered yet as a possible access network to interact with the Evolved Packet System.

The solution comprehends using a double tunneling of PMIP and DSMIP protocols that cover the mobility of the wireless router/Satcom endpoint and the mobility of the UE. In both cases the PDN GW in the terrestrial network acts as an anchor that keeps the binding between the home address of the UE and the local IP address (CoA) in the WLAN. The IP packets are encapsulated and sent through the satellite network by using the DVB-RCS protocol.

Further work on the integration of DVB-RCS with the Evolved Packet Core is needed. Especially in the area of policy and QoS control there is further work to do. To get some more practical feedback on the challenges of integrating an EPC with a DVB-RCS access, we are planning to implement a test network that combines an Evolved Packet Core trial environment with a simulated DVB-RCS link.

References

1. ETSI EN 301 790 Digital Video Broadcasting (DVB): Interaction Channel for satellite distribution systems
2. 3GPP TS 23 401 General Packet Radio Service (GPRS) enhancements for Evolved Universal Terrestrial Radio Access Network (E-UTRAN) access
3. IETF RFC3775 MIPv6
4. ETSI TS 102 602 Satellite Earth Stations and Systems (SES); Broadband Satellite Multimedia; Connection Control Protocol (C2P) for DVB-RCS
5. 3GPP TS 23 402 Architecture enhancements for non-3GPP accesses
6. IETF RFC 5555 DSMIPv6
7. IETF RFC 5213 PMIPv6
8. IETF RFC5844 PMIPv6 over IPv4
9. IETF RFC3963 Network Mobility (NEMO) basic support protocol
10. 3GPP TS 23 203 Policy and Charging Control architecture
11. Satcom Integration with IMS based Core Networks: Nokia Siemens Networks, SES Astra, http://telecom.esa.int/telecom/www/object/index.cfm?fobjectid=28885
12. Satcom Integra Multi-service IP next generation satellite networks: Thales Alenia Space, Ericsson, http://telecom.esa.int/telecom/www/object/index.cfm?fobjectid=29662t
13. Olsson, M., Sultana, S., Rommer, S., Frid, L., Mulligan, C.: SAE and the Evolved Packet Core: Driving the mobile broadband revolution. Academic Press
14. ETSI TR 101 895 Satellite Earth Stations and Systems: Broadband Satellite Multimedia. IP over satellite

A Packet Reassembly and Segmentation Protocol for Low Rate Applications in Bluetooth Sniff Mode

Jiangchuan Wen and John Nelson

Department of Electronic and Computer Engineering,
University of Limerick, Limerick, Ireland
{Jiangchuan.Wen,John.Nelson}@UL.ie

Abstract. In this paper, a Packets Reassembly and Segmentation (PRAS) protocol is proposed, to be used in conjunction with the Bluetooth sniff mode, to re-assemble small host controller interface (HCI) (ACL) data packets to larger ones so that the link controller can use a larger baseband packet type (e.g. 3-DH5) as appropriate. The associated Bluetooth operations and control procedures of the PRAS protocol are given. The analysis shows that this protocol reduces Bluetooth's use of small size baseband packets and significantly enhances packet transmission efficiency with lower overhead in Bluetooth sniff mode.

Keywords: Bluetooth, Packets Reassembly and Segmentation protocol, Sniff mode, Packet transmission efficiency, Wireless Sensor Networks.

1 Introduction

Nowadays, Bluetooth [1] devices frequently have to use small payload packets to deliver low rate data in WSNs and waste energy by performing the required polling operations to maintain channel synchronization. Sniff mode is a low power mode on a Bluetooth BR/EDR Controller, which can reduce the unnecessary polling operations and allow devices to enter a low power state. The Bluetooth protocols don't provide the opportunity to take full advantage of sniff by adopting more efficient baseband packet payloads. Hence, a new protocol is required and the result is the Packets Reassembly and Segmentation (PRAS) protocol.

2 The PRAS Protocol

The kernel PRAS protocol functionality is as follows: 1) when the Bluetooth device uses sniff mode and the BR/EDR controller caches small size HCI ACL data packets, the link manager (LM) can re-assemble the small size packets before delivery; 2) when the Bluetooth receiver receives a re-assembled packet, it can be segmented and restored to the original small size HCI ACL data packets; 3) the operations above shall be negotiated by a LM command and implemented in the controller.

N. Venkatasubramanian et al. (Eds.): Mobilware 2011, LNICST 93, pp. 119–120, 2012.

3 LMP Negotiation and Re-assembled Packet's Identifier

The PRAS protocol can be an extended feature in the BR/EDR controllers by a new LM Protocol (LMP) command LMP_PRAS. The re-assembled packet shall be encapsulated in a Bluetooth baseband packet and identified by the other Bluetooth device. We recommend using an LLID value of '00' in the payload header, which is currently undefined in the Bluetooth standard, to indicate that a re-assembled L2CAP message is being transported in the payload.

4 Packets Reassembly and Segmentation Process

During the sleep slots of the sniff interval period, the PRAS protocol re-assembles the HCI ACL data packets stored in a buffer for each common user ACL link (ACL-U). The payload re-assembly process in the baseband buffer is shown in Fig.1.

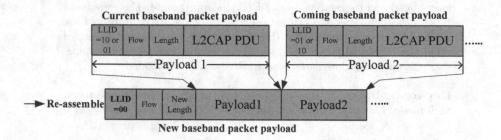

Fig. 1. The PRAS protocol payload re-assembled process

When the controller receives a packet with the LLID set to '00', the LM and HCI shall segment the packet's payload and restore the original packets.

5 Evaluation the PRAS Protocol and Conclusion

This protocol transparently exchanges the L2CAP PDUs and it doesn't affect other operations (e.g. encryption) in the LMP. The overhead of PRAS protocol is very low and only adds a two byte payload header.

The target application is low rate data Bluetooth-based sensor networks. The PRAS protocol can reduce the number of slot operations of the Bluetooth BR/EDR controller and enhance packet transmission efficiency, thereby improving power efficiency with sniff mode.

Reference

1. Bluetooth SIG.: Specification of the Bluetooth system, Version 4.0. (2010)

Running Android Applications
without a Virtual Machine

Arno Puder

San Francisco State University
Computer Science Department
1600 Holloway Avenue
San Francisco, CA 94132
arno@sfsu.edu

Abstract. Android has gained significant popularity in the smartphone market since its introduction in 2007. While Android applications are written in Java, Android uses its own virtual machine called Dalvik. Other smartphone platforms, most notably Apple's iOS, do not permit the installation of any kind of virtual machine. App developers who want to publish their applications for different platforms are required to re-implement the application using the respective native SDK. In this paper we describe a cross-compilation approach, whereby Android applications are cross-compiled to portable C code. With this approach it is not necessary to have a Dalvik virtual machine deployed on the target platform. We describe different aspects of our cross-compiler, from byte code level cross-compilation, memory management, to API mapping. A prototype of our cross-compiler called XMLVM is available under an Open Source license.

1 Introduction

Android is a software stack for mobile devices initially developed by a company called Android, Inc. before being bought by Google in 2005. Since 2007, members of the Open Handset Alliance (OHA) collaborate on the development of Android which nowadays has become one of the main development platforms for smartphone applications. Although Android employs Java as a programming language as well as a subset of the standard J2SE API, it does not make use of Oracle's (formerly Sun Microsystem's) virtual machine technology for technical and political reasons. Android features its own virtual machine, called Dalvik [5], for running Android-based applications. In contrast to the Oracle virtual machine, Dalvik is based on a register-based byte code instruction set. Running Android applications therefore requires the Dalvik virtual machine on the target platform.

Developers targeting smartphones ideally want their applications to be available on as many platforms as possible to increase the potential dissemination. Given the differences in the way applications are written for smartphones, this incurs significant effort in porting the same application to various platforms. The

N. Venkatasubramanian et al. (Eds.): Mobilware 2011, LNICST 93, pp. 121–134, 2012.
© Institute for Computer Sciences, Social Informatics and Telecommunications Engineering 2012

Dalvik virtual machine is not available on all smartphone platforms of interest. In particular, Apple explicitly forbids the use of virtual machine technology on their iOS devices, making it impossible to run applications that rely on Dalvik.

In this paper, we introduce a cross-compilation approach, whereby an Android application can be cross-compiled to portable C code. The solution we propose not only cross-compiles on a language level, but also maps APIs between different platforms. Since C is allowed for iOS development, Android applications can therefore be cross-compiled to Apple's devices. The benefit of our approach is that only skill set for the Android platform is required and only one code base needs to be maintained for both devices.

This paper is organized as follows: Section 2 provides an overview of Android and iOS as well as the deficiencies of previous work. Section 3 presents our cross-compilation framework that can cross-compile Android applications to iOS devices. In Section 4, we discuss our prototype implementation of this framework as well as a monitoring application that was cross-compiled using our toolchain. Finally, Section 5 provides a conclusion and an outlook to future work.

2   Background

We first provide a brief overview of Android and iOS from a programmers perspective highlighting the differences in their programming models (Section 2.1) followed by a discussion on the shortcomings of previous work (Section 2.2).

2.1   Overview of Android and iOS

Although smartphones are relatively similar with respect to their hardware capabilities, they differ greatly in their native application development models. Android is a mobile operating system running on the Linux kernel. Android is not exclusively targeting smartphones, but is also available for netbooks and settop boxes. Next to Android, Apple claims a firm position in the smartphone market with their proprietary iOS platform. Its user interface is called Cocoa Touch which is an extension of the Cocoa framework that is used on Apple desktop and laptop computers.

Targeting Android as well as iOS devices requires significant skill sets and overhead. Whereas Android uses Java as the development language, Cocoa Touch uses Objective-C. Those two languages are radically different. While Java features strong typing and garbage collection, the version of Objective-C used on iOS devices supports dynamic typing, but no garbage collection.

Similarly, differences exist in the APIs and programming models defined by Android and Cocoa Touch. An Android application consists of a set of so-called *activities*. An activity is a user interaction that may have one or more input screens. An example for an activity is to select a contact from the internal address book. The user may flip through the contact list or may use a search box. These actions are combined to an activity. Activities have a well-defined life cycle and can be invoked from other activities (even activities from other applications). Besides a variety of widgets, Android also allows the declarative description of user interfaces. XML files describe the relative layout of a user interface which not only simplifies internationalization but also allows to render the user interface on different screen resolutions.

The only official language offered by Apple for iOS devices is Objective-C. Similar to C++, Objective-C is an object-oriented extension of the C programming language. Analogous to Smalltalk, an object can be sent any message. Since the version of Objective-C used for iOS devices does not integrate a garbage collector, the programmer has to use a low-level reference counting mechanism for memory management. The design of Cocoa Touch makes extensive use of Objective-C's dynamic typing. Cocoa Touch offers a variety of UI elements. However, unlike Android, Cocoa Touch offers no layout manager: all UI elements have to be positioned in terms of absolute coordinates on the screen at design time.

2.2   Previous Work

We have worked on cross-compilation in the past [10]. Our cross-compiler, called XMLVM, translates Java byte code instructions represented in XML to a high-level programming language. In the past, the exclusive target for cross-compiling Android applications were iOS devices. For this reason, Java byte code instructions were cross-compiled to the native programming language for iOS devices, namely Objective-C. XMLVM mapped Java classes to Objective-C classes. While this proved to be a simple mapping, it also led to various problems. For one, Objective-C allows overriding but not overloading of methods. Since Java supports both, method names need to be name mangled with their signature when generating Objective-C method names. While name mangling solves the problem of method overloading in Objective-C, the one-to-one mapping of the object models leads to other problems. E.g., Objective-C does not allow to override instance members, so the following Java program cannot be cross-compiled with the Objective-C backend of XMLVM:

```
1 // Java
2 class Base {
3     int x;
4 }
5
6 class Derived extends Base {
7     int x;
8 }
```

Another shortcoming stems from the fact that Apple did not include a garbage collector in the version of Objective-C used for iOS applications. XMLVM's backend make use of iOS' reference counting mechanism by inserting retain and release instructions into the generated Objective-C code. One issue with this approach are cyclic data structures which cannot be reclaimed via reference counting. In order to avoid memory leaks, it is the programmer's responsibility to break cycles by using java.lang.ref.WeakReference. Instances of WeakReference are ignored by the garbage collector when constructing the reachability graph. Another problem is caused by multi-threaded applications: because it is impossible to know what other threads are doing with individual objects, the inserted reference counting instructions need to be conservative and retain objects for the duration of their use. This leads to significant overhead because the majority of the generated code is related to the retaining and releasing of object references.

Because of these shortcomings we decided to replace the Objective-C backend with a code generator for the C programming language. Since C is a strict subset of Objective-C, the cross-compiled code can still be targeted for iOS devices. Generating C code also allows support for the full Java language as well as compile-time optimizations. The following section gives a detailed overview of the C code generator in XMLVM.

3   Cross-Compilation Framework

In this section we introduce XMLVM, a flexible, byte code level cross-compiler, that allows to translate an Android application to iOS devices. In Section 3.1 we give an overview of the XMLVM toolchain. Section 3.2 explains our byte code level cross-compiler to the C programming language. In Section 3.3 we outline the API mapping and finally in Section 3.4 we discuss the integration of a Garbage Collector.

3.1   Toolchain

We chose Android as the canonical platform. This means that a developer only needs to be familiar with the Android system and can then cross-compile an Android application to other smartphones. There are several reasons for choosing Android. First of all, we believe that there is a wide skill set for the Java programming language and there are powerful tools to develop for Java. We view this as an advantage over Objective-C.

The design of Android itself offers various advantages. For one, Android was not exclusively designed for smartphones, but for a wide range of mobile devices. Android's API allows to explore the device's capabilities to give the application the chance to adapt accordingly. Android offers layout managers that can adapt to different screen resolutions at runtime. Cocoa Touch on the other hand expects the programmer to position every widget in terms of absolute coordinates. Since Apple offers with the iPhone 3GS, iPhone 4, and iPad three devices with different screen resolutions, the burden is placed on the programmer who has to manually design three UIs. Since Android applications can more easily adapt to different devices, it makes them ideal candidates to be cross-compiled to other platforms.

The XMLVM toolchain is a byte code level cross-compiler. The output of a Java compiler is first translated to an XML document to allow easy transformations based on XSL stylesheets, as will be shown in the following subsection. XMLVM makes use of Android's Dalvik virtual machine [5] for representing byte code instructions. Dalvik is based on a register-based virtual machine which allows for the generation of more efficient code in the target language compared to Oracle's stack-based virtual machine instructions [8]. On the basis of the intermittent XML representation we generate code in the target language, which in our case is C. In the following examples we focus on the register-based format of XMLVM as the starting point of the cross-compilation. The following three subsections explain in detail the cross-compilation process, the API mapping via a compatibility library as well as memory management via garbage collection.

3.2   Byte Code Level Cross-Compilation

A unique property of our toolchain is that we cross-compile from byte code to high-level programming languages. We make use of the byte code instructions introduced by the Dalvik instruction set to allow more efficient code generation. In a previous project we have used a similar approach to cross-compile byte code to JavaScript for AJAX applications [9]. Using byte codes has several advantages. For one, byte codes are much easier to parse than Java source code. Several high-level language features such as generics are already reduced to low-level byte code instructions. The Java compiler also does extensive optimizations to produce efficient byte codes. To illustrate our approach, consider the following simple Java class:

```
1 // Java
2 public class Account {
3     int     balance;
4     boolean overdraftProtection;
5
6     // ...
7
8     void deposit(int amount) {
9         balance += amount;
10    }
11 }
```

Class `Account` has a method called `deposit()` that adds a given amount to the `balance` of an account. The source code is first compiled to a Java class file via a regular Java compiler. The binary class file is then fed into our XMLVM tool. The first transformation performed on the resulting XMLVM is to convert the stack-based byte code instructions to register-based instructions introduced by Dalvik [5]. The conversion from a stack-based to a register-based machine has been researched extensively [3,11]. Internally, XMLVM generates the following XMLVM document based on class `Account`:

```
1  <vm:xmlvm ...>
2    <vm:class name="Account" ...>
3      <vm:field name="balance" type="int" />
4      <vm:field name="overdraftProtection" type="boolean" />
5      <vm:method name="deposit" ...>
6        <vm:signature>
7          <vm:return type="void" />
8          <vm:parameter type="int" />
9        </vm:signature>
10       <dex:code num-registers="3">
11         <dex:iget class-type="Account" field="balance" vx="0" vy="1" />
12         <dex:add-int vx="0" vy="0" vz="2" />
13         <dex:iput class-type="Account" field="balance" vx="0" vy="1" />
14         <dex:return-void />
15       </dex:code>
16     </vm:method>
17   </vm:class>
18 </vm:xmlvm>
```

The reason our tool is called XMLVM is because the structure of the class file as well as the byte code instructions of a virtual machine are represented via appropriate XML tags. On the top-level, there are tags to represent the class definition (line 2), field definitions (lines 3 and 4), method definition (line 5), and the signature of the method (line 6–9). The children of tag <dex:code> (line 10) represent the byte code instructions for method deposit(). The attribute num-registers denotes the number of registers required to execute this method.

In the following we give a brief overview of the byte code instructions generated for method deposit(). Upon entering a method, the last n registers are automatically initialized with the n actual parameters. Since method deposit() has three registers labeled 0 to 2, register 2 will be initialized with the one actual parameter of that method (the amount). The implicit this-parameter counts as a parameter and will therefore be copied to register 1. The byte code instructions read and write to various registers that are referred to via attributes vx, vy, and vz, where vx usually designates the register that stores the result of the operation. The first instruction <dex:iget> (*instance get*) loads the content of field balance of the account object referenced by register 1 into register 0 (line 11). The <dex:add-int> (*add integer*) instruction in line 12 will add the integers in registers 0 (the current balance) and 2 (the actual parameter) and store the sum in register 0. This instruction performs the operation $vx = vy + vz$. The <dex:iput> (*instance put*) instruction in line 13 performs the opposite of <dex:iget>: the content of register 0 is stored in field balance of the object referenced by register 1.

Once an XML representation of a byte code program has been generated, it is possible to cross-compile the byte code instructions to arbitrary high-level languages such as C, by simply mimicking the register machine in the target language. Individual registers are mapped to variables in C. Since a register can contain different data types, we introduce a C-union that reflects these data types:

```
1 // C
2 typedef union {
3     JAVA_OBJECT o;
4     JAVA_INT    i;
5     JAVA_FLOAT  f;
6     JAVA_DOUBLE d;
7     JAVA_LONG   l;
8 } XMLVMElem;
```

Registers can only store object references, integers, floats, doubles, and longs. Shorter primitive types such as bytes and shorts are sign-extended to 32-bit integers. With the help of the union XMLVMElem, it is possible to use XSL stylesheets [12] to produce code in the target language. In the following we show how the aforementioned byte code instruction <dex:add-int> is mapped to C source code:

```
1 <!-- XSL template -->
2 <xsl:template match="dex:add-int">
3     <xsl:text>    _r</xsl:text>
4     <xsl:value-of select="@vx"/>
5     <xsl:text>.i = _r</xsl:text>
6     <xsl:value-of select="@vy"/>
7     <xsl:text>.i + _r</xsl:text>
8     <xsl:value-of select="@vz"/>
9     <xsl:text>.i;</xsl:text>
10 </xsl:template>
```

Register variables are always prefixed with _r followed by the register number. The definition of these helper variables are based on union XMLVMElem. These variables are automatically generated by other XSL templates during the code generation process. With the help of these variables, the effect of individual byte code instructions can easily be mapped to the target language. Applying all XSL templates to the XMLVM of class Account shown earlier yields the following C source code:

```
1 // Generated C
2 void Account_deposit___int(JAVA_OBJECT me, JAVA_INT n1)
3 {
4     XMLVMElem _r0;
5     XMLVMElem _r1;
6     XMLVMElem _r2;
7     _r1.o = me;
8     _r2.i = n1;
```

```
9     _r0.i = ((Account*) _r1.o)->fields.balance;
10    _r0.i = _r0.i + _r2.i;
11    ((Account*) _r1.o)->fields.balance = _r0.i;
12    return;
13  }
```

The code in line 10 was generated by the XSL template for the `<dex:add-int>` instruction explained earlier. Every method of a class is mapped to a C function whose name is mangled from the class and method name as well as the method's signature. For each class, a so-called *Type Information Block* (TIB) is generated (see Figure 1). The TIB contains all relevant meta-data about a class such as fully qualified name, base class, all implemented interfaces, etc. When a class is instantiated, enough memory is allocated for all the instance members plus a pointer to the TIB. Since XMLVM cross-compiles byte code to C, there is no notion of dynamic class loading as usually found in a Java VM. A particular challenge poses the Java reflection API. In order to support dynamic method invocations via the reflection API, XMLVM creates method dispatchers for each class.

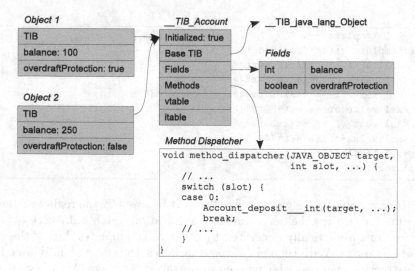

Fig. 1. Type Information Block

Since XMLVM cannot load classes dynamically at runtime, all classes that are needed for an application need to be known at compile time. XMLVM performs a static dependency analysis to determine the transitive closure of all referenced classes. Since XMLVM operates under the *Closed World Assumption* (i.e., all referenced classes are known *a priori*) it is possible to perform powerful compile-time optimizations, especially for method invocations. Java distinguishes between two different dynamic method invocations on byte code level: `<dex:invoke-virtual>` is used for calling methods on an object, where as <dex:invoke-interface> is used to invoke methods via an interface type. The reason for two different invoke instructions has to do with the fact that Java allows single inheritance for classes but multiple inheritance for interfaces. For the former it is possible to build a so-called vtable which essentially is an array of function pointers. An <dex:invoke-virtual> instruction references a vtable index to the appropriate implementation of a method. Because of the Closed World Assumption it is known at compile-time whether a method is overridden in a derived class or not. If a method is not overridden, it can be called directly without the need of allocating an entry in the vtable.

Similar optimizations can be done for <dex:invoke-interface>. Here XMLVM computes an itable (analogous to the vtable) for interface methods. Because of the Closed World Assumption it is possible to compute an itable that can be indexed via one indirection. The technique is known as selector coloring and is described in [4]. The overhead of performing an <dex:invoke-interface> is identical to performing an <dex:invoke-virtual>.

The following code excerpt shows how a method invocation in Java (line 2) is represented in XMLVM (lines 5–10) and how it is mapped to C code. If method deposit() is not overridden in a derived class, it can be invoked via a direct function call (line 13). Otherwise method deposit() needs to be invoked via a vtable (lines 16–17). First, FPTR is defined as a function pointer of the proper type that reflects the signature of method deposit(), then the vtable is accessed via the TIB. In this particular example the function pointer for method deposit() is stored at vtable index 11.

```
1 // Java
2 account.deposit(amount);
3
4 <!-- XMLVM -->
5 <dex:invoke-virtual class-type="Account" method="deposit" register="0">
6   <dex:parameters>
7     <dex:parameter type="int" register="1" />
8     <dex:return type="void" />
9   </dex:parameters>
10 </dex:invoke-virtual>
11
12 // C (direct)
13 Account_deposit___int(_r0.o, _r1.i);
14
15 // C (via vtable)
16 typedef *(void (*)(JAVA_OBJECT, JAVA_INT)) FPTR;
17 (FPTR ((Account*) _r0.o)->tib->vtable[11])(_r0.o, _r1.i);
```

3.3 API Mapping

Any Java program builds upon external API. The most common are the APIs defined as part of J2SE such as data structures. XMLVM leverages the Open Source project Apache Harmony for these purposes. Since much of the J2SE API is itself written in Java, we simply cross-compile this to C as well. On system-level, Apache Harmony uses native Java methods to access functionality of the underlying operating system. In XMLVM we have implemented those native methods based on the Posix API. E.g., the Java thread API is mapped via the native methods to pthreads.

Other APIs such as the one defined by Cocoa Touch are platform specific. Such API needs to be accessible from a Java application. E.g., if a Java-based iOS applications needs to place a label on the user interface, a Java-based API of class `UILabel` is required. The following shows the Java version of class `UILabel` that is part of the XMLVM library:

```
1 // Java
2
3 package org.xmlvm.iphone;
4
5 class UILabel extends UIView {
6     //...
7     void setText(String label) { /* Ignored */ }
8 }
```

We call classes such as `UILabel` *wrapper classes* since their only purpose is to provide a Java API against which the developer can implement an application. For that reason, the method implementation of wrapper classes can be left empty. Wrapper classes are treated special by XMLVM's cross-compiler. The implementation of a method in a wrapper class is ignored and instead special comment markers are emitted. The programmer can inject manually written code between these comment markers. The following code excerpt demonstrates this concept for method `UILabel.setText()`:

```
1 // Objective-C (generated with injected code)
2
3 void org_xmlvm_iphone_UILabel_setText___java_lang_String(JAVA_OBJECT me,
4                                                          JAVA_OBJECT n1)
5 {
6     //XMLVM_BEGIN_WRAPPER
7     NSString* text = toNSString(n1);
8     org_xmlvm_iphone_UILabel* thiz = me;
9     UILabel* label = thiz->fields.wrappedObject;
10    [label setText:text];
11    [text release];
12    //XMLVM_END_WRAPPER
13 }
```

Note that while the generated wrapper code is C, the code injected by the developer between the comment markers (lines 6–12) is Objective-C. This is necessary because the wrapper effectively wraps an Objective-C object. The code above essentially converts a `java.lang.String` instance to an Objective-C `NSString` via a helper function (line 7) and retrieves the wrapped Objective-C `UILabel` instance (line 9). The field `wrappedObject` is part of the `UILabel` instance and points to the native Objective-C object. Next, the `setText:` message is sent to the Objective-C object (line 10) and finally the `NSString` instance is released (line 11).

Exposing the Cocoa Touch API in Java is the prerequisite for our *Android Compatibility Library* (ACL). The purpose of the ACL is to offer the Android API to an application while using the Java-based Cocoa Touch API for its own implementation. The ACL is therefore written in Java and maps the Android API to the Cocoa Touch API. It offers the same API to the application as Android does but is implemented using the Cocoa Touch wrapper classes. The following code excerpt shows how an Android `TextView` is mapped to a Cocoa Touch `UILabel`:

```
1 // ACL (Java)
2 package android.widget;
3
4 public class TextView {
5     private UILabel label;
6     // ...
7     public void setText(String text) {
8         label.setText(text);
9     }
10 }
```

Therefore, an application using an `android.widget.TextView` is effectively using a `UILabel` on iOS devices via the ACL. The above code excerpt is also cross-compiled to C and is part of XMLVM's implementation of the ACL. In other cases, such as Android's layout manager, we cross-compile source code from the Android project that is available under an Open Source license. This way the layout manager can be used on iOS devices. Other UI idioms cannot easily be mapped such as Android's physical "Back" and "Menu" buttons. Mapping those features is left for future work.

3.4   Garbage Collector

XMLVM makes use of the Boehm Garbage Collector [1]. The Boehm GC is a conservative garbage collector using a mark-and-sweep algorithm. It allows finalization code to be invoked when an object is collected. Whenever a class is instantiated, the `GC_MALLOC()` function of the Boehm GC is used to allocate memory thereby registering the new object with the GC. Making use of `GC_MALLOC()` is therefore all that is necessary in terms of memory management for self-contained Java applications cross-compiled to C.

However, special attention needs to be given to wrapper objects such as UI widgets from Cocoa Touch. Although version 2.0 of the Objective-C programming language introduced a garbage collector, Apple decided to remove this feature for iOS devices. Apple's reason for doing so is most likely related to the undeterministic behavior of a garbage collector that might disrupt the user experience. Instead of garbage collection, an iOS developer has to resort to a reference counting mechanism for memory management.

Base class NSObject of the Cocoa Touch library offers methods retain and release, that increment and decrement respectively the reference count of an object. Objects are created with reference count of 1 and when the reference count drops to 0, the Objective-C runtime automatically deallocates the object. It is the iOS developers responsibility to retain and release objects according to the object ownership rules of Cocoa Touch.

Wrapper classes such as the aforementioned UILabel act as a bridge between the generated C code and native objects from Cocoa Touch. In the following we refer to the term "C object" as the cross-compiled version of a Java object. As depicted in Figure 2, each Objective-C object that needs to be accessible from Java (such as UILabel), needs to be wrapped by a C object. The C object will retain the Objective-C object to claim ownership and register a finalizer with the GC. When the C object is destroyed by the GC, the finalizer will release the wrapped Objective-C object as well. Special attention needs to be paid to associations between Objective-C objects. Whenever a wrapped Objective-C object holds a reference to another wrapped Objective-C object, the association needs to be mirrored among the wrapping C objects as well (see Figure 2). If this were not the case, the GC could not construct a correct reachability graph since it is unaware of Objective-C associations.

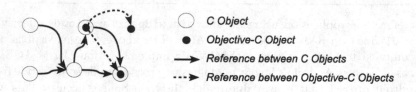

     ○   *C Object*

     ●   *Objective-C Object*

     ⟶   *Reference between C Objects*

     ⤏   *Reference between Objective-C Objects*

Fig. 2. Wrapper objects

4   Prototype Implementation

We have implemented a prototype based on the ideas described in this paper. We make use of BCEL [2] and JDOM [6] to parse Java class files and build up the XMLVM files. Saxon [7] is used as the XSL engine to apply the stylesheets that are responsible for the code generation. The implementation of the Java to C cross-compilation is fully Java compatible including garbage collection, threading, and reflection API. Our tool does not offer the same kind of completeness for the API mapping. Considering that both the Android and the Cocoa Touch API consist of thousands of methods, XMLVM currently maps approximately 30% of the API. However, the currently supported API already allows for complex applications.

Fig. 3. Layout mapping example

XMLVM has been used to cross-compile Android applications to the iOS by various companies. In the following we highlight one of these applications to demonstrate the power of cross-compilation. A German consulting company implemented a monitoring application for IBM datapower devices. A datapower device is a SOA appliance that can be monitored via SOAP requests over HTTPS. The monitoring application was written for Android and cross-compiled to iOS devices using XMLVM. The Android version makes extensive use of layout manager, Android-specific UI widgets as well as custom widgets, HTTPS requests and XPath queries to SOAP replies. All this functionality was successfully cross-compiled to iOS devices.

Figure 3 depicts the original Android version of the monitoring application on the left side and the cross-compiled iOS version to the right. Apart from the obvious mapping of labels, buttons and images, the Android version makes use of a radio button group. The corresponding widget under iOS is called a segmented control that serves the same purpose. Since a segmented control is wider than higher in contrast to Android's radio button group that is aligned vertically, the cross-compiled layout manager places the segmented control underneath the graph-drawing custom widget. As can be seen in Figure 3, the custom widget is automatically stretched in the iOS version to the full width of the screen.

5   Conclusion and Outlook

The popularity of smartphones makes them attractive platforms for mobile applications. However, while smartphones have nearly identical capabilities with respect to their hardware, they differ substantially in their programming environment. Different programming languages and different APIs lead to significant overhead when porting applications to various smartphones. We have chosen Android as the canonical platform. Our byte code level cross-compiler XMLVM can cross-compile an Android application to portable C code that can be run on iOS devices, therefore not requiring the Dalvik virtual machine on the target platform. We have demonstrated that a cross-compilation framework is feasible, thereby significantly reducing the porting effort.

In the future our goal is to support debugging of cross-compiled applications. The idea is that a Java application that was cross-compiled with XMLVM can be debugged with any standard Java debugger such as the one integrated in Eclipse. In order to accomplish this, an implementation of the JWDP (Java Wire Debug Protocol) needs to be available on the target platform. We plan to use the Open Source Maxine project that features a Java implementation of JWDP. With the help of the Java-to-C cross-compiler we will cross-compile Maxine to C to support debugging on any Posix compliant platform. The challenge of this task will be to interface with the generated C code to determine the memory layout (such as stack and heap) at runtime.

XMLVM is available under an Open Source license at `http://xmlvm.org`.

References

1. Boehm, H.: Bounding space usage of conservative garbage collectors. SIGPLAN Notices 37(1), 93–100 (2002)
2. Dahm, M.: Byte code engineering. Java Informations Tage, 267–277 (1999)
3. Davis, B., Beatty, A., Casey, K., Gregg, D., Waldron, J.: The case for virtual register machines. In: IVME 2003: Proceedings of the 2003 Workshop on Interpreters, Virtual Machines and Emulators, pp. 41–49. ACM, New York (2003)
4. Dixon, R., McKee, T., Vaughan, M., Schweizer, P.: A fast method dispatcher for compiled languages with multiple inheritance. SIGPLAN Notices 24, 211–214 (1989)
5. Google, Inc. The Dalvik virtual machine, `http://en.wikipedia.org/wiki/Dalvik_virtual_machine`
6. JDOM. Java DOM-API (2004), `http://www.jdom.org/`
7. Kay, M.: Saxon: The XSLT and XQuery Processor, `http://saxon.sourceforge.net/`
8. Lindholm, T., Yellin, F.: The Java Virtual Machine Specification, 2nd edn. Addison-Wesley Pub. Co. (April 1999)
9. Puder, A.: A Cross-Language Framework for Developing AJAX Applications. In: PPPJ. International Proceedings Series. ACM, Lisboa (2007)
10. Puder, A.: Cross-Compiling Android Applications to the iPhone. In: PPPJ. International Proceedings Series. ACM, Vienna (2010)
11. Shi, Y., Casey, K., Ertl, M.A., Gregg, D.: Virtual machine show-down: Stack versus registers. ACM Trans. Archit. Code Optim. 4(4), 1–36 (2008)
12. W3C. XSL Transformations (1999), `http://www.w3.org/TR/xslt`

A Framework for Building and Operating Context-Aware Mobile Applications

Aaratee Shrestha, Bettina Biel, Tobias Griebe, and Volker Gruhn

University of Duisburg-Essen, Gerlingstrasse 16, 45127 Essen, Germany
{aaratee.shrestha,bettina.biel,
tobias.griebe,volker.gruhn}@paluno.uni-due.de

Abstract. A context-aware mobile framework must support and handle complex context data which is dynamically manipulated in the distributed mobile network. Research in this area has focused on the efficient design of such a framework. However, there are still key problems such as dynamic adaptation, reusability, interoperability, high energy and memory consumption. Our approach to solve the problems of Context-Aware Mobile Applications (CAMA) is to design a framework architecture by using Service Oriented Architecture (SOA). The reusable, loosely-coupled local and external services allow CAMA to communicate with the CAMA Framework, OS and external service providers using minimum interfaces. The framework supports interoperability, dynamic adaptability and context handling in a frequently changing environment. In this work-in-progress paper, we define SOA, usability and testing requirements for a prototype CAMA and the CAMA Framework. We conclude that our approach will enhance mobile framework architecture to provide solutions to the key problems of CAMA.

Keywords: context-awareness, context-aware mobile applications (CAMA), service oriented architecture (SOA).

1 Introduction

Mobile technology has been broadly adapted in business and entertainment domains with increasing demand. Users can access context data, workflows and systems anywhere anytime. A robust mobile framework that can handle different context data, process it and make it accessible to lightweight applications for users without time, place and network restrictions is an important requirement.

Context is the "situational information of entities such as person, places or objects, that are relevant to the interactions between a user and an application" [6]. We define CAMA as context-aware mobile applications where context data and services are manipulated in dynamic environments. We agree with Pauty [15], that "the services are aware of the current context of the user and self-adapt to context changes". Thanh [19] states, that mobile services are realized by combining different SOA services. SOA features are essential in an environment depending on non-robust connections and multi-device user access to services [18]. Also, SOA provides the advantages of flexibility, implementation abstraction and

N. Venkatasubramanian et al. (Eds.): Mobilware 2011, LNICST 93, pp. 135–142, 2012.
© Institute for Computer Sciences, Social Informatics and Telecommunications Engineering 2012

interoperability [13,17,2], that are very important in dynamic mobile computing platforms. SOA can address multiple client devices in distributed environments where the client heavily relies on the interaction with a server system. The server exposes only one interface to various clients and acts as provider of autonomous interfaces [16]. Because of these advantages over traditional mobile web services, our framework is motivated to implement SOA.

In this work-in-progress paper, our first step towards a solution is to introduce the example of a Calendar-Location-Weather (CLW) application and then summarize its requirements. We explain how our framework is designed to overcome the general challenges and problems of context-aware frameworks. Our framework supports key SOA features such as reusability, interoperability, loose coupling as well as dynamic adaptability and context handling in dynamic environments. The contribution of this paper is an architecture design by using the CLW example of a CAMA, usability and testing requirements. The structure of this paper is as follows. Section 2 covers the CLW application scenario, followed by a summary of requirements of the CAMA framework in section 3. We present the current architecture design in section 4 and compare it to related work in section 5. A conclusion and future work is found in section 6.

2   The Calendar-Location-Weather (CLW) Application

Imagine a user wants to be woken up in the morning to travel from Essen to Berlin to attend a meeting. He opens the CLW application, enters the event's name, date, time, location, means of transportation (train) and saves it. Weather forecast and related services are enabled by him as well. The CLW will wake him up on time, give weather information and, if it rains, it reminds him to take an umbrella. In case the train is late, it will inform him and provide a list of alternatives (e.g., other trains, buses, renting a car). The CLW application will alarm the user when it is time to go to catch the train at Essen main station.

The CAMA framework stores the event data in the Context Database and communicates with external provider's databases. The framework checks the

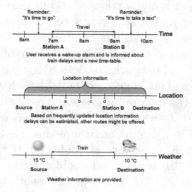

Fig. 1. The CLW application integrates three types of context information

date whether it matches the calendar date in the Context Database using the Inference Rule Set. The Inference Rule Set supplies commands to update the data of the CLW application and queries location and weather updates, e.g., the German railways or a weather forecast.When the context changes, it is displayed at the current location map and the weather information.

3 Requirements of the CAMA Framework

Mobile SOA. Using SOA for mobile architectures is an emerging area and several researches have been done in different aspects of context-awareness. In this research, we analyzed the specific problems related to CAMA while using SOA, which was considered during the design of framework architecture. High level requirements based on business goals and the usage context are: instant access to relevant applications, services and data required by mobile device users through a highly usable unified user interface of composite CAMA. These are not supported by traditional framework approaches as explained by IDC Research Report [11]. Monitoring of the mobile context of user and environment is frequently needed, as it changes continuously. In traditional frameworks, this is difficult for the reasons of tight coupling, non-interoperability and modes of operation as described by Ennai et al. [7]. Interoperability and reusability of local and remote context data and services are often required by mobile device users such that a large number of CAMA are using the same context data and services multiple times. Transferring large amounts local context data is difficult when there arise any problems with the device such as network, memory, battery. In present mobile devices, storage space and computing capability are increased. Yet, problems exist to deploy large complex applications and data on a mobile device as explained by Tergujeff et al. [18].

Usability of CAMA. CAMA running in our proposed framework should be highly usable. Usability is closely related to other qualities, such as performance, robustness, fault-tolerance, security, modifiability and adaptability. Hence, we decided to design the framework architecture using the Software ArchiTecture analysis of Usability Requirements realizatioN (SATURN) method [1]. During this research, the method is applied in an iterative architecture-based development process with alternating analysis and design activities.

In SATURN, requirements are expressed through scenarios, which are described and/or selected from pattern-based knowledge base of generic scenarios. Regarding usability, we selected the scenarios *Canceling Commands*, *Feedback*, *Context-Aware Interaction*, *Positioning* and added *Evaluating the application*.

Evaluating the scenarios, the open questions are (1) which structure and behavior of components and interfaces can realize the use cases of a scenario; and (2) how responsibilities can be distributed between the CLW application, the CAMA framework and the mobile platform.

Testing CAMA. Due to the high dynamics of changing context and service topology, testing CAMA imposes a novel set of requirements to the design of the

CAMA framework, the design of test cases and the testing process. CAMA depend on multiple internal and external services whose availability may change at any moment, either inducing a service discovery process or rendering the application inoperative. Test engineers must design functional test cases and sufficiently control the CAMA's execution environment including context data. Rather than concentrating on the system under test, the testing of a CAMA requires the test environment to produce and manipulate context data on demand.

As it is complicated to artificially reproduce context information for testing purposes, the design of the CAMA framework needs to implement features to facilitate testing of CAMA. The key questions regarding an integrated testbed in the architecture design are: (1) how context information can be generated; (2) how test cases need to be designed to react properly to changing context information; and (3) what test coverage criteria need to be applied.

Test cases require the artificial setting of position data and the creation of weather, traffic and travel information. Besides the local sensor readings, most of this information is derived from the context-aware system of the CAMA framework which in turn consumes data from external sources. Hence, the CAMA framework needs to employ a testing mode which allows the artificial provisioning of context information, overriding the actual context data, to create a valid and reproducible test environment.

4   Mobile Framework

The framework architecture is designed to support the customized CAMA development for different mobile platforms and features service-oriented functionality. Its design is focused on the dynamic adaptability to frequent and unpredictable changes in context and user requirements to provide continuously available services. The integration of context-aware data and services is executed in real-time. Therefore, our framework architecture as seen in Fig. 2 is designed to fulfill some of the requirements to solve the above addressed problems and challenges. Mobile applications act as clients and may heavily rely on context data and context-aware services. Different components of the architecture play a vital role for accessing the requested data. The components of our mobile framework are briefly discussed as follows.

The *Service Provider* creates a mobile service and publishes its interface in Fig. 2 label (2) and access information to the Service Registry. The Service Provider sends the context data (21) received from the Context Interpreter to the Service Consumer. The sub-components of Service Provider such as *Publishing Manager, Service Interface Handler and Service Manager* helps to publish service interfaces. The Publishing Manager is responsible for publishing the service interface of different services. Service Manager decides in which category the service should be listed in the Service Registry and list all potential service recipients. It decides which service to expose, regarding the service charges and how to make trade-offs between security and availability. It is responsible for what Service Level Agreements (SLAs) are required to use the service. Service

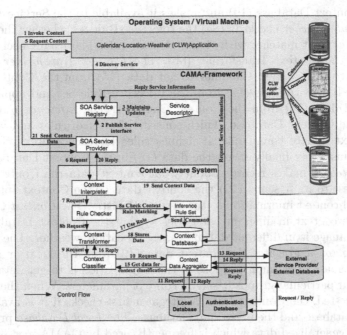

Fig. 2. CAMA Framework Architecture and CLW Application

Interface Handler acts as an interface for the service contract request between service provider and service consumer using the SLA.

The *Service Consumer* (e.g., CLW Application) of a client locates entries in the Service Registry with the help of a find-bind mechanism (1,2,3,4) and requests the Service Provider to invoke one of its services. After the discovery of a service in the Service Registry, the Service Consumer sends a service request (5) that is executed by the Service Provider. The *Service Registry* is a reference database containing information about services, service definitions, interfaces and parameters. The *Service Descriptor* is a database containing data and metadata maintained and updated (3) by the Service Registry.

The Service Provider, Service Consumer and Service Registry utilize SOA for using the services from the Context Database. For the communication and the request/response mechanism of SOA, the framework uses HTTP based Representational State Transfer (REST) protocol, which has advantages on the client side in mobile communication compared to the SOAP/WSDL protocol like in traditional frameworks as discussed by [7] where communication is more focused between multiple backend systems. According to [14] REST implementation of the data transmission proved to be more efficient compared to SOAP. Our CAMA framework utilizes the REST implementation as it features lightweight, flexible contracts and interfaces – a uniform way to interconnect with web resources and a balance between security and usage of resources.

Context Interpreter sends the request (6) to the Rule Checker, and checks for valid context when the Service Provider requests context data. It collects data from the Context Database (19) and makes it available to the Service Provider (20). The *Rule Checker* checks in (8a) the Inference Rule Set whether the rule for the specific context matches with the predefined rule. The Rule Checker sends requests to the Context Transformer (8b). The *Context Transformer* sends a request (9) to the Context Classifier to get data (15) from the Context Data Aggregator. It uses the rule (17) from the Inference Rule Set and applies it on the received data (16) from the Context Classifier. The *Inference Rule Set* is a part of the Context Database, which consists of a set of rules and facts and sends context update commands. It defines rules for each context. Then the Context Transformer finally stores the data (18) in the Context Database. The *Context Database* makes records about what context data the Context Interpreter request to it. It sends (19) the context data to the Context Interpreter and updated context information to the Service Registry. The *Context Classifier* classifies the context in different categories so that the Context Database can store and manage it in different databases, e.g., location, weather. The *Context Data Aggregator* aggregates the context data (12) from the local or the (14) external database. The main purpose of this aggregation is to get detail information about particular groups based on context parameters. When the context data is requested, the Context Data Aggregator first checks if it is available in the Local Database and then External Database. The *Local Database* provides a small set of generalized data which is frequently used by CAMA, e.g., calendar database located on the mobile device.

CAMA framework retrieves context data at first from the Context Database. The data is processed and stored in the Context Database from the Local Database. If data is not found in the Context Database, it searches the External Database and the External Service Provider as they provide more detailed context information. The Authentication Database holds the user credentials and manages secure login and access. The context services originate across various channels. The CAMA framework provides automatic session management such as session-time out, secure access of external service provider and multiple service providers.

5   Related Work

The traditional SOA framework on the client has been proposed by Tergujeff et al. [18] does not address context-awareness. Gehlen et al. [8] present a client proxy that executes requests and routes responses, but it does not support real-time change of context. A mobile middleware for CAMA on rule-based data monitoring is discussed by Costa et al. [5] but specific concerns (e.g., lack of user context, integration of services, etc.) have not been addressed. A mobile web service framework is described by Kim et al. [12]. However, it does not support hosting and migrating services in a context-aware environment. A traditional SOA framework that moves all the processing to the server and leaves only user interactions and user interface on the client side is mentioned by Kozel and Slaby [13]. In contrast, our solution is more focused on lightweight client-side processing. A reflective middleware for dynamic adaptability proposed by

Ghim et al. [9] does not address SOA features and uses mobile agents instead. A dynamic framework for context-aware mobile services by Chang et al. [4] describes a problem classification and a complexity model of context-aware mobile services into 3D dynamic problems. Our approach uses another classification of context, that is less complex.

CARISMA [3] mainly deals with the conflict between profiles of applications, that are kept as meta-data of the middleware and consist of passive and active parts. Policies are used to provide context services. CARISMA addresses issues related to the usage of context for dynamic adaptation of applications, but there are no application interfaces with local and external services and it mainly focuses on policy conflicts.

SOCAM [10] middleware is built on top of the OSGi service platform, and its architecture presents a formal context model based on ontology. It provides support for the tasks of dealing with context by context reasoning. External or internal context can be used by services directly or by Context Providers. The Context Interpreter consists of the Context Reasoner and the Context Database, which contains instances of the current ontology. The context is updated by a triggering mechanism. SOCAM has been deployed mainly for intelligent vehicle environment which may not be suitable for other mobile environments.

Conventional mobile distributed systems using web services have proven successful for the design of SOA in mobility, yet they could not overcome the challenges of context-awareness. Therefore, our SOA framework for lightweight and flexible CAMA is a more suitable solution.

6   Conclusions and Future Work

In this work-in-progress paper, we defined mobile SOA, usability and testing requirements for our mobile framework implementing a SOA based on a specific CAMA, i.e. the CLW application expressed through a scenario. Our CAMA framework architecture design provides a number of solutions to the problems introduced by context-awareness. We showed the conceptual design of the SOA and the context-aware mobile framework architecture. By using a SOA-architecture, we met requirements regarding instant access to applications, services and data and frequent monitoring of the mobile context of user and environment.

In our current work, we focus on the architecture design of the context adaptation and aim at realizing the usability and test requirements striving for a highly usable unified user interfaces of CAMA. Open questions and motivational future work comprise the data transfer on p2p interactions with near-by mobile devices, managing network problems and processing requests without context data in the Context Database and metadata in the Service Registry.

References

1. Biel, B., Grill, T., Gruhn, V.: Exploring the benefits of the combination of a software architecture analysis and a usability evaluation of a mobile application. Journal of Systems and Software 83(11), 2031–2044 (2010)

2. Bosch, J., Friedrichs, S., Jung, S., Helbig, J., Scherding, A.: Service orientation in the enterprise. Computer, 51–56 (2007)
3. Capra, L., Emmerich, W., Mascolo, C.: CARISMA: context-aware reflective middleware system for mobile applications. IEEE Transactions on Software Engineering 29(10), 929–945 (2003)
4. Chang, C.-C., Tseng, J.C.R., Lin, K.-J.: A dynamic capability framework for context-aware mobile services. In: Proc. of the 10th IEEE Conf. on E-Commerce Tech. and the 5th IEEE Conf. on Enterprise Computing, pp. 183–189 (2008)
5. Costa, P., Pires, L.F., Sinderen, M.V., Filho, J.P.: Towards a services platform for mobile context-aware applications. In: Proc. of 1st Intl. Workshop on Ubiquitous Computing, pp. 48–61 (2004)
6. Dey, A.K.: Understanding and using context. Personal Ubiquitous Comput. 5(1), 4–7 (2001)
7. Ennai, A., Bose, S.: MobileSOA: a service oriented web 2.0 framework for context-aware, lightweight and flexible mobile applications. In: EDOCW (2008)
8. Gehlen, G., Mavromatis, G.: Mobile web services based middleware for context-aware applications. In: Proc. of 11th European Wireless Conference 2005, pp. 784–790 (2005)
9. Ghim, S.-J., Yoon, Y.-I., Choe, J.-W.: A Reflective Approach to Dynamic Adaptation in Ubiquitous Computing Environment. In: Kahng, H.-K., Goto, S. (eds.) ICOIN 2004. LNCS, vol. 3090, pp. 75–82. Springer, Heidelberg (2004)
10. Gu, T., Pung, H.K., Zhang, D.Q.: A service-oriented middleware for building context-aware services. J. Netw. Comput. Appl. 28, 1–18 (2005)
11. IDC. Worldwide mobile enterprise applications 2006-2010 forecast and analysis. IDC Research (2006)
12. Kim, Y.-S., Lee, K.-H.: A lightweight framework for mobile web services. Journal Computer Science – Research and Development 24, 199–209 (2009)
13. Kozel, T., Slaby, A.: Mobile devices and web services. In: Proc. of 7th WSEAS Intl. Conference on Applied Computer Science, pp. 322–326 (2007)
14. Mulligan, G., Gracanin, D.: A comparison of soap and rest implementations of a service based interaction independence middleware framework. In: Proc. of the 2009 Winter Simulation Conference, pp. 1423–1432 (2009)
15. Pauty, J., Preuveneers, D., Rigole, P., Berbers, Y.: Research challenges in mobile and context-aware service development. In: Proc. of Future Research Challenges in Software and Services (2006)
16. Praher, C.P.: Mobile service oriented architecture in the context of information retrieval. Master's thesis, University of Linz (2008)
17. Schroth, C., Janner, T.: Web 2.0 and SOA: Converging concepts enabling the internet of services. IT Professional, 36–41 (2007)
18. Tergujeff, R., Haajanen, J., Leppanen, J., Toivonen, S.: Mobile SOA: Service orientation on lightweight mobile devices. In: Proc. of IEEE Intl Conf. on Web Services, pp. 1224–1225 (2007)
19. Thanh, D., Jorstad, I.: A service-oriented architecture framework for mobile services. Special issue on Situated Interaction and Ubiquitous Computing, 65–70 (2005)

Secure Middleware for Mobile Phones
and UICC Applications

Ioannis Kounelis[1], Hao Zhao[2], and Sead Muftic[2]

[1] Institute for the Protection and Security of the Citizen (IPSC)
Joint Research Centre – European Commission, Ispra (Va), Italy
[2] School of Information and Communication Technology
Royal Institute of Technology (KTH), Stockholm, Sweden
{kounelis,hzhao,sead}@kth.se

Abstract. In this paper we describe our concept, design and current prototype implementation of a new middleware for mobile phones and UICC. The purpose of the middleware is to be used as an interface between applications, loaded in mobile phones, and functionalities of the corresponding supporting modules (applets) stored in UICC. At the moment, our middleware supports only security and mobile payment functions. Our primary goal was to explore the features that multi–application chips provide and to create a new way for handling of sensitive information when stored and used in mobile phones. Another goal is to extend the middleware to hide technology details of underlying UICC and their applets, so that applications developed on the top of the middleware are independent of the underlying mobile phone technologies. We plan to extend the current version of our middleware module to be used with other UICC applications and alternative mobile operating systems.

Keywords: UICC, middleware, mobile phones.

1   Introduction and Goals

In recent years mobile phones have become a necessity in our everyday life. Since the number of mobile phones used globally exceeded 5 billion in July 2010 [1], one can understand the importance of mobile technologies. Mobile phones have evolved a lot since their first release and nowadays they are not just communication devices to make calls and send SMS messages.

A significant number of today's mobile devices has a complete operating system enabling them to execute all sorts of applications. From Symbian and BlackBerry's O.S. to the iPhone's O.S. and Android, mobile devices provide powerful platforms for communications, but also for execution of applications. Browsing the Internet is simpler than ever. With GPRS/3G/4G and wireless Internet connections, mobile phones can easily connect to the Internet and enhance browsing experience.

However, along with the new capabilities and opportunities come extended needs and demands, especially for security. One of the first and the most important is secure

N. Venkatasubramanian et al. (Eds.): Mobilware 2011, LNICST 93, pp. 143–152, 2012.

storage of data in mobile phones. At the moment, most of the applications loaded and executed in mobile devices, regardless of the phone's manufacturer, use the phone's memory (or memory card) to store data. It is similar to the use of a hard disk in PCs. However, the trend is to store data and use security functions based on capabilities of new, Javacard chips in mobile phones, called Universal Integrated Circuit Card (UICC) [9].

One of the goals of our research was to design and implement middleware that will provide to mobile applications a new, safer and more secure way of handling data operations, by using UICC [12]. Therefore, our middleware is a layered structure, at the top providing high–level Application Programming Interfaces (APIs) to mobile phone applications and at the bottom level communicating with UICC applets based on Application Programming Data Units (APDUs).

Besides secure storage, functionalities are also provided by the UICC to enable mobile applications to securely execute their functions and use their internal data. Such functionalities include financial transactions (credit card payments, electronic cash, etc.), security enhancements (private and public key generation, storage and verification of certificates, encryption, etc.) and administrative commands.

2   Interactions with Mobile Applications

High level applications, which are available to mobile phone users, use high-level programming APIs provided by the upper-end of the middleware. On the other hand UICC applets "understand" only APDU commands. Therefore, in order to make communications between mobile applications and UICC applet as smooth as possible, we introduced the middleware layer.

The middleware provides high level APIs to mobile application developers. These APIs do not require from application developers any knowledge of UICC internal functions and therefore they can be easily used through corresponding APIs. Moreover, the middleware communicates with UICC and applets using APDUs. So, middleware in fact performs communications between the mobile applications and the UICC by "translating" application-enabled APIs to card-level APDUs.

There are two basic approaches to implement the middleware. The first one is to extend an existing application with some extra features that will provide this functionality. The second approach is to create a separate module – the middleware that will provide communication between an application, which wants to use UICC functions and data storage in chip, and the UICC itself.

2.1   Middleware as a Separate Module

In this case the middleware is designed and implemented as a module separate from any application. It runs simultaneously with the application that use UICC functionalities. This means that there are two different layers in which the middleware provides communication. The upper layer deals with communication between the application and the middleware, while the lower layer deals with communication between middleware and UICC and its applets.

When considering communication at the upper layer, we actually need two functionalities:

– To pass data, sent to the UICC, between the application and the middleware or to execute some function of the underlying applets, in a secure way
– To receive feedback, positive or negative, of the communication process, i.e. whether data was successfully sent to the UICC or not and the result of the invoked operation.

At the lower layer we handle APDU commands exchanged with the UICC and its applets. In order to do that, an application must first create a connection with the UICC in order to communicate with an applet. This connection supports exchange of APDU messages in a format standardized by ISO 7816-4 [2]. Each connection has a logical channel reserved for its use. Our current implementation supports up to twenty logical channels for communication with the UICC chip, so our middleware truly supports multi–application UICC [8, 9]. The details of upper and lower layer communications depend also on the operating system of the mobile phone.

2.2   Middleware Integrated with an Application

An alternative approach is to create the middleware not as a separate module, but as an extension of an application that uses it. This means that the application calls middleware's APIs internally without using external invocation methods. The advantage of this approach is that upper layer communication and exchange of data between the application and the middleware can be done directly without the need to adjust to the mobile phone's operating system. As for the communication towards UICC, the approach is exactly the same as when the middleware is used as a separate module.

This approach makes the communication between the middleware and the application much easier to implement. No extra connection is needed between the two entities and transfer of data towards the UICC is performed smoothly. Moreover, since the middleware is integrated into the application, it can be completely adjusted to the application's specific needs and as a result, it is more efficient and effective during its use and operations.

3   Design Principles

Designing the middleware requires a different approach than creating a standard application. As it is intended to be used by mobile phone application developers, it does not provide any user interface, but it needs availability to easily connect to and communicate with other mobile applications. Therefore, some requirements are immediately obvious from this approach.

Developers do not need to know how the middleware works. It is not necessary to have knowledge of the internal logic of the middleware and of the way it implements its internal methods. This new way of using UICC and their applets should not change the way the user interacts with a phone. As Saltzer and Schroeder's Psychological Acceptability design principle suggests, if the new security features change the way of interaction and make it harder, users will simply avoid using them [3].

Moreover, the process must be transparent to the upper layer applications. The upper layer should not understand any difference between receiving and storing data to the UICC and manipulating data internally by its own applets. As a result, the middleware must provide friendly, easy to use and simple interface especially at the upper, API level.

The middleware must have no semantic knowledge of any data that it parses and passes in both directions. It must treat all data in the same way and not be dependent on different types of variables and values. This enables the middleware to handle data which are encrypted at the upper layer. Nonetheless it should have no knowledge of any passwords or keys that are used for authentication or cryptography. Implementing the middleware in this way makes it much more secure, flexible and easy to use.

Another important property of the middleware is to try to access and use UICC as infrequently as possible. UICC's lifetime is highly dependent on the frequency of its use. Although new UICCs tend to have bigger endurance to read/write cycles (100,000 cycles for [14]) we consider essential that the middleware should be designed in such a way that it reads and stores data on the chip as few times as possible.

4   Implementation Example

Within this research and development, we not only designed our middleware, but we also implemented and tested a prototype version of it. As our tool for designing and developing the middleware we used Java ME. Java ME is the most used independent development and operational platform. It is currently used in over 8000 devices and it is supported by many different vendors (Nokia, Sony Ericsson, LG, Samsung, and many others) [4]. Moreover, it has the Security and Trust Services API (SATSA), which enables communication with the UICC with the use of APDUs [5].

In order to test the middleware in a real case scenario we used our Secure Mobile Wallet application [6]. We extended the Wallet with middleware functionality as described in section 2.2. As a result, interactions between the Wallet and the middleware are performed internally. On the lower layer, communication towards the UICC is achieved with the use of the SATSA-APDU package.

An example of how the middleware is used can be seen in Figure 1. An upper layer application wants to retrieve some values from the UICC. In order to do so, it calls the corresponding methods from the middleware. The first time the middleware is called it establishes a connection with the UICC and leaves it open throughout the execution time of the upper layer application. Afterwards, since the connection is open, the middleware communicates with the UICC and fetches the data buffer, which contains the values that are requested. Then it parses the buffer and returns to the upper layer application the correct value.

In our implementation we provide the following API categories to the upper layer: Identification Data, Financial Data, Mobile Application Data, Security Data, System Data, PIN Commands and Middleware Operations. Each category further consists of a different set of buffers which store corresponding data. For example, the Identification Data category consists of the Wallet Owner, the Wallet Issuer and the SAFE System data buffers. Each of these buffers handles specific values, like the ones shown in figure 1. Each buffer has a different access method that can require authentication before giving read/write rights to the upper layer. Therefore strong access control can also be enforced.

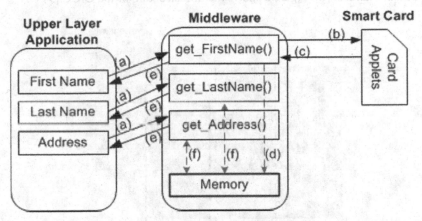

Fig. 1. An example use of the middleware. The upper layer application wants to retrieve three attributes from the UICC. To do so it calls the corresponding methods from the middleware. a) Call corresponding middleware method. b) Request data buffer which contains the desired variable. c) Send the requested buffer. d) Save the buffer in the memory. e) Parse the buffer, return the value. f) Read the buffer from the memory

For our middleware we introduced internal working memory. So, when the middleware reads a buffer from the UICC, it stores it temporary in its memory. As a result, when the middleware needs to fetch another value that belongs to the same buffer, it will first check if it has already stored that buffer in its memory and then read the data from there. This leads to a significant decrease in the number of transactions with the UICC and hence makes the whole process a lot faster to complete while at the same time it extends the UICC's lifetime.

The decision of how to manipulate the memory is left to the mobile application developers. For example, they may choose not to use the memory at all or use it as much as possible in order to minimize the transactions with the UICC. This can depend on the hardware specifications of the UICC. If the UICC can support a very large number of read/write cycles, [13] for instance supports 500,000 cycles, use of memory buffers may not be needed.

5   Interactions with UICC

UICC is the new generation of chips used for mobile communications, usually known as Subscriber Identity Module (SIM). It is introduced by organizations like ETSI, ISO and GSM that promote next generation of SIM chips as an open and service-oriented platform. UICC is no longer a closed environment and technology, but a multi-application hardware and software environment [7]. It allows other applications, besides standard SIM application, to reside and run on the same chip. SIM and other applications are parallel and managed simultaneously by the card operating system, i.e. Global Platform [8]. Figure 2 shows the infrastructure of the UICC [9].

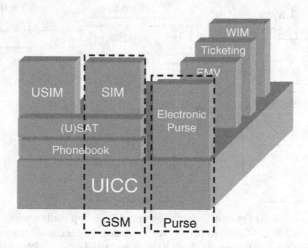

Fig. 2. The Internal Structure of UICC and Its Applications (adopted from [9])

Another significant innovation of UICC technologies is that they are now enabled by the Java virtual machine. So, all UICC internal applications are developed using Javacard Framework, which is much smaller and more compact compared with other platforms, for instance Java EE. These on-card Java applications are called Javacard applets. Even though the on-card Javacard language and environment is a subset of full Java language and environment, it integrates some other technologies specially created for SIM chips, called SIM Toolkit. The SIM Toolkit is a set of international standardized commands. Using it Javacard applets can construct their own Graphical User Interface [10]. Javacard technology and SIM Toolkit make it easier to develop a complete application for UICCs.

Javacard applets reside on the UICC and they are accessed by the middleware. Actually, Javacard applets stored in UICC support and respond to the middleware's requests. The middleware provides high level APIs to upper layer developers by "translating" them into sequences of corresponding APDUs. After that, it sends those APDUs to Javacard applets. All APDUs are predefined and standardized. In our implementation, we have two types of APDUs: for standard functions of Javacard applets we use standard APDUs [8]. However, for our Wallet application that uses our Wallet applet, there are no standard APDUs, so we have created our own APDUs supporting secure mobile payment functions and data handling. Only the middleware and the specific applet loaded in the UICC understand the meaning of these APDU commands, so they can successfully communicate with each other. When the UICC receives an APDU, the command is analyzed by the on-card operating system and then the corresponding applet is activated. The applet executes specific function that the APDU requires and sends back the response. The whole process is completed within the UICC; data are passed back to the middleware through a secure channel, so UICC provides support to and guarantee full data security. The complete process is shown in Figure 3 (adopted from [11]).

The secure channel that is created between the UICC and the reader (handset) is based on authentication using each one's set of Master keys. The middleware residing in the handset uses connection tools (SATSA for example) sending APDUs to UICC chips. The master keys of the chip are pre-set in the connection tools. During the authentication the security requirements, i.e. encryption, integrity, are negotiated. Finally, with a set of temporary keys, deriving from the Master keys, the session keys are established. This whole process is transparent to the upper layer and is described in the GlobalPlatform Card Specification [8].

There are two different approaches in order to load the applet into the UICC. The first one is to load the applet before the UICC SIM card is removed from the plastic housing. The application is loaded into the card with other applications, i.e., communication applications. This is done by the network operator during the chip personalization process.

The second approach is to load the applet using the OTA protocol. OTA protocol is designed to load and manage applications in UICC modules after they are delivered to subscribers. The back server sends a set of commands to the UICC module in order to update either the applications or the data. OTA protocol provides the possibility for service providers to maintain their applications OTA, whenever it is necessary.

To implement the OTA protocol, several issues should be solved. These are: over-the-air barrier to transport applications; methods to update applications and data in UICC modules; approaches to manage applications remotely. The solutions for these issues are all standardized. The barrier used to transport applications can be standardized message services like SMS. 3GPP TS 11.11 specifies commands for UICC modules that are operating files and if these commands are carried in class 2 SMS messages, the UICC modules can recognize and execute them. Global Platform Card Specification V2.2 [8] specifies the administration operations to the applications. To prevent the OTA administration approach being used illegally, 3GPP TS 03.48 specifies the security mechanisms.

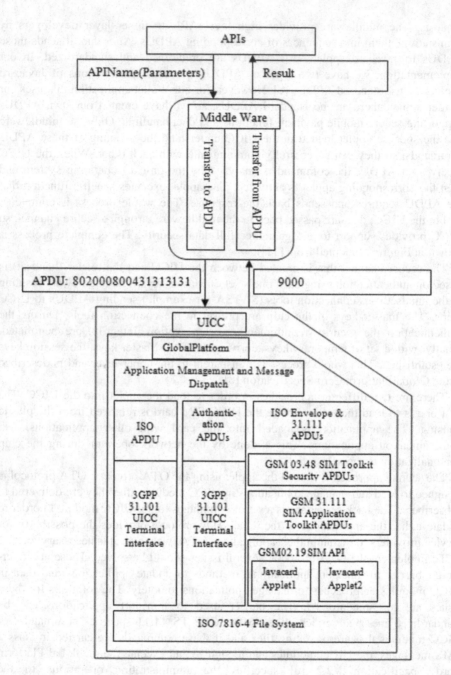

Fig. 3. The Process of Exchanging Data between the Upper Layer and the UICC

6   Conclusions

With the design and even prototype implementation of our middleware, we are now able to store data in a secure way on the UICC module and retrieve it with ease. We also implemented many functions and data handling operations for secure mobile financial transactions. The process of using those APIs is transparent to upper layer applications what makes the middleware very easy to use. No extra knowledge is needed in order to take advantage of its capabilities. Moreover, the whole process is as "light", from a computational point of view, as possible, so that no extra hardware capabilities are needed.

Users of mobile phone applications that are based on our middleware can now securely store data on their UICC and take advantage of the capabilities it provides. They can be confident that data cannot be retrieved by an unauthorized person. In addition, they can take advantage of the UICCs mobility. Namely, users can transfer their UICC to another phone and all the data will be available to them as if nothing changed. This gives users the possibility to enjoy true mobility of their mobile phone applications.

7   Future Research

During this research we implemented the middleware using Java ME which was built into an existing application (Secure Mobile Wallet). Further research, however, could involve the process of making the middleware totally independent from any specific mobile phone application. It should be created as a standalone functional module that communicates with other applications in a secure way and then stores and retrieves data from the UICC.

Moreover, besides secure storage, various additional functionalities should also be added. The middleware should be able to provide an interface for all the functionalities that are supported by all applets stored on the UICC. It should be also possible to support over–the–air applet management functions, such as the possibility to load and unload new applets or to check the available memory.

Finally, further research could also focus on implementing our middleware for other platforms. Although Java ME is the most ubiquitous application platform for mobile devices, the fast spread of Android, as well as the already popular iPhone O.S., makes the need of creating a middleware that is able to run with those operating systems absolutely necessary. Unfortunately, by the time this paper was written, there were no standardized APIs for the above operating systems supporting exchange of APDUs with a UICC. However, it is most likely that such APIs will be soon available to developers.

References

[1]   Wireless Intelligence, http://www.wirelessintelligence.com (accessed January 26, 2011)

[2]   International Standards Organization (ISO): Identification cards – Integrated Circuit Cards – Part 4: Organization, security and commands for interchange. International Standards Organization, ISO 7816-4 (2005)

[3]   Bishop, M.: Computer Security: Art and Science, pp. 348–349. Addison-Wesley, Boston (2003)

[4]   Oracle: Java Platform Micro Edition Software Development Kit 3.0 for Windows, http://www.oracle.com/technetwork/java/javame/downloads/sdk30-jsp-139759.html (accessed January 26, 2011)

[5]   Java Community Process: Security and Trust Services API (SATSA) for JAVATM 2 Platform, Micro Edition. Java Community Process, JSR-177 (2007)

[6]   Zhang, F.: Secure Applications for Financial Environments (SAFE) System. Licentiate Thesis Report, pp. 66–73 (2010)

[7]   European Telecommunications Standards Institute (ETSI): UICCs: Secured Packet Structure for UICC-based Applications. ETSI TS 102.225 V7, http://www.etsi.org (accessed September 21, 2010)

[8]   Global Platform: Global Platform Card Specifications, version 2.2, http://www.golbalplatform.org/secificationscard.asp (accessed September 23, 2009)

[9]   Lenhart, G.: The UICC Platform. ETSI Technical Committee UICC Platform, http://portal.etsi.org/scp/summary.asp (accessed September 23, 2009)

[10]   Guthery, S.B., Cronin, M.J.: Mobile Application Development with SMS and the SIM Toolkit, pp. 131–155. McGraw-Hill Professional (2001)

[11]   Guthery, S.B., Cronin, M.J.: Mobile Application Development with SMS and the SIM Toolkit, p. 117. McGraw-Hill Professional (2001)

[12]   Kounelis, I.: Design and Implementation of Secure Mobile Phone Middleware for UICC Chips. M.Sc. Thesis, ICT/KTH (June 2010)

[13]   STMicroelectronics: ST21Y144, Smartcard MCU with 114 Kbytes High Density EEPROM (March 2007), http://www.st.com (accessed May 5, 2011)

[14]   Shanghai Huanhong Integrated Circuit Co.: SHC 1206, http://www.arm.com (accessed: May 5, 2011)

An Investigation of Different Computing Sources for Mobile Application Outsourcing on the Road

Mohammed Anowarul Hassan and Songqing Chen

Dept. of Computer Science
George Mason University
mhassanb@gmu.edu, sqchen@cs.gmu.edu

Abstract. Mobile applications are growing fast due to pervasive usage of mobile devices. With inherently limited on-device resources, plenty of research has been conducted on job partitioning/outsourcing strategies to execute mobile computing tasks on external sources, such as public clouds or nearby computers. However, little is known about the performance difference to mobile users on these external computing sources.

In this paper, considering the user's response time and the battery power consumption on mobile devices, we first show that outsourcing mobile applications to public clouds may not outperform outsourcing to nearby residential computers, particularly for delay sensitive applications. To facilitate efficient mobile outsourcing to residential computers, we propose to build a framework RoseMic (ROad-SidE-MobIle-Computing). In RoseMic, a resource overlay network is built with users' idle residential (home) computers. To encourage the sharing of idle residential computers, RoseMic also includes a credit based incentive mechanism that can be enforced automatically without users' interferences in order to defeat collusion attacks. To demonstrate the performance of RoseMic, we run several real-world applications. The results show that RoseMic outperforms Amazon EC2 by 3 times and 4 times on average in terms of response time and the battery power consumption, respectively.

1 Introduction

With the fast development of micro-chip and wireless technologies, mobile devices are gaining increasing popularity. According to International Data Corporation, the total number of hand-held devices sold in 2009 is 1,127.8 million [4]. Among them, 174.2 millions (15.5%) are smartphones, which is a 15.1% increase from the previous year.

The pervasive usage of mobile devices has enabled fast growth of mobile applications. Compared to traditional mobile phones that are mainly used for voice communications, today a smartphone is capable of common tasks that were only possible on desktop computers, such as surfing the Internet, taking and editing pictures, gaming, document processing, etc.

However, mobile devices, albeit their fastly increasing CPU speed and memory size, are not as capable as modern desktop computers when running these applications. In particular, mobile devices are ultimately constrained by the limited

N. Venkatasubramanian et al. (Eds.): Mobilware 2011, LNICST 93, pp. 153–166, 2012.

battery supply and a prolonged computation process or a computing intensive application can quickly exhaust the limited battery power.

To address the fundamental challenge posed by the limited on-device resources for computing-intensive tasks, plenty of research has been conducted on designing various job partitioning/outsourcing strategies [7,12,15] to outsource mobile computing tasks to external sources. Today external computing sources are widely available, such as public clouds or nearby surrogate computers. However, little has been done to investigate the outsourcing performance to mobile users on different computing sources. This is particularly important for some delay sensitive mobile applications. In practice, a mobile user in motion may only have sporadic WiFi connections with very short connection duration. For example, previous work [14] has shown that with a typical WLAN with 200 meters of range, a user in motion with a speed up to 120 Km/h can have Internet access for about only 6 - 12 seconds. It is thus very desirable for a mobile user to complete the outsourcing and get the result back as soon as possible, best in this time frame.

In this paper, we set to investigate where to effectively outsource mobile applications on the road. Considering the response time to the user and the battery power consumption on mobile devices that are critical to mobile users in motion, we first show that outsourcing mobile applications to clouds may not outperform outsourcing to nearby residential computers, particular for delay sensitive applications. Thus, to facilitate efficient mobile outsourcing to road-side residential computers, we propose to build a framework RoseMic (ROad-SidE-MobIle-Computing), aiming to reduce the user's response time and battery power consumption. In RoseMic, a resource overlay network is constructed with participating users' idle residential (home) computers. Furthermore, to encourage users to participate in this resource overlay, an incentive mechanism is built and enforced automatically without any user's interference in order to defeat collusion attacks.

To demonstrate the performance of RoseMic, we have built a prototype and experimented RoseMic with several real-world applications, including text searching, face detection, and image processing. The results show that RoseMic not only outperforms on-device computing by 8 times and 10 times in terms of response time and the battery power consumption, respectively, but also outperforms Amazon EC2 by 3 times and 4 times on average, respectively.

The remainder of the paper is organized as follows. We present our motivation in Section 2 and RoseMic overview in Section 3, followed by the detailed design in Section 4. We present some preliminary evaluation results in Section 5 and discuss related work in Section 6. We make concluding remarks in Section 7.

2   Motivation

Previous research has proposed that mobile devices can outsource computing intensive jobs to public clouds or surrogate computers. To test the performance of outsourcing to the public clouds and nearby residential computers, we have conducted some preliminary experiments with Amazon EC2 and our local computers. The experiment is to find a string in a text file. Three approaches have been tested out.

- **Android:** This is to perform computation on the mobile device itself. In the experiment, we use Google Nexus one SmartPhone with Android 2.2 Operating System and 1 GHz CPU and 512 MB RAM.
- **Amazon EC2:** This is to send the data file and the computing task to Amazon EC2. We rent EC2 and follow the instructions to get our rented portion initialized first. Our portion of slice uses a CPU of 5 GHz and 1.7 GB of memory. The wireless network speed is 300 Kbps on average.
- **Residential Computers:** This is to send the data file and the computing task to nearby computers. In the experiment, we use the Android phone to send to the local computer in the same network via 802.11b with a speed of 10 Mbps. The local computer has a CPU of 2 GHz and 3.2 GB of RAM.

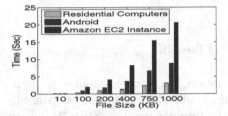 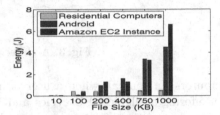

Fig. 1. Response Time   **Fig. 2.** Energy Consumption

Figure 1 shows the user response time when the same program is executed with different approaches along the increase of the file size. It also shows that although EC2 has a much faster CPU, the local machine outperforms EC2 by about 7 times and the performance on EC2 is even worse than the performance when it is executed on the mobile device itself. Figure 2 further shows the corresponding energy consumed on the mobile device for executing the program with different approaches. Not surprisingly, outsourcing to nearby computers consumes the least amount of energy on Android based on Power Tutor [5].

We have also conducted experiments with several other applications and obtained similar results. These results show that when outsourcing mobile computing tasks, the network tranferring time, i.e., the available bandwidth, has to be taken into consideration and sometimes this may be a dominant factor. Under such situations, outsourcing to nearby residential computers may be more beneficial than to public clouds.

3 Overview of ROad-SidE-MobIle-Computing (RoseMic)

RoseMic is proposed to assist mobile computation outsourcing by leveraging nearby residential computers. In RoseMic, we assume that data transferring in this procedure can only be done through WiFi instead of cellular connections considering its cost and relatively small bandwidth.

Figure 3 depicts the architecture of RoseMic. As shown in this figure, there is a resource overlay that a participating mobile user can leverage for computing in motion. The resource overlay consists of normal users' residential (home)

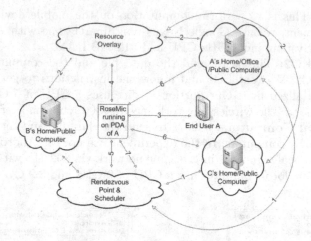

Fig. 3. Architecture of RoseMic

computers. In general, when a user is in motion, her home computer is often idle, offering available CPU cycles and WiFi connections that can be utilized. A user can register her home computer in the resource overlay (**Step 2**) before her departure through the rendezvous points (**Step 1**). At present, we assume there is one to one map between the mobile user and her home computer on the overlay. It is easy to expand to the one to many case.

When the user is on the road and wants to execute some computing intensive application, she submits the job to the RoseMic client running on her mobile device (**Step 3**). The RoseMic client will contact the overlay (**Step 4**) by visiting a well-known bootstrapping site. Such contact could be done through the cellular connection if WiFi is not available. In the response to this request, the user is directed to the rendezvous point (**Step 5**). Based on the geographical location of the mobile user, a list of nearby residential computers on the overlay are identified by the rendezvous point. The rendezvous point also maintains the credit information for each user. The scheduler running on the rendezvous point further selects some of these computers based on its scheduling policy. The scheduler can take a lot of factors into consideration, such as the current load on the machines, the distance to the user, the available credit of the requesting machine, etc.

Once the list of residential computers in the connectivity range is determined, the list of the machines is sent back by the rendezvous point to the mobile user (**Step 5**). From now on, all communications are done through WiFi connections. Based on the list, the mobile user connects to these nearby computers and can start the execution. If the RoseMic scheduler decides to execute the job on-device, then it does so and returns the result to the user (**Step 3**). If outsourcing is more economical, RoseMic then submits the job to the most appropriate residential computer and waits for the result (**Step 6**). The RoseMic then also returns the result to the user's application (**Step 3**). Upon the completion of the task, RoseMic automatically sends the completion information to the rendezvous point so that the credit scores of the involved users are updated (**Step 7**). That is, the credit of the mobile user who requests the computation outsourcing should be deducted accordingly and the credits of owners of the computing machines should be increased.

Note that in practice RoseMic does not prevent the user from leveraging public clouds when necessary. For example, when there is no nearby residential computers available, public cloud can be used.

4   Design of RoseMic

The previous section shows that RoseMic consists of (1) a resource overlay, (2) an incentive model and (3) a scheduler. In this section, we further present our design of these three parts.

4.1   Resource Overlay Network

To utilize nearby residential computers, in RoseMic, a resource overlay network is constructed by mobile users' residential computers that would otherwise be idle. Note that our assumption is that there is a one-to-one map between a mobile user and her residential computer on the overlay. That is, there is a same id used to identify the mobile device and the corresponding overlay computer. In addition, a rendezvous point is used to store the credit made by the corresponding overlay computer for each mobile user. Basically, the rendezvous point provides directory services and maintain a database of record <id, location, status, credit> for each user. Note the location is the geographical location of the mobile user's residential machine, and the status is the load state on that machine. The location is denoted as a pair of <latitude, longitude>. The status could be one of the following: idle, medium, busy, and is determined simply based on the CPU utilization on the machine. In the following context, we assume the node and the residential computer are interchangeable unless noted otherwise.

Node Joining. If a user wants to register her node to offer services, she can instruct the joining node to first contact the bootstrapping site via a Web browser (assume the same Web site www.RoseMic.org). In the response, the rendezvous point (RP) is returned to the joining node. Subsequently, the joining node contacts the RP for joining. In the joining request to the RP, the id and location information is also required. However, we do not assume GPS or GPS-capable functions on the home computer. Instead, we rely on the Google Geolocation service by enabling the "sharing your location" in the web browser. Such a request leverages Google Geolocation service to identify the location of the requesting computer based on nearby access points and other wireless information [3].

With the id and location information, the RP can retrieve its available credit from the database. Furthermore, the RP sets this computer status to idle initially, and sorts the available computers based on their location. After joining the resource overlay network, the joining node does not keep its connection with the RP. Instead, a participating node sends periodic heartbeat message to the RP to notify it aliveness.

Node Departure. A user's residential computer may depart from the resource overlay network for many reasons. For example, the user may want to use her computer exclusively or it may simply crash. Accordingly, we classify node departure into two categories. The first is normal departure. In a normal departure, the node notifies the RP about its un-availability and requests to be taken off from the available list maintained by the RP. Correspondingly, the RP removes this node from the available computer list. Since a participating node periodically sends keepalive message to the RP, it is easy to deal with abrupt departure. Basically, if there is no keepalive message received for a certain timeout period, the node is assumed to be dead. Correspondingly, the node is removed from the available list.

4.2 Credit-Based Incentive Model

To encourage the contribution of idle CPU cycles and bandwidth from residential computers, we propose to build a credit-based incentive mechanism on the overlay. The motivation behind users' offering their residential computers is as follows. While a user is in motion, her residential computers is often idle. So is the residential WiFi connection. Thus, a user in motion can use other users' computers for computation as a return of offering her computer and WiFi connection for others when she is on the road. To guarantee fair sharing, users who offer CPU cycles from their computers get credits that they could use in the future (when they need to use other users' computers or WiFi connections).

To keep track of the credit of each user, the credit is stored on the RP. To deal with collusion attacks, RoseMic also includes a credit system. While more details will be provided later, the high level idea is: upon the completion of a task, a transaction module in RoseMic automatically reports to RP about the computing tasks conducted on the relevant computers. Basically, the transaction module reports 1) the `id` of computing requester, 2) the `ids` of the computers used, 3) the amount of CPU cycles and bandwidth being used from each of the involved computers. The RP uses this information to calculate the credits that should be deducted from the requester and distribute these credits to the involved `ids` proportionally.

For example, if user A uses the residential computer of C, the credit of user C should be increased by the equation 1:

$$credit_C^A + = \alpha \times C_A + \beta \times D_A, \tag{1}$$

where C_A represents the total CPU cycles used by user A, D_A represents the total bandwidth usage by user A, denoted by the amount of data transferred to the computer of C from A's mobile device for the computation. Based on the same principle, user A's credit is reduced. Note in equation 1, α and β are normalization factors that can be determined experimentally and/or based on the resource demand and supply. Initially, each user has no credit but we allow negative credits in the system.

Our credit-based incentive model is enforced without direct involvement of the users. This is to deal with collusion attacks that some users may launch to claim credits for bogus transactions. Unless our transaction module in RoseMic is attacked and modified, no collusion attacks could be launched. In addition, we can also enforce that a user cannot use other users' computer unless her computer is on the resource overlay in order to deal with free-riders.

4.3   RoseMic Scheduler

The RoseMic scheduler is responsible for finding the most appropriate residential computers for the mobile user who requests the computation outsourcing service. In our current design, the scheduler runs on the RP.

In finding the most appropriate computers to execute the task, the RoseMic scheduler considers the following:

1. User's credit: A user with a high credit score has a high priority to get her job outsourced. This is to encourage more users to participate in the resource overlay network.
2. Job Type: When requesting the computation outsourcing, the mobile user also indicates the job type. Based on both the CPU and the bandwidth demand and the data locations, nearby residential computers or the user's home computers are determined.
3. Bandwidth: In searching for the most appropriate residential computers for outsourced computation, the computer with the highest bandwidth is always selected first if other conditions are the same.
4. Node Status: Since RoseMic targets delay-sensitive applications, the status of selected computers may affect the response time. Furthermore, it is also important for the RP to maintain load balance across different residential computers on the resource overlay.

Considering the above factors, RP employs its optimization function by comparing the predicted response time of different task assignment strategies. It takes a number of input and outputs the best execution strategy.

Algorithm 1. RoseMic Scheduler(I,J,L)

1: $LC \leftarrow$ The set of available computers nearby including the mobile device and home computer of the user calculated from I,J and L
2: $LCF \leftarrow$ empty set
3: **for** each node i in LC **do**
4:    **if** $J_c \leq i_c$ **then**
5:       add i to LCF
6:    **end if**
7: **end for**
8: **for** each node i in LCF **do**
9:    $i_{dt} \leftarrow J_D - i_{ds}$
10:    $candidate\_value_i \leftarrow (i_c - J_C) \times \gamma - (i_{dt} \div i_{bw}) \times \sigma - (|L - i_l| \div i_{bw}) \times \lambda$
11: **end for**
12: **return** node i $= \max\{\forall\, i \in$ LCF$: candidate\_value_i\}$

In the above algorithm, I represents the user's `id`, from which the credit of the user can be retrieved. If multiple users compete for the same residential computers, user with higher credit gets the priority. L is the location, which is needed to find the nearby computers available for computation outsourcing. J represents the job type. J_C indicates the CPU cycle demanded, and J_D indicates the amount of data needed to the transfered for computation. LC is the list of the available computers, which holds the following informations for each node in that list: 1) i_c: computation power available on node i; 2) i_l: location of node i; 3) i_{bw}: bandwidth of the channel from the mobile device to the node i; 4) i_{ds}: amount of data stored in prior for a job J in the node i; 5) i_{dt}: amount of data needed to be transferred from the mobile device to node i. γ, σ and λ are constants to add weight on different components. Note that we assume profiling can be used to obtain these parameters for mobile applications.

Note that we include the mobile device and the home computer of the user as potential candidates to execute computation as well, because computation may be economical to execute entirely on the mobile device or the user's home computer, where most of the data may reside.

As shown in the algorithm, in the first step, RoseMic reduces the set of available computers nearby LC to the set of feasible computers LCF. If any node has enough CPU to execute the job, it is a candidate and added to set LCF. The candidate value for each node i is calculated based on the latency, bandwidth, amount of data needed to be transferred and computation power available on that node. The scheduler then selects the node with highest candidate value to outsource the computation.

5   Preliminary Evaluation

To evaluate the performance of RoseMic, we conduct experiments with a RoseMic prototype and compare its performance against when executing on the mobile device as well as executing on the public cloud Amazon EC2. In these experiments, the credit system is not being evaluated as these experiments are conducted locally as proof-of-concept.

5.1   Experiment Setup

We use Google Android Nexus One with 1 GHz CPU and 512 RAM as the mobile device for the local execution. We use computers with dual-core CPU with 2GHz and 2 GB RAM to emulate overlay residential computers. The remote EC2 Ubuntu instance has a 5 GHz CPU with 1.7 GB of RAM. We use Power Tutor [5] to measure the power consumed by the applications running on the smartphone. The WiFi is 10 Mbps and the average bandwidth from the Android Phone to EC2 instance is around 300 Kpbs on average.

We have conducted experiments with three applications, 1) Text Searching, 2) Face Detection, and 3) Image Sub-Pattern Searching.

In the experiments, we emulate a 3 user model and they have identical residential computers and mobile devices. The latitude and longitude of the first user's residential computer is 38.901222 and -77.26526, while the other two users' residential computers are at 38.846224 (Lat.) and -77.306373 (Lon.). The EC2 instances rented are at Northern Virginia Data Center of Amazon. We profile each application to deduce the average CPU cycle and data transfer requirement and we run each application in the following different environments.

- **On-device***(OD)***:** This is to run the application on the mobile device directly.
- **Computation+Data***(CD)***:** This is to outsource the computation program and the data. The RoseMic client running on the mobile device gets connected to the resource overlay and the rendezvous point to explore the neighboring residential computers and outsource the computation with the data file.
- **Computation+Data+Node Failure***(CD+F)***:** This is to consider the node failure in the above environment to study the impact of node failure. When a node fails, we contact the resource overlay and the rendezvous point once again to find another neighboring residential computer and restart the job. To emulate node failure case, we deliberately turn off one computer in the middle of an on-going computation when the computation is 90% completed. Then RoseMic detects the failure based on timeout and it contacts resource overlay and rendezvous point to find another nearby residential computer.
- **Computation***(C)***:** This is to outsource only the computation for these applications. This is to emulate the scenario when the selected residential computer is the user's home computer, which has the data of the task and the mobile device only needs to transmit a small portion of data.
- **Computation+Node Failure***(C+F)***:** This is to consider the node failure in the above environment. Note that here for both the failed node and the new node, we outsource only the computation. We emulate the node failure case as we have done for CD+F.
- **EC2** *(EC2)***:** We outsource the computation to the remote amazon EC2 instance with 5 GHz of CPU and 1.7 GB of memory. We assume that EC2 is always available and 100% reliable.

We use Java and outsource the computation class in byte code format and use java dynamic class loader to execute the computation. We assume the computing environment is set in advance. In these experiments, we mainly focus on the response time and the energy consumption on the mobile device.

5.2   Experiment Results

In this section, we describe the performance of the different approaches we have tested for the three applications. We repeat each experiment five times and present the average of the results.

Text Search. In this experiment, the user searches a string in a text file and the frequency of occurrence of that string is returned to the user. This simple string counting application takes an input file of 2.6 MB. We use string matching to find the total number of occurrence of that string in that text file.

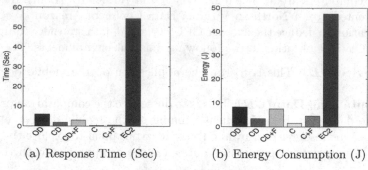

(a) Response Time (Sec)   (b) Energy Consumption (J)

Fig. 4. Text Search

Figure 4 shows the performance of the application when it is executed on the Android and the computation is outsourced. Figure 4(a) shows the response time of the execution. Figure 4(b) shows the corresponding energy consumption on the mobile device. In this application, if the data needs to be outsourced, it is 2.6 MB. Otherwise, only the computing program needs to be outsourced, which is 1 KB.

As shown in Figure 4, outsourcing to EC2 results in the worst performance in terms of both the response time to the user and the amount of energy consumed, which are significantly larger than if the application is executed on the mobile device itself. On the EC2, the response time is over 50 seconds. If we consider the average connection time of a mobile user with a roadside WiFi ranges between 6-12 seconds [14], this is impossible for a mobile user to get the result in time in the same communication session although EC2 has a faster CPU speed (note that Amazon Northern Virginia Center is in the same region where these experiments are conducted). This would be a critical problem for delay sensitive mobile applications that a user waits to get the result back.

Figure 4 also shows that although outsourcing to nearby residential computers demands some bandwidth for file transferring, the response time and the total energy consumption on the mobile device are 69% and 59% less than that when the application is executed on the mobile device itself, respectively, indicating the benefit of the outsourcing.

As residential computers may not be reliable for many reasons (e.g., a user comes home and wishes to use her computer dedicatedly), we also study the node failure for this application. Figure 4 shows with node failure, the performance of outsourcing still outperforms the on-device computing in terms of both the response time and the total energy consumed on the mobile device, although there is a 76% and 200% increase compared to if there is no node failure.

Face Detection. In this experiment, we take a picture of a human face and try to match it with all the pictures in a folder previously taken. We use Cross-Correlation Function [2] to find the correlation between an image pair. Based upon that, we detect a particular person. We have each image in a different jpg file. The correlation between the files has been calculated by taking input from three different streams for 3 RGB values. The resultant size for the reference images is 575 KB in total and the newly taken image size is 145 KB. So the total size of the data file is 720 KB, and the computation program is 3 KB.

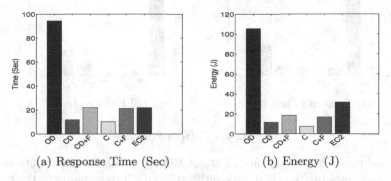

(a) Response Time (Sec)   (b) Energy (J)

Fig. 5. Face Detection

Figure 5 shows the performance results when the program is executed in different environments. For this application, Figure 5(a) shows that executing on the Android takes the longest time of about 94.5 seconds. In all the outsourcing scenarios, the response time is significantly reduced. Not surprisingly, the corresponding energy consumption is the largest for the on-device execution.

While in all the outsourced computation scenarios, both the response time and the energy consumption are reduced, the reduction when the program is outsourced to the nearby residential computers is more pronounced than when the program is outsourced to EC2: on the residential computer, the response time is about 10.25 seconds and 11.90 seconds without or with the data transferred. This indicates that it is possible for the user to get the result back with the same connection when the user is in motion. Correspondingly, the energy consumed is only about 23% and 36%, respectively, when the computation is outsourced to nearby residential computers.

Even when there is node failure, Figure 5 shows that both the response time and the energy consumption increases by 107% and 127% compared to their counterpart without any node failure, the results are still comparable or better than those when outsourcing to EC2, in terms of response time and energy consumption, respectively.

Image Pattern Search. In this experiment, we take a picture and try to find the picture as a part of another large picture in a folder previously taken. We use Cross-Correlation Function [2] and 2D Logarithmic Search [13] to find the sub-image. We have each image in a different jpg file. The correlation between the files has been calculated by taking input from three different streams for 3 RGB values. The resultant size for the reference image is 1.7 MB and the newly taken image size is 260 KB.

Figure 6 shows the performance results when the program is executed in different environments. For this application, Figure 6(a) shows that executing on

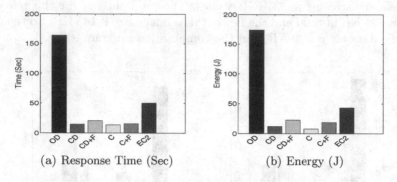

(a) Response Time (Sec)   (b) Energy (J)

Fig. 6. Image Pattern Search

the Android takes the longest time of about 163.9 seconds. In all the outsourcing scenarios, the response time is significantly reduced. Correspondingly, the energy consumption is the largest for the on-device execution.

While in all the outsourced computation scenarios, both the response time and the energy consumption are reduced, the reduction when the program is outsourced to the nearby residential computers is more pronounced than when the program is outsourced to EC2: on the residential computer, the response time is about 13.37 seconds and 14.52 seconds without or with the data transferred. Correspondingly, the energy consumed is only about 10% and 11%, respectively, when the computation is outsourced to nearby residential computers without or with the data transferred respectively.

When there is node failure, Figure 6 shows that both the response time and the energy consumption increases by 40% and 136% compared to their counterpart without any node failure. These results are still much better than those when outsourcing to EC2.

Summary: The experimental results show that while computation is outsourced to local residential computers, the overall performance is better than when the computation is outsourced to EC2, though EC2 is much more powerful than nearby residential computers in terms of the CPU speed. The average gain for the response time is about 8 times and 3 times compared to if the computation is executed on Android or outsourced to EC2. The corresponding energy reduction is 10 times and 4 times, respectively.

We also note that EC2 performs the worse than on-device execution in *Text Searching* but performs better in the other two applications. This is due to the nature of the applications. *Face Recognition* and *Image Pattern Searching* applications are more CPU intensive than *Text Searching*. Thus, even executing on Android is faster than outsourcing to EC2, where data transferring becomes a dominant factor.

Note that the above results are case studies because a different user who has a different distance to EC2 or have conducted experiments on EC2 at different times or have conducted experiments with different applications with different data size and bandwidth may have different results.

6   Related Work

Outsourcing computing tasks from mobile devices to powerful computing resources, also referred to as remote execution, has been researched for over a decade [7,12,15,8]. The increasingly popular and pervasive usage of mobile devices makes this imperative. To outsource the computation, two classes of approaches have been studied. The first is to create the computing environment without modifying the applications. For example, work [9] proposes a full virtual machine clone technique that can enable the applications to be run without any modification on the cloud. This approach, however, has to consider the significant overhead of cloning the mobile environment, which may be expensive and delay the computing process, whether on the public computing clouds or nearby surrogate computers [16].

Instead of cloning the computing environment, the second approach is to partition the job between the mobile device and external computing resources [7,8,10]. Many of existing studies mainly aim to simplify such a process. Balan et al. [7,8] propose to augment the computation and storage capabilities of mobile devices by exploiting the nearby (surrogate) computers. Rudenko et al. [15] suggests that if the total energy cost of sending the task else where and receiving the result back is lower than the cost of running it locally, then remote process execution can save battery power. Flinn et al. [12] also propose a similar idea, in which remote execution simultaneously leverages the mobility of mobile devices and the richer resources of large devices. Studies [17,10] demonstrate the ability to partition the application and associate classes and thus outsourcing them. MAUI [11] is recently proposed to partition the program dynamically and submit it on surrogate computers.

Nevertheless, there is little research on where mobile applications should be outsourced. We consider this problem because the response time and the battery power consumption are critical to mobile users in motion. In addition, RoseMic leverages the idle CPU cycle and bandwidth sharing to assist mobile application outsourcing on the road. This is different from SETI@home [6] and BONIC [1], where participants purely voluntarily contribute their CPU cycles to a scientific problem. In RoseMic, participants share CPU and bandwidth with each other in a P2P fashion in order to get services.

7   Conclusion

The pervasive usage of mobile devices demands a flexible and effective computation outsourcing mechanism. While a lot of work has been conducted on job partitioning/outsourcing, in this study, we have investigated the effectiveness of outsourcing to nearby residential computers, particularly for delay-sensitive applications. To reduce the user response time and the energy consumption on mobile devices, we have designed a framework RoseMic to effectively support mobile computation outsourcing. We have experimented with several applications and our preliminary results show that our approach can more effectively improve the user response time and reduce the energy consumption on mobile devices than outsourcing to public clouds.

Acknowledgement. We appreciate constructive comments from anonymous referees. The work is partially supported by US NSF under grant CNS-0746649 and and AFOSR under grant FA9550-09-1-0071.

References

1. Boinc, http://boinc.berkeley.edu/
2. Cross Correlation, http://en.wikipedia.org/wiki/Cross-correlation
3. Google Geolocation Service,
   http://code.google.com/p/gears/wiki/GeolocationAPI
4. International Data Corporation : Press Release (January 28, and February 4, 2010),
   http://www.idc.com/
5. Power Tutor, http://ziyang.eecs.umich.edu/projects/powertutor/index.html
6. Seti Home, http://setiathome.berkeley.edu/
7. Balan, R., Flinn, J., Satyanarayanan, M., Sinnamohideen, S., Yang, H.-I.: The case of cyber foraging. In: Proceedings of the 10th ACM SIGOPS European Workshop, Saint-Emilion, France (July 2002)
8. Balan, R.K., Gergle, D., Satyanarayanan, M., Herbsleb, J.: Simplifying cyber foraging for mobile devices. In: Proceedings of the 5th International Conference on Mobile Systems, Applications, and Services (MobiSys), San Juan, Puerto Rico (June 2007)
9. Chun, B.G., Maniatis, P.: Augmented smartphone applications through clone cloud execution. In: Proceedings of the 12th Workshop on Hot Topics in Operating Systems (HotOS), Monte Veritá, Switzerland (May 2009)
10. Chun, B.G., Maniatis, P.: Dynamically partitioning applications between weak devices and clouds. In: Proceedings of ACM Workshop on Mobile Cloud Computing & Services (MCS), San Francisco, CA, USA (June 2010)
11. Cuervo, E., Balasubramanian, A., Cho, D.K., Wolman, A., Saroiu, S., Chandra, R., Bahl, P.: Maui: Making smartphones last longer with code offload. In: Proceedings of the 8th International Conference on Mobile Systems, Applications, and Services (MobiSys), San Francisco, CA, USA (June 2010)
12. Flinn, J., Narayanan, D., Satyanarayanan, M.: Self-tuned re-mote execution for pervasive computing. In: Proceedings of the 8th Workshop on Hot Topics in Operating Systems (HotOS), Schloss Elmau, Germany (May 2001)
13. Jain, J.R., Jain, A.K.: Displacement measurement and its application in interframe image coding. IEEE Transactions on Communications 29 (December 1981)
14. Ott, J., Kutscher, D.: Drive-thru internet: Ieee 802.11b for "automobile" users. In: Proceedings of IEEE InfoCom, Hong Kong (March 2004)
15. Rudenko, A., Reiher, P., Popek, G.J., Kuenning, G.H.: Saving portable computer battery power through remote process execution. In: Proceedings of Mobile Computing and Communication Review, MC2R (1998)
16. Satyanarayanan, M., Bahl, P., Caceres, R., Davies, N.: The case for vm-based cloudlets in mobile computing. IEEE Pervasive Computing 8(4) (October 2009)
17. Nahrstedt, K., Gu, X., Messer, A., Greenberg, I., Milojicic, D.: Adaptive offloading inference for delivering applications in pervasive computing environments. In: Proceedings of IEEE International Conference on Pervasive Computing and Communications (PerCom), Dallas-Fort Worth, Texas (March 2003)

Mobility-Tolerant, Efficient Multicast in Mobile Cloud Applications[*]

Ju Wang[1], Hui Chen[1], Kostadin Damevski[1], and Jonathan Liu[2]

[1] Virginia State University, Petersburg, VA 23806, USA
[2] University of Florida, Gainesville, FL
jwang@vsu.edu

Abstract. Interactive mobile applications require a highly available multicast service for information dissemination and collaboration, while being able to withstand mobility-induced network connectivity problems. However, efficient and reliable wireless multicast has remained a difficult challenge. We propose a novel wireless multicast scheme that allows more efficient and mobility-proof multicast in mobile cloud environments. Our scheme uses a distributed caching and deferred acknowledgement (ACK) technique to reduce delivery ACK traffic during a multicast session. Packets with pending ACK are cached in selected network nodes to provide fast re-delivery. A distributed multicast tree construction algorithm is also utilized to provide fast topology repair under dynamic network conditions. The tree maintenance requires each node to keep track of its 2-hop neighborhood connectivity. Our scheme's ability to overcome frequent network topology changes leads to a low message exchange overhead to correct local topology errors.

Keywords: multicast, mobile cloud, reliability, mobility, fail-recovery, MAC protocol, wireless network.

1 Introduction

Cloud computing with mobile devices [10–12] enables many new exciting applications that were unavailable in the past. For example, a mobile cloud could be made of smart phones to process real-time data (e.g., video and audio feeds, GPS coordinates). Other mobile cloud applications might involve realtime control/actuation (e.g., to physically turn on a ventilating fan) in wireless powered sensor networks. Such new applications need a capable and reliable communication infrastructure (both wireless and wired portions) to move large amount of data between mobile nodes in a timely manner.

One challenge in the intersection of mobile and cloud computing is the lack of mobility-tolerant middleware services. Reliable wireless multicast service would greatly enhance many mobile cloud applications. For instance, a mobile application utilizing a cloud of street video cameras can support a wide range

---

[*] This material is based upon work supported by the National Science Foundation under Award No.1040254.

N. Venkatasubramanian et al. (Eds.): Mobilware 2011, LNICST 93, pp. 167–180, 2012.
© Institute for Computer Sciences, Social Informatics and Telecommunications Engineering 2012

of image-based searching tasks (e.g. missing children, terrorist suspects). Such applications would depend on a reliable multicast service to distribute target pictures to all cloud nodes. Other wireless-based applications can also benefit from the service tremendously. Network-wide information dissemination, such as distributing new program/firmware across a re-programmable sensor network, could be performed more efficiently.

However, multicast in wireless mobile networks is expensive and significant network resource and energy must be committed to overcome a wide range of communication problems, from device failures, short term link lost, to packet delivery failures due and node movements. The fundamental challenge of multicast reduces to the efficient construction and maintenance of a multicast tree. The problem has been studied by many researchers [1, 3, 6] for both wired and wireless networks as an instance of the Minimum Connected Dominant Set (MCDS) problem, and recent work focuses on distributed multicast protocols [7]. Distributed solutions are attractive since localized decision making is more adaptive to a changing mobile environment.

When reliable packet delivery is added to the requirement, the problem becomes even more challenging. An intuitive solution requires all target nodes to acknowledge the receipt of each multicast packet. The multicast source is forced to schedule retransmissions until all nodes confirm a packet reception. If the multicast network contains more than one level of relay structure, the ACK traffic must be relayed back to the source node through the same network (but in reverse direction). To further complicate the matter, node movements during the multicast session will cause topology change and possibly interrupt the ACK process. The ACK from a moving node might have to be relayed to its original parent node to avoid unnecessary retransmission. All scenarios considered, significant amount of network traffic would be induced to an already congested network.

We observed that multicast traffic is sessional by nature: multicasting a video frame at the application layer will result in a stream of multicast packets from the same source node. Such traffic pattern is utilized in our design to improve reliability at a moderate message cost. Our solution consists of two key techniques:

1. We use a distributed caching and deferred ACK protocol to reduce the required ACK messages while still providing reliable tracking of data delivery. Multicast packets are cached throughout the network to provide a swift retransmission of dropped packets. The readily available of large flash memory in today's mobile devices provides significant cache benefit. Specifically, we are able to save significant ACK-related messages through the deferring scheme.
2. For route construction, we use a modified Distributed Local-Gain-Maximizing (DLGM) algorithm [17] to form a decentralized multicast tree that avoids network flooding. The scheme utilizes a multicast session concept so that multicast packets belongs to the same session can be handled with efficiency by reusing the routing path of a previous packet. Our DLGM-s algorithm, short

for DLGM-with-Session, is designed to handle multicast failure caused by node movements and reuse routing decision from previous packets. The uniqueness of our algorithm is that the multicast tree is formed during the media access stage and the algorithm is executed by all nodes to determine whether or not it should relay, delay, or ignore a new multicast packet. The algorithm is inherently distributed and adaptive to topology changes. Each node's local decision takes into account a dynamic multicast-gain calculated from the local connectivity and relaying activities at nearby nodes.

The rest of this paper is organized as follows: Section 2 provides a summary of related work; Section 3 shows the architecture of the proposed scheme and its packet delivery performance; Section 4 provides a qualitative analysis of reliability against device mobility for the relevant methods; Section 5 concludes this paper.

2 Related Works

Cloud computing [8] originates from service-oriented computing where hardware and software resources are provided as services and applications are regarded as consumers. Recently, the cloud computing model is extended to utilize mobile devices (such as smart phones) as hardware farms [13] at the cloud side to augment its computing capabilities. Mobile cloud applications can leverage all of the advantages from the conventional cloud concept, such as computation offloading to data centers [11]. In [14], an Android based smart phone and the Elastic Compute Cloud service of Amazon Web Services (http://aws.amazon.com/ec2/) is used to create a mobile cloud traffic light detector application. The smart phones are used mainly as video capture devices, and Amazon's cloud receives and processes the video frames.

Reliable multicast in a traditional network requires two all-to-one transmissions per packet: the Confirm-To-Send (CTS) stage and the ACK stage. Both consume considerable network resources. Several solutions were proposed in the past to use certain delay strategies to avoid CTS/ACK collision, or use selective CTS/ACK replying to reduce the problem to a manageable scale. However, most of this work is performed within a single hop network and there is no consideration to support multicast session. We observe that many practical multicast tasks would consists of many packets from the same source. We thus believe that, instead of replying ACK immediately, a deferred ACK scheme at the session level could allow a node to reduce ACK traffic without compromising the overall network trackability.

On the routing side, many existing multicast protocols construct a multicast tree through network flooding. However, simple flooding is known for its low efficiency due to many overlapped transmissions. Traditional multicast protocols are mostly best-effort type of services without delivery confirmation to save bandwidth.

The construction of the multicast tree can be formulated as an instance of the Connected Dominant Set (CDS) problem. CDS is known as an NP-complete problem and many heuristic algorithms have been discussed [5], some of which are distributed solutions for ad-hoc networks [4, 6, 7]. The method by Wieselthier et al.[15] shows that discovering the minimum-size multi-point relay set (MSMRS) is NP-hard. Qayyum et al. proposed MRP (Multipoint Relay Protocol)[3] where each relay node must select some of its 1-hop neighbors to further relay the multicast packet. A source-initiated CDS is thus formed as the broadcast packet is relayed throughout the multipoint relays.

The algorithm discussed in [5] is based on a generalization of Chvatal's greedy algorithm for the set cover problem. The algorithm obtains a dominant set S first, then it grows the dominant set by searching S's neighbor nodes and including vertexes of the highest degree. The MCDS algorithm requires the global knowledge of the network topology, which is expensive to implement in a distributed environment. Wan [4]shows that at least $O(nlogn)$ messages are required.

Wu and et.al. [1] [2] use a two-stage algorithm that takes an opposite approach. Their algorithm initially obtains a relative redundant CDS by choosing nodes whose neighbor sets are not completely overlapped. This is followed by a prune process to eliminate as many locally redundant nodes as possible while maintaining the required connectivity. The mark process and the original two prune rules require N^2 neighbor knowledge and is a purely discrete algorithm. Wang et.al, [17] use a concurrent CTS method to reduce the CTS overhead and DLGM algorithm to construct a hidden routing tree. The work presented here could be considered as an extension of this work in multicast session scenarios.

3   Overview

We assume a hybrid ad-hoc wireless network architecture that consists of three types of nodes: (1) A central node (C-Node) for monitoring and controlling purpose; (2) a set of stationary relay nodes (R-node) whose sole purpose is to facilitate routing and packet forwarding; (3) and a dynamic set of mobile nodes (M-node) who provide application specific computing, sensing, and actuating resources needed in mobile cloud applications. The concept of R-node is commonly used in the Wireless Sensor Network (WSN) community to alleviate the packet routing problem, similar to wireless access point in WLAN or base station in cellular networks. In addition to the fixed R-nodes, any M-node could claim itself as an R-node based on its position in the topology. Compared to other work, one distinct difference of our network architecture is that M-node assume a critical role in packet routing and delivery confirmation. As will be demonstrated later, such design greatly enhances the network's ability to operate even in high node mobility situations. Figure 1 shows a mobile cloud application at our institute where the proposed network architecture will be used to create a smart high-tunnel greenhouse. The demonstration network consists of wireless sensor devices, both static and mobile, to collect crop growth information and control irrigation/ventilation/pesticide delivery.

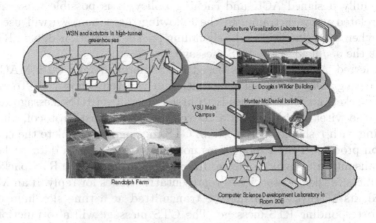

Overview of the proposed research instrument.

Fig. 1. Smart High-tunnel Mobile Cloud Demonstration Network

3.1   Problem Description

Many events can interrupt packet delivery during a multicast session: a node might be temporary out of reach, a packet might be dropped due to interference, or a node might experience hardware failure. To simplify our discussion, we exclude situations when packet delivery is physically impossible, which translates to the assumption that all nodes are connected and there is no permanent node loss. It is further assumed that all nodes are aware of the existence of some other nodes in the network and their ID, though the global network topology is unknown.

To achieve reliable multicast, the network must have a proper packet tracking ability and retransmission mechanism. Traditionally multicast packets are not cached other than in the source node, thus all packet delivery confirmations must be forwarded to the source node. If some packets need to be retransmitted, the process will start from the source node and possibly go through the entire network again even if many nodes might have already received it. In our scheme, the problem is solved by using dedicated multicast cache (M-cache) at all nodes for packet caching. Given that today's mobile device have access to gigabyte-level inexpensive flash memory for secondary storage this caching mechanism is practically achievable. The wide availability of cached copies of multicast packets is what makes the proposed scheme reliable and efficient.

3.2   Node Behavior: Deferred ACK

The rationals behind a deferred ACK scheme is the assumption that the multicast session might consist of many packets. Since a previous packet could be acknowledged through a piggy-back ACK from a later multicast packet (of the same session), it is unnecessary for all nodes to ACK for every new packet.

With carefully designed ACK and caching policy, it is possible to save much of ACK related network traffic. In the following discussion, we will use a dot notation when a specific field of the signalling packet is mentioned, e.g., RTS.seq represents the *seq* field of the RTS message.

The deferred ACK protocol is based on a modified RTS-CTS MAC layer function to regulate transmission activities in a given 2-hop cell. To relay a multicast packet, an R-node r needs to first transmit an RTS message to start acquiring the wireless channel. In a conventional multicast protocol, all nodes neighboring with r should reply with an CTS message to complete the channel-reservation process. If the R-node does not receive all CTSs, a data packet will not be transmitted to avoid collision. In our new protocol, the RTS packet will contain an *ctslist* field to specify m representative nodes for reply. If an M-node is selected, its CTS packet should be transmitted at a time slot indicated in the the corresponding RTS message. The CTS message will also function as a piggy-back ACK for its expected data packet. We hence use the term CTSACK for the modified CTS message.

After the RTS stage, the R-node will wait for $m + 2$ time slots to collect CTSACKs where the first m slots are reserved for the polled M-nodes, and the last two slots are open to any new nodes that just joined the current cell. Each CTSACK message also contains a source ID field so the R-node can update its local topology as well as the delivery status for cached packets. The R-node also interprets $CTSACK.seq + 1$ as the next expected packet of the respective M-node. If the $CTSACK.seq + 1$ is less than the sequence number of the current pending packet, an implicit retransmission requests would be entered for the corresponding packet into transmitting queue. Finally the R-node decides whether the current DATA packet should proceed, or a the RTS must be repeated.

The M-node behavior after receiving a RTS is fairly straightforward:

On Receiving an RTS

1. If the sender is not my uplink node, skip,
2. If the sender is not in my neighbor list, prepare a CTSACK message with subtype TU (topology update) and content for one of the two free CTS slots.
3. Otherwise, if the local node ID is listed in the ACK responder field of the received RTS, prepare CTSACK and transmit it at the designated slot. The current expected packet sequence number is included in the CTSACK.

For both R-node and M-node, a newly arrived multicast packet will be added to the local M-cache. For each entry in the M-cache, a node v maintains two lists: a ACK list and a CTS list to keep track of the status of its M-nodes. The ACK list contains all M-nodes that are associated to v. The CTS list will be changed if a node change its association or is not interested to a particular multicast packet. The ACK list is initialized to CTS list and updated accordingly when an CTS packet is observed. The pseudo-code in Figure 2 described the detailed protocol of the R-node to manage the multicast cache and determine its retransmission activity.

R-Node Protocol
$st \in \{READY, mRTS, rRTS, DATA, IDLE$
$T_0 :$ timer; $recv_{count} :$ integer; $WSIZE :$ integer

    (st==READY) and (have new packet in M-cache)
      send RTS
      set $T_0 = m + 2$ CTS **slot and start** T_0
      --→ $st := mRTS$
    (st == mRTS) and (T_0 not expired) and (received a CTSACK packet)
      seq = CTSACK.seq
      if cache[seq+1] does not exist
        insert rtxUP event
      else
        insert rtxlocal event
      src = CTSACK.src
      cache[seq]->ack[src] = 1
      cache[seq]->ackcount ++
      if (cache[seq]->ackcount > 1/2 * N) mark replaceable flag
      CTScount++
      if (CTScount > 1/2 * m)
        --→ $st := DATA$
    (st==DATA)
      send data packet
      st:=IDLE
    (T_0 expired)
      if (CTScount < 1/2 m)
      --→ $st = rRTS$
      TUTrigger -=1
      else reset TUTrigger
    (st == rRTS)
      determine the new list of ACK[wait] list
      append the code ids in
      the MRTS packet.
      reset T_0 **and re-send MRTS packet**
      st:= mRTS
    st==IDLE & rtxlocal event
      select the oldest packet from
      cache that is marked for retranmission
      remove its retx flag
      add the packet into tranmission buffer
      st := READY
    st=IDLE & rtxUP event
      compile the missing packet ids
      and send request to upstream.
    st=IDLE TUtrigger==0
      broadcast topology update 'hello' message

Fig. 2. R-node behavior. N is the size of local cell. m is the length of ACK list field. The protocol requires at least 50% of polled nodes to ACK.

3.3 Routing Behavior

Defining cell $N(v)$ as node v's neighbor set, the multicast routing problem is formulated to a MCDS problem [4, 6, 7]. Denoting graph $G(V, E)$ for the underlying network and $s \in V$ the multicast source node, the problem of seeking the optimum multicast tree is to find the smallest tree T, such that

$$\bigcup_{v \in T} N(v) = V$$

and

$$s \in T$$

We now discuss how a distributed multicast scheme would be constructed by maximizing the local multicast gain.

Since a distributed routing solution can't assume the knowledge about the global topology $G(V, E)$, we seek to maximize the number of newly covered nodes per transmission during a multicast session. The basic routing method is the DLGM (Distributed Local Gain Maximum) algorithm in [17]. The main modification here is the mechanism to reuse past routing decisions. For clarity, we summarize some of the key features of DLGM.

Unlike other routing methods where each node must maintain a list of neighbor node for local relay, DLGM rely on each nodes making individual decision based on a locally calculated gain factor. To maximize multicast coverage, the self-nominated relaying nodes should cover as many new nodes as possible. Meanwhile, the relaying nodes should be sufficiently separated each other to allow parallel relaying actions. Such design has obvious advantageous in a highly dynamic environment where the bulk of effort for routing tree update could be spared.

The DLGM algorithm requires that each nodes keep track of multicast status in its neighbor area. For each node $v \in V$, we denote its direct neighbor set by $N(v)$. At each node v, we maintain (1) $N(v)$, and (2) $N(u)$ for each $u \in N(v)$. That is, each node knows the network topology of its 2-hop neighborhood. The 2-hop neighbor set surrounding v is denoted by $N^2(v) = N(v) \bigcup_{i \in N(v)} N(i)$.

The modified DLGM algorithm will be executed by all nodes when receiving a data packet to decide whether the received packet will be relayed, delayed or discarded (the protocol behavior is based on an arbitrary node v). The algorithm utilizes previous relaying experience to accelerate decision making. For a new packet from node u, node v will examine weather the N^2 neighbor of u has been changed since last relay. If nothing has been changed, v will delay the same $d_{backoff}$ slot before MRTS. The assumption is that other nodes in $N(u)$ will make a similar decision to use their old delay slot. Since there is no conflict among the delay selection in the previous packet, the probability of no collision is high with the local topology unchanged.

Distributed Local Gain Maximizing with Session (DLGM-S)

- For each node $i \in N(v)$, define a multicast gain function $g(i)$ as the number of nodes in $N(i)$ that are not marked. Initially all nodes are not marked, thus $g(i) = |N(i)|$.

- When receiving an MRTS packet from a node u, mark all nodes in $N(u)$ as received.
- For each node $i \in (N(v) \bigcap N(u))/v$, update their $g(.)$ function accordingly. Particularly, $g(u)$ will become zero.
- If there exists a node $i \in (N(v) \bigcap N(u))/v$ such that $g(i) >= g(v)$, node v will mark a delay flag. and wait.
- wait for the data transmission from node u to complete.
- **If $N^2(u)$ topology is intact, and the past packet from u is relayed without collision**
  - *wait $d_{backoff}$ slot as determined in the previous multicast packet.*
  - *enter MRTS stage for the pending packet.*
  - *If MRTS collision, redraw $d_{backoff}$ and mark collision flag.*
- *if $N^2(u)$ changed since last packet, or there were MRTS collision in the last relay attempt*
  - *backoff a random period from $d_{backoff} = [1 \ g(u)]$ slots;*
  - *otherwise send an MRTS to relay the multicast packet.*

3.4   Protocol Analysis

In this section, we demonstrate some properties of the DLGM algorithm by proving two facts: (1) the deferred ACK algorithm is correct, in the sense that all nodes will receive the multicast packet as long as the network is connected, and (2) the DLGM-S algorithm provides the local greedy propagation.

Proposition 1: Let $G(V, E)$ be the graph representation of a wireless network under consideration, S be the multicast source node and M be the data packet; then for $\forall v \in V$, v will receive M in a finite period of time.

Proof: The proof for a stationary network is given in [17], hence we focus on the scenario where node v missed a packet after its movement or other topology change. Assume that v is associated to a new upstream node u, and u has completed broadcasting of p before v join. According to the deferred ACK protocol in Fig 2, node u employ a round robin selection for its *ctslist*, which imply that each of its neighbor, including v, will be selected to CTSACK at some time. Since node v's $CTSACK.seq$ field serve as the last received packet at node v, this gives node u a chance to lookup its local cache and schedule a future retransmission (see the *rtxlocal* and *rtxUp* state in Fig 2. If the local cache in u does not contain such packet (due to replacement), the retransmission request will be passed up to node u's upstream until the request can be served.   ∎

Proposition 2: Let node S be the multicast source node and M the data packet. Let $N(S)_1$ be S's neighbor and $N(S)_2$ be S's two-hop neighbor set. After S sends out M, the next relaying node r must have the largest degree in $N(S)_2 - N(S)_1$.

Proof: Since the extension in DLGM-S is concentrated on the determination of waiting slot. It inherit most of the features in DLGM, including the logic to determine local relay behavior. In particular, each node still must track the delivery status of its neighbors, thus the proof in [17] still apply. A new cases need to be addressed where $N(u)$ is changed at the time of relay decision at node *v*. This could be argued in a similar fashion as in [17] under the assumption that the join of a new node needs to be broadcasted from node *u*, thus all exisiting neighbor of *u* will learn the topology change at the same time.   ∎

3.5 Performance Evaluation

The performance of the proposed protocol stack is evaluated by simulations. The goal is to observe and compare the performance of the proposed scheme under different network configurations such as network size, density, and mobility.

As in [17]. our simulations consider a 1000*1000 square meters area. To exclude noise of extreme topology, the testing network is generated such that a specified network size and node density requirement are satisfied. To determine the connectivity of a generated network, a uniform radio transmission range $R \in [50100]$ *meters* is assumed. Any pair of nodes is connected if their distance does not exceed R.

3.6 Multicast Cost

We are first interested in the multicast transmissions attempts during a multicast session in a static setting. Note the transmission number T_x does not include the RTS/CTSACK signaling packets.

We increase the number of network nodes m from 10 to 150 in the simulated area. Randomly generated topologies are used to test relevant multicast protocols including MPR and the DLGM/CTSACK methods.

Figure 3.(a) shows the overall multicast transmit time for networks of different size. The average connectivity is fixed as $D = 4$. The size of *ctslist* is denoted by the variable *beta*. We set p to 0.75 and 0.4 to represent two relaying behaviors: with *beta* = 0.75 representing a relatively conservative protocol where the R-node demand 75% of its neighbors to reply. *beta* = 0.4 being a moderate aggressive protocol where the R-node only require 40% of its neighbors to transmit data packet. Our DLGM with $p = 1$ achieves another 5% reduction in the total delay time. The size of *ctslist* offers an effective control of protocol behavior over large dynamic range. A small *beta* value allow a R-node to quickly enter to data transmission stage, but might suffer increased probability of collision since other R-nodes might also have collected its needed CTS votes. With *beta* = 1 the most stringent media reservation policy is enforced, and the collision is minimized.

3.7 Transmission Energy Expenditure

To study the protocol behavior over different network topologies, we take a close look at the transmission number T_x, which has strong correlation to the total energy expenditure in a multicast session and how fast multicast can be done. Figure 4 shows T_x of the proposed scheme for two network topologies of different node density. One topology has a node density of $D = 4$ and contains $m = 30$ nodes, and the second topology has $D = 4$ and $m = 60$. The result set for

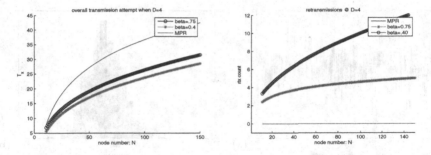

Fig. 3. transmission cost (a)tx attempt for D=4 ,(b) rtx for D=4

each case represents 500 randomly generated network topologies of the specified average network density.

Figure 4.(a) shows T_x-vs-topology for the first result set. It is observed that the performance of the multicast protocol varies significantly from topology to topology even when the total node number and degree are the same. The lowest transmission cost is observed at topology #27 with T_x as three time slots. This best-case topology is isomorphic to a degree 4 complete tree. It is worth noticing that $T_x = 3$ is the lowest transmission cost achievable for a network with $d = 4, m = 30$ (since $2 < log_4(30) < 3$). The longest transmission delay observed in this set of simulations is 20 time slots. Topologies with long delay usually have a long single chain and a cluster of nodes forming a clique. The existence of clique increases the average node degree, while the long single chain causes the long multicast time.

Figure 4.(b) shows the distribution of T_x. The observed distribution approximates a well-defined Gaussian function with a mean multicast time $\overline{T_x}$ of 12. Figure 4.(c) and (d) show the results for networks with 60 nodes ($N = 60$). The corresponding best scenario result is 7 time slots, and the worst case result is 36 time slots. A similar Gaussian distribution is observed.

4   Fault Recovery and Handoff Processing

Node failures/mobility might cause packet delivery problems to an extended network portion for ongoing and consequent multicast sessions. As shown in [17], packet loss could be caused by the poor handling of node movement even the network is physically connected. Ramani et.al, [16] reported that the break-and-reconnect period of 802.11 networks in infrastructure mode could be several seconds. Large portion of the delay is due to DHCP exchanges between the moving node and the new R-node. During the handoff period, a node will be unable to receive any packets (the decoding of overheard packet require the knowledge of the encryption key).

A more complicated scenario is that an R-node itself goes through a handoff process. As a relay vehicle moves away from its own gateway, the uplink channel quality will degrade and eventually the node needs to re-establish a connection

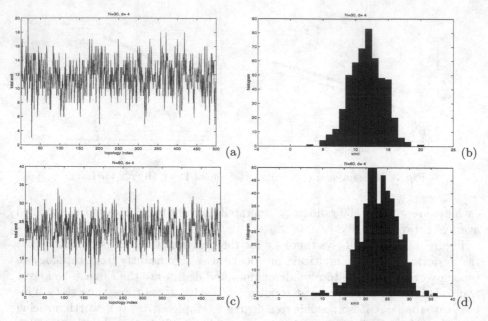

Fig. 4. (a) transmission attempts for D=4, m=30; (b)histogram of transmission time for D=4, m=30; (c) transmission attempts for D=4, m=60;(b) histogram of transmission time for D=4, m=60;

to a new gateway. This might force all downstream vehicles to execute a secondary handoff procedure. The aggregated delay will be far too long for certain applications, such as unmanned aerial vehicle control.

For simplicity, our analysis only consider the topology changes caused by the movement of one node. The node detected the topology change is denoted as node x, and the node that causing the topology change is denoted as y. To keep the multicast tree intact, the recovery protocol must satisfy two conditions: (1) the current 2-hop neighbor of node x must be reconnected, and (2) node y must be covered by some other nodes.

4.1   Recovery Analysis for MPR

In the worst case, MPR protocol would have to recalculate the entire MPR set whenever there is a topology change. Thus theoretically MPR is capable of self-healing to topology change and fault-tolerant. The retransmission policy could be integrated to MPR for dropped packets.

When node y moves out of its current position, all nodes that use y as MPR relaying node must update their MPR set, including x. These nodes will solicit to their current neighbor to obtained new 2-hop information. They will then execute the MPR algorithm to establish a new local MPR set to assure connectivity. This procedure requires a message cost of $D.M^2$ where D is the maximum node degree and M is the maximum size of 2-hop neighbor.

To reconnect y to a new R-node, y will broadcast a "request-to-join" packet to its new neighbors. All nodes that receive this packet will execute the MPR algorithm to include y in their multicast tree, which will count for another $D.M^2$ message exchange.

4.2 Recovery Analysis for DLGM-s

The handoff procedure for DLGM is briefly described in [17], here we reexamine the basic mechanism and provide some recent results. Still assuming that node y leaves its current neighbor, the method in [17] could not fix the topology error until some packet delivery failures in y's neighbors. This is because the DLGM algorithm does not specify a fixed R-node among mobile nodes, hence there is no fixed upstream node for any nodes. According to RTS/CTSACK signaling procedure, y's upstream node x will find that node y fails to respond to the MRTS packet and thus can determine y's absence. However with the deferred ACK and reduced *ctslist* in the R-node, it would take several packets drop before x realized that y is missing. A improvised procedure allow y's neighbor to act at the earliest time to reduce the packet drops in the transient period:

– let node $z \in N(x)$ share a non-empty neighbor as y: $N(y) \bigcap N(z) \neq \emptyset$.
– If $\exists w \in N(y) \cap N(z)$ such that $seq(w) < seq(local) + 1$, node z can presumably decide x's absence.
– x will remove y from $N(z)$.
– X broadcast y's absence.
– For each node u in $N(x)$, y will be removed from the $N()$ of u's neighbor $N(u)$.

The above procedure will generate exactly $M(x)$ messages where $M(x)$ is x's degree. The $M(x)$ messages will trigger updating process in the original $N^2(x)$ neighbor. It can be shown that the N^2 information around x's two-hop neighbors will remains consistent after this procedure. Compare to the procedure in [17], the topology repair occurs almost immediately after a node left. Re-connecting y to its new neighbors remain the same. This stage of updating requires $2 * M^2 + M + 1$ packets. Thus the overall message complexity is still in the order of $O(M^2)$ per single node topology change.

5 Conclusion

We proposed a completely distributed, reliable MAC-layer algorithm for wireless multicast. The uniqueness of our method is that each node decides its behavior (to relay a message or not) based on the realtime neighborhood status. Our simulations show that this method is more efficient than other schemes especially when the network topology is highly dynamic.

References

1. Wu, J.: Dominating-Set-Based Routing in Ad Hoc Wireless Networks with Unidirectional Links. Trans. Parallel and Distributed Systems 13(9), 866–881 (2002)
2. Dai, F., Wu, J.: An Extended Localized Algorithm for Connected Dominating Set Formation in Ad Hoc Wireless Networks. IEEE Trans. Parallel and Distributed Systems 15(10), 908–920 (2004)
3. Qayyum, A., Viennot, L., Laouiti, A.: Multipoint relaying for flooding broadcast messages in mobile wireless networks. In: Proceedings of the Hawaii International Conference on System Sciences (HICSS 2002) (January 2002)
4. Wan, P.-J., Alzoubi, K.M., Frieder, O.: Distributed construction of connected dominating set in wireless ad hoc networks. In: Proceedings of Infocom 2002 (2002)
5. Guha, S., Khuller, S.: Approximation Algorithms for Connected Dominating Sets. Algorithmica 20(4), 374–387 (1998)
6. Alzoubi, K.M., Wan, P.-J., Frieder, O.: Distributed Heuristics for Connected Dominating Set in Wireless Ad Hoc Networks. IEEE ComSoc/KICS Journal on Communication Networks 4(1), 22–29 (2002)
7. Stojmenovic, I., Seddigh, M., Zunic, J.: Dominating sets and neighbor elimination based broadcasting algorithms in wireless networks. In: Proc. IEEE Hawaii Int. Conf. on System Sciences (January 2001)
8. Armbrust, M., Fox, A., Griffith, R., Joseph, A., Katz, R., Konwinski, A., Lee, G., Patterson, D., Rabkin, A., Stoica, I., et al.: Above the clouds: A berkeley view of cloud computing. EECS Department, University of California, Berkeley, Tech. Rep. UCB/EECS-2009-28 (2009)
9. Pering, T., Want, R., Rosario, B., Sud, S., Lyons, K.: Enabling Pervasive Collaboration with Platform Composition. In: Tokuda, H., Beigl, M., Friday, A., Brush, A.J.B., Tobe, Y. (eds.) Pervasive 2009. LNCS, vol. 5538, pp. 184–201. Springer, Heidelberg (2009)
10. Lyons, K., Pering, T., Rosario, B., Sud, S., Want, R.: Multi-display Composition: Supporting Display Sharing for Collocated Mobile Devices. In: Gross, T., Gulliksen, J., Kotzé, P., Oestreicher, L., Palanque, P., Prates, R.O., Winckler, M. (eds.) INTERACT 2009, Part I. LNCS, vol. 5726, pp. 758–771. Springer, Heidelberg (2009)
11. Li, X., Zhang, H., Zhang, Y.: Deploying Mobile Computation in Cloud Service. In: Jaatun, M.G., Zhao, G., Rong, C. (eds.) CloudCom. LNCS, vol. 5931, pp. 301–311. Springer, Heidelberg (2009)
12. Chun, B., Maniatis, P.: Augmented Smartphone Applications Through Clone Cloud Execution. In: Proceedings of USENIX HotOS XII (2009)
13. Zhang, X., Schiffman, J., Gibbs, S., Kunjithapatham, A., Jeong, S.: Securing elastic applications on mobile devices for cloud computing. In: Proceedings of the ACM Workshop on Cloud Computing Security, pp. 127–134 (2009)
14. Angin, P., Bhargava, B., Helal, S.: A Mobile-Cloud Collaborative Traffic Lights Detector for Blind Navigation. In: Eleventh International Conference on Mobile Data Management, pp. 396–401 (2010)
15. Wieselthier, J.E., Nguyen, G.D., Ephremides, A.: Algorithms for Energy-Efficient Multicasting in Static Ad Hoc Wireless Networks. Mobile Networks and Applications (MONET) 6(3), 251–263 (2001)
16. Ramani, S., Savage, S.: Syncscan: Practical Fast Handoff for 802.11 Infrastructure Networks. In: Proc. of IEEE7 INFOCOM (March 2005)
17. Wang, J., Wang, X.: An energy-efficient,distributed wireless multicast protocol based on concurrent CTS and N^2 connectivity. Wireless Network 16, 2031–2048 (2010)

Virtual Device: Media Service Fitness, Selection and Composition

Niall Murray, Brian Lee, A.K. Karunakar, Yuansong Qiao, and Enda Fallon

Software Research Institute,
Athlone Institute of Technology, Ireland
{nmurray,ysqiao,akkarunakar}@research.ait.ie,
{blee,efallon}@ait.ie

Abstract. The motivation for the virtual device is to facilitate the seamless use of application services residing on different devices in the vicinity of the user. Due to heterogeneity of devices in the user's pervasive environment, multiple potential combinations to support a required task may exist. This work aims to determine the best possible media services considering all instances. The best services are selected and composed to satisfy a user task. Recent works propose using user preferences, environment capabilities and similarity between requested and available services to determine service fitness. We consider potential local and remote content sources and destination devices, with similarity, user preferences and environment capabilities to determine fitness. Services are selected for composition based on fitness. We model and simulate this issue and explain the results of our experimentation. Optimal multimedia service composition from varying devices provides the user with the best possible multimedia consumption and production experience.

Keywords: Virtual device, Atomic service fitness, service composition, media service selection.

1 Introduction

Future multimedia networks will be a ubiquitous communication platform where users will enjoy continuous multimedia services in any location on any device [1]. Today users are surrounded by technology that is heterogeneous, pervasive, and variable [2]. Consequently a user has a rich set of media services available to them when undertaking multimedia tasks in a multimodal, device independent manner. The virtual device supports user tasks such as audio video communication by combining media services from different devices. These devices include; small hand held multifunctional devices with limited processing and display capabilities, enhanced single function dedicated devices or powerful multifunctional multimedia systems (e.g. PDA, PCs, HDTV's, Network Speakers, surround sound systems).

Considering these devices, overlaps may exist in the types of services provided. The fitness (suitability) of individual services is calculated to distinguish between instances. By selecting and composing the blue-chip services of different devices, the

N. Venkatasubramanian et al. (Eds.): Mobilware 2011, LNICST 93, pp. 181–194, 2012.

virtual device supports user task satisfaction beyond what a user companion device can offer. The principles of Service Oriented Architecture (SOA) provide the basis for a suitable approach. The focus of this paper is one of those principles, service composition [3].

A service is defined as an indivisible, self contained application unit that performs a processing function on multimedia content. Internet accessible consumer devices provide one-to-many services. The virtual device supports the user task by composing the best service(s) of different devices within the context of the same session. The "single service for every device" vision of the webinos project [4] fits neatly into this paradigm.

Fig. 1 below illustrates the types of services we refer to. It also includes what we define as content manipulation services, which is outside the scope of this work.

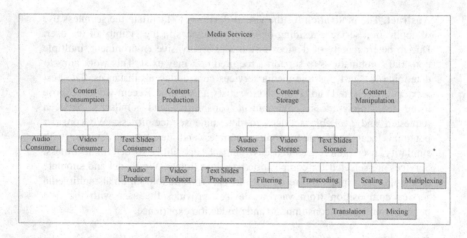

Fig. 1. Multimedia Content Service types

Concurrent services require strict functional and/or timely synchronization [5]. It is a multi-source, multi-destination service composition challenge. A natural method on which to model task or composite multimedia service composition is using graph theory as has been done in [6][7][8][9][10].

This work focuses on how to achieve the maximum quality media service composition by considering context. If this selection process is not performed properly, the search will generate non optimized results, causing a low Quality of Service (QoS) perception from the consumer point of view [11]. Simply choosing the most powerful device or service does not always result in the most efficient and most favourable user experience. It may not be the user's preferred mode of communication. In addition, there is no advantage in choosing a powerful display device if a very limited video production device is producing the video content. Unnecessary execution of manipulation content services in Fig. 1 can be minimized through intelligent decision making.

We propose the consideration of local and remote content consumption and production services in selecting local services, in conjunction with user preferences and device resources. Considering remote services enables early elimination of unusable services and we suggest that it facilitates reduced media processing costs and delays i.e. if we can match a particular encoding format source and destination between distributed compositions – no transcoding service would be required. Finally, it provides a method to overcome the dependency [12] on service users' feedback.

The overall contributions of this paper are:

1. Defining the service selection and composition problem to include local and remote services as well as user preferences and device resources.
2. We model and define the fitness of a service as a function of device resources, user preferences, availability, encodings and potential remote services.
3. We present the results of our experiments displaying the benefits of using our proposed algorithm.

This paper is organized as follows: Section 2 defines our problem with the aid of a sample scenario. Section 3 describes how the service composition problem is modelled in terms of local services, user preferences, device resources and remote services. Section 4 presents the algorithms for service composition. Section 5 explains our experimentation and simulation results. Section 6 outlines related work. Finally in section 7 we conclude this paper, discuss our contributions and outline future work.

2   Problem Definition

We envisage public and private environments consisting of multiple mobile and stationary nodes. These nodes provide one or more content related services as per Fig. 2a, which shows an audio-video camera providing five possible services. All nodes are Internet connected devices where resident services can be invoked by peer nodes. These devices may include; small hand held multi-functional devices with limited processing and display capabilities, enhanced single function dedicated devices or multifunctional multimedia systems.

Consider the following scenario defined as real time communication between distributed compositions. Brian is talking with John on his virtual device enabled smart phone and is walking from his office to his car. John is working from home and is using the microphone from his personal computer and surround sound speaker system to converse with Brian. Also in John's study are a PC connected camera and a large display screen. Once Brian sits in his car and places the phone in the holder, his call is automatically transferred from his handheld device to the services available in his car. He is now using the microphone embedded in the sun visor, speakers from the car radio system and can see John on the LCD panel integrated into the car panel. John can also now see Brian because of the camera built into the steering wheel. Local services from Brian's perspective are the services resident on devices within his vicinity that he uses to communicate with John (e.g. the microphone embedded in the visor). Remote services from Brian's perspective are the services available to John for communication (e.g. microphone in his personal computer).

Considering this scenario and Fig. 2b, many of the devices in a user's vicinity may provide similar functional services. Differences may exist between these services in terms of capabilities, availabilities, user preferences and usage costs. In the scenario outlined, the user may want to use a number of different types of services (e.g. video and audio consumption and production services) in a communication session. Consequently there are multiple constraints in terms of what the user requires, and multiple choices in terms of devices providing different services to solve these problems. Like [2], we consider determining the quality of compositions a variant of a 0-1 Knapsack problem, named multiple dimensional, multiple choice 0-1 Knapsack. The multiple dimensions refer to the multiple constraints and the multiple choices refer to choosing one among a set of similar items. In optimizations research this problem has been proven to be NP-complete [13].

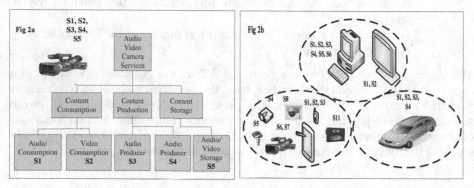

Fig. 2. (a) shows how a video camera device can provide many content related services. **(b)** shows a flavour of some of the devices providing one-to-many services denoted by S_i that could be used in service composition to create the virtual device.

Our work aims to achieve the best service composition by selecting the highest scoring instances of the individual service types, through consideration of local and remote services, device resources and user preferences.

3   Service Composition System

To compose services from distributed devices, a number of steps are required. Many of these steps are outside the scope of this document but for completeness we air some views on potential approaches. As per Fig. 3 below, it is assumed that an Internet scale network exists. Devices provide their content production, storage, consumption and manipulation services for execution by peers. The following entities are the basis for the system.

- *User Companion device*: it is assumed that a task requiring atomic service composition is initiated from the user companion device. It is likely that the user companion device will always be in the vicinity of the user and hence, in the vicinity of devices providing atomic services.
- *Atomic service*: an application level service that provides content processing functionality in one of the four defined areas of consumption, production, storage and manipulation.

- *Service component devices*: mobile or stationary devices hosting any of the four types of content services of Fig. 1. The user companion device can also provide atomic services for composition.
- *Coordinator*: it coordinates the discovery and selection of the atomic services. It is typically a mobile or stationary device that has high computation and processing ability and is in the vicinity of devices supporting a rich set of atomic services. The selection of the coordinator device has been addressed in [14][15]. The coordinator executes the algorithm introduced as part of this work.
- *Composite service*: multiple atomic services composed to satisfy a user task.
- *Task*: an application level user request that is satisfied by an atomic service or composite service.
- *Service composition specification*: is a specification of a user defined task. Considering the sample scenario in section 3, it is a specification of the atomic services required for real time communication between distributed compositions.

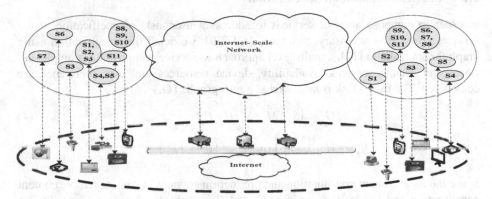

Fig. 3. Internet-Scale Network where devices provide their services for composition to support communication between distributed compositions

3.1   Network Model

This network can be represented by a graph, G. Each node N, in the graph represents a device that provides one-to-many services. F represents a set of links between each of the nodes.

$$G = \{N, F\} \tag{1}$$

The resources of a device reflect the non functional characteristics. The resources $R(n)$ are quantifiable [16] values such as CPU (X), battery power (P), network bandwidth (B) and memory (M). These resources are used to calculate the fitness of the service component device that supports the service. This also provides a measure of service availability. The value of $R(n)$ for each device is a function of local device values X_L, P_L, B_L and M_L and the maximum values of X_{max}, P_{max}, B_{max} and M_{max} considering all devices that provide services.

$$R(n) = f(X, P, B, M) \tag{2}$$

$$R(n) = \left(X_L \Big/ X_{max} + P_L \Big/ P_{max} + B_L \Big/ B_{max} + M_L \Big/ M_{max} \right) \div 4 \text{ ,where } 0 \le R(n) \le 1$$

The services available on a particular node $S = \{S_1, S_2,...S_k\}$ is a set of Fig. 1 type services. The services supported by a device n are denoted by $S_i(n)$ where $ST(s)$

$$S_i(n) = \{ST, E, A\} \quad \text{, where } 0 \le i \le k \tag{3}$$

represents the service type as per Fig. 1, E represents the content compression formats supported and $A(s_i)$ represents the availability status of the service. It is assumed that all nodes in the network can exchange information.

3.2   Service Composition Specification

In order to compose a set of services to address a user task, a specification of the services required is necessary. Similar to [6][7][9], we detail this specification using graph theory. Like in [17], a multi level approach to service composition is employed. Local and remote services, availability, device resources and user preference are considered. The user's task is modelled as a task graph, TG.

$$TG = \{S_L, M_i, S_r, U, F\} \tag{4}$$

$$S_L \subset (C_L \cup P_L) \text{ and } S_r \subset (C_r \cup P_r)$$

S_L are the local content consumption and production services. S_r are the remote content consumption and production services. C_L and P_L are the local content consumption and production services respectively whilst C_r and P_r are the remote content consumption and production services respectively. M_i represents content manipulation services. F represents the data flows between P_r to C_L and P_L to C_r potentially through M_i intermediary manipulation services. U is a set of user preferences related to consumption and production services for the task. User preferences are specified as part of the task description and explicitly provided by the user once available services are determined. The novel aspect of this work is the use of P_r and C_r to decide the combination of P_L and C_L selected. It is assumed that nodes providing services for composition are physically located close to each other.

Real time communication between distributed compositions will result in multiple concurrent bi-directional content streams. The aim is to select a set of local services, mapping from TG to G, considering user preferences, device resources, local and remote services to achieve the best context based composition.

For all nodes N, multiple services may exist providing similar functionality. Selection of different instances of the same service types, results in different mappings from the service specification to device's services. Between services, different values exist in how closely a service instance matches a service request. A user may prefer one service instance over another. Different values of *R(n)* will exist between devices that host the same service types. Considering these factors, the goal is to select the best possible composition set for the user.

3.3   Local Atomic Service Fitness Calculation Considering Local Information

A two step suitability function is used to calculate the fitness of atomic services of the same type. We consider the QoS function of Perttunen et al. [18] an excellent base to perform this task. This model is extended to produce atomic service type league tables based on atomic service fitness. We assume a reasonably small number of atomic services for each service type are discovered; otherwise per service fitness calculation could become an exhaustive process. Equation 5 shows each of the parameters used to generate atomic service fitness. The maximum value for each of these parameters is one; hence highest potential atomic service value (ASV) is one. A league table is created based on the ASV for each of the services (i) within each atomic service type (t).

$$ASV_t(s_i) = R(n) \times W_t(s) \times Sim(RS_i, AS_i) \times U(s_i) \times A(s_i) \qquad (5)$$

- *R(n)* as previously introduced denotes the device resources of the service component device hosting the service.
- $W_t(s)$ [18] is a user inputted weight associated with a particular service type specified by the user. It signifies how important a user views one particular service type e.g. the user may feel audio is a more important service to have over video in a given context, hence a higher weighting is selected for audio.
- $Sim(RS_i, AS_i)$ [18] is a similarity function comparing the requested service (RS_i) and available service (AS_i). Certain user preferences like preferred screen size are considered as part of the similarity function execution. This parameter is not applicable for all service types. If it is not applicable, a default value of one is applied.
- $A(s_i)$ represents if an atomic service is available for use as part of a composite service. In [18], the availability function is a measure of current availability state, usage policy, lease information, queue for usage and user groups. For simplicity, only current availability state is considered here.
- $U(s_i)$ is the user preference for a particular atomic service instance. The incorporated user preference model is derived from [16]. Users specify a preference value reflecting their approval or disapproval for a particular service instance. An option of "Avoid this service instance" facilitates the user to specify that they do not wish to instantiate a particular service instance.

Table 1. User Preferences Table

Importance Level	Preference Value
Desired Service Instance	1.0
Satisfactory Service Instance	0.7
Acceptable Service Instance	0.3
Avoid this service Instance	0.0

3.4   Local Atomic Service Fitness Calculation Considering Remote Services

The next contribution of this paper involves a comparison of all atomic service tables with the equivalent remote services. The benefits of this step are: (1) it ensures all required services can be supported i.e. what the user would like to do is actually possible, considering real time communication between distributed compositions. (2) It checks for commonalities in terms of encoding formats between the potential local and remote content sources and destinations. Considering this removes the necessity for execution of some of the intermediary manipulation services (e.g. transcoding), thus reducing processing costs and delays. For local services that have commonalities with a remote side, we add an additional weight to the $ASV_t(s_i)$ which results in the final service value ($FSV_t(s_i)$). Local sources that have a remote "partner" service and support a common encoding are given a default value of 1 for use in service fitness calculation. Local sources that have a remote "partner" service but do support a common encoding format are given a default value of 0.5 for use in service fitness calculation. Finally, local services that do not have a remote "partner" service are given a default value of 0 for use in service fitness calculation. If a partner service does not exist, this means that this service cannot be used in the communications session; hence the value of 0 is assigned. As shown in table 2, $FSV_t(s_i)$ is the product of the respective weightings and $ASV_t(s_i)$.

3.5   Atomic Service Composition

The final league tables comprise atomic services ordered in terms of $FSV_t(s_i)$. These tables represent the set of all available atomic services for the communication session. The top scoring services in each table are selected for composition. These services make the selected service set (SSS). If during the session, a particular service becomes unavailable (for example due to node mobility), the next most suitable service type can be easily retrieved from the respective table. Hence this system provides an efficient service failure recovery mechanism. Only one service is selected from each of the service tables at any one time. The resultant selected composition is a set of the highest scoring services calculated based of $FSV_t(s_i)$. The overall rating for this composition is the sum of the max $FSV_t(s_i)$ for each atomic service type.

4   Service Fitness and Composition Algorithms

This section outlines in pseudo code the various steps of the two algorithms. Service discovery provides the coordinator with information regarding available atomic services to satisfy the user task. This information is used to calculate the service availability $A(s_i)$ and device resource capabilities $R(n)$. It also provides the available service information (AS_i) required for $Sim(RS_i, AS_i)$. The user inputs their user preferences $U(s_i)$, weightings for service type $W_t(s)$ and the requested service information (RS_i). Considering these inputs from the discovery and user, it is possible to execute Algorithm 1 and calculate $ASV_t(s_i)$ as per equation 5.

Algorithm 1. Generation of Atomic Service Value (ASV$_t$(s$_i$))Tables
1.   List of required atomic services (RAS) to satisfy task
2.   List of local discovered atomic services (DAS) to satisfy task
3.   Create a fitness table for each required atomic service type
4.   For each RAS type
5.   For each DAS type, If match(RAS, DAS) // service types match
6.   Determine Sim(RS$_i$, AS$_j$)// similarity
7.   Determine A(s$_i$) // service availability
8.   Determine R(n) //resource capability from [X,P,B,M]
9.   Determine U(s$_i$) // user preference
10.   Determine W$_t$(s) // atomic service weighting
11.   Calculate ASV$_t$(s$_i$)
12.   Upload score & details to fitness table
13. Return FitnessTable

Additional differences may exist between atomic service types in terms of compression formats supported. This information is used to further calculate the fitness of the local atomic services considering the formats of the remote services. Algorithm 2 compares the services in the tables generated in Algorithm 1 with the remote services. The aim is to find remote "partner" services for each of the local atomic service types e.g. a local video consumption device could partner with one-to-many remote video production services. If no "partner" service is found, the score for this service instance is set to 0 as it is not possible to support this service type in the communication session. If a partner service is found, a comparison in terms of encoding formats supported is executed. If a common encoding exists, an extra weight is added to this particular local service as per lines 6 and 7 of Algorithm 2. Table 2, column "Algorithm 2 (Encoding Match)" shows that encoding matches were found for the following services: HDTV, panel display, smart phone display and hence the weighting value of one. No encoding match was found for the PC Display and as a result it is given the weighting of 0.5. The highest scoring atomic services in each of the final set of fitness tables are selected for composition as discussed. The composition is the highest quality mapping from *TG* to *G*.

Algorithm 2. Comparison of Atomic Services with Remote Services and Optimal Service Composition
1.   Local atomic service fitness tables to satisfy task
2.   Remote atomic services
3.   For each Service Type table
4.   For each Remote AS, check service type //e.g. video consumer
5.   If partner(DAS, RAS) // service types
6.   If (encodings match) //
7.   Update FSV$_t$(s$_i$) // see table 2
8.   return All Fitness Tables
14.   For each FSV table
15.   SelectTopScoringService()
9.   Compose Set of setOfTopScoringServices

5   Simulation Results and Analysis

Simulations are performed on a Windows Vista Ultimate OS with 4.00 GB RAM and Intel® Core™ 2 Quad Q6600 @ 2.4GHz. The simulated environment models ten devices that can potentially provide one-to-many services within the vicinity of the user. Table 2 below shows a sample generated league table for a video consumption atomic service showing all execution points of Algorithms 1 and 2. As mentioned previously, the maximum value for each of the parameters is one, hence the highest possible scores of $ASV_t(s_i)$ and $FSV_t(s_i)$ is also one. Inspecting the values, considering resource capability $(R(n))$ and similarity with requested service $Sim(RS_i, AS_i)$, the PC Display service scores as the strongest candidate. All instances are available and given the same weighting, hence $A(s_i)$ and $W_t(s)$ are equal to one. It is not until Algorithm 2 and encodings matching takes place that the HDTV service scores highest and rises to first position in the table with the PC Display moving to second place. Based on this execution, the HDTV video consumer service is selected as part of the composition to satisfy the user task.

Table 2. Video Consumption $FSV_t(s_i)$ Fitness table after execution of Algorithm 1 and 2

AS Type: Video Consumer	R(n)	Sim(RS_i, AS_i)	A(s_i)	U(s_i)	W_t(s)	ASV_t(s_i)	Algorithm 2 (Encoding Match)	FSV_t(s_i)
HDTV	0.93	0.857	1.0	0.7	1.0	0.56	1.0	0.56
PC Display	1.0	0.928	1.0	0.7	1.0	0.65	0.5	0.325
Panel Display	0.85	0.5	1.0	0.3	1.0	0.127	1.0	0.127
Phone Display	0.73	0.333	1.0	0.3	1.0	0.073	1.0	0.073

Figure 4a below reflects the ratings of the services as their information is processed through each of the stages of Algorithms 1 and 2. $R(n)$ reflects the resource capabilities of the devices supporting the services. The $Sim(RS_i, AS_i)$ function determines the similarity between the user request and the available services. $U(s_i)/A(s_i)/W_t(s)$ are the user preferences, availability and weightings for each of the services. Once these five parameters are executed, $ASV_t(s_i)$ is calculated which reflects Algorithm 1 processing. Algorithm 2 performs the encoding matching check which as illustrated results in a changing of places between the HDTV and PC Display services. Because a common codec exists between the HDTV and remote video production service, an extra weighting is given to the HDTV display service which results in it becoming the highest scoring service in the video consumer service table.

As mentioned earlier, the composed services are a set of the highest individual scoring atomic services. For explanation purposes, Fig. 4b compares the fitness of the highest scoring SSS with a set comprised of medium scoring atomic services, and two compositions with sets of low scoring atomic services. Comparing the highest SSS with services (s1,s6,s10,s14) and lowest SSS with services (s4,s8,s12,s17) have scores of 3.2 and 0.7 respectively as shown in Fig. 4b. This clearly demonstrates the validity of the algorithms and the approach taken as part of this work.

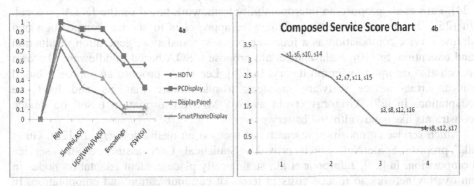

Fig. 4. 4a reflects the change in scores after each of the steps of equation 4. **4b** compares the scores of a set of high fitness services with a set of medium fitness services and a set of low fitness services calculated. One atomic service from each of: Audio Consumption set (s1,s2,s3,s4,s5), Video Consumption set (s6,s7,s8,s9), Audio Production set (s10, s11, s12, s13) and Video Production set (s14, s15, s16, s17) are selected for each composition.

6   Related Work

A broad range of related work involving task based service composition in pervasive environments and MANETS, content delivery and adaptation, the connection of devices in pervasive environments exists.

Similar to our work, Sousa et al., in [2] describe an approach to finding the best match between the user's requirements and the environments capabilities. Hossain et al., in [19] determine the best possible composition as a function of gain (the extent of which a media service satisfies a user in a particular context) and cost of the service. In [20], Karmouch et al. define service composition in MANETS as a distributed constraint satisfaction problem. Similar to us they use a QoS model based on the work of Pertuttan et al., [18]. We borrow facets of and extend this model with device capability and consideration of the remote services. Mukhtar et al., define an approach for task composition considering user preferences and device capabilities [16]. In [9], they use graph theory to define the user task. In [12] Atrey et al., use how regularly a service has been composed with another service to determine a reputation for a service. In [21] Jiang et al., address service composition based on prospect of minimum disruption. None of these works consider the potential atomic remote services to select local atomic services.

In relation to selection of the coordinator device, Karmouch et al., in [15] implement a broker based distributed service composition protocol which extends the work of Chakraborty et al., [14] for service composition. Basu et al., [7] define graph based approaches to distributed application composition approaches in MANETS.

[22][23][24] propose different approaches for connecting devices in pervasive environments. In [22], Schuster et al., provide a service orientated architecture for virtual device composition utilizing middleware on all devices. In [23], Senthivel et al., construct ad hoc service overlay networks (SON) based on service requests. In [24], Park et al., propose an interoperability framework based on the JXTA protocol. In [25], Ibrahim et al., survey middleware approaches to service composition and define service composition as a four step process: translation, generation, evaluation and execution. In [10], Kalasapur et al., propose a SOA based middleware platform which also incorporates graph theory. In [26], Lee et al., propose an approach based on a virtual device software manager, a middleware manager and hardware adaptation. In [27], Grigoras et al., address MANET formation based on device constraints like bandwidth and battery power.

Much service composition research has focused on media delivery. In [28], Gu et al., propose SpiderNet which provides Statistical QoS assurances for service composition. In [29], Jafarpour et al., strategically place content adaptation nodes in an overlay network to reduce costs in terms of communication and computation. In [30], Qian et al., determine lowest delay in service oriented multimedia delivery in pervasive environments. Xu et al., [31] propose a distributed Storage-assisted Data-driven overlay network to support P2P Video-on-Demand services.

In [32] Nahrstedt et al., introduce and discuss challenges with web services based approaches to multimedia delivery. SPovNet [33] is an overlay based solution that facilitates the spontaneous deployment of distributed network applications and services. In [34], Kim et al., discuss an emerging trend of media orientated service composition with SON's and outline challenges. They also dicuss virtualized resource components as a futuristic solution. In [35], Buford et al., suggest an Internet-scale P2P Overlay to facilitate expanding the capability of a device.

To the best of our knowledge, the use of remote potential services has not been a driver to calculate fitness, select and compose local atomic services. In [6], Nahrstedt et al., discuss a novel scoring function based on importance of objects in media streams to decide what is displayed on what portion of a shared screen. In our work, it is the capability and the availability of services in the remote composition that we use as an eliminator for irrelevant service components as part of the composition process.

7   Conclusion

This paper has presented a framework to calculate service fitness and select services for composition. This novel approach uses the remote potential capabilities as input to deciding the local service composition in addition to user preferences and resource capabilities. We formally model the user task taking into consideration all of the aforementioned factors. A two step suitability algorithm produces league tables for required atomic services based on service fitness. The result provides a user with an optimized selection of services, whilst providing an efficient service failure recovery mechanism. The simulation and experimentation show how each of the factors considered; local services, remote services, resource capability and user preferences affect the service scoring and how the best possible set of services are selected. In future work, we aim to define group synchronization schemes to address requirements of cluster applications where multiple correlated media stream with variable end-to-end delays exist.

Acknowledgments. We would like to recognize the assistance of Enterprise Ireland through its Applied Research Enhancements program in the financing of this Research. Also Dr. Mark Daly, a lecturer in the AIT School of Engineering for his assistance and advice with system modelling.

References

1. Murray, N., Qiao, Y., Lee, B., Karunakar, A.K., Fallon, E.: Design Considerations for Future Multimedia Systems: A Comparison of Approaches Based on SIP and the Advanced Multimedia System. International Journal of Ambient Computing and Intelligence 3(1), 20–32 (2011)
2. Sousa, J.P., Poladian, V., Garlan, D., Schmerl, B., Shaw, M.: Task-based Adaptation for Ubiquitous Computing. IEEE Transactions on Systems, Man, and Cybernetics – Part C: Applications and Reviews 36, 328–340 (2006)
3. Erl, T.: SOA Principles, http://www.soaprinciples.com/
4. webinos (Secure Web Operating System Application Delivery Environment), FP7-ICT-2009-5 – Objective 1.2, http://webinos.org/
5. Nahrstedt, K., Balke, W.-T.: A Taxonomy for Multimedia Service Composition. In: 12th ACM International Conference on Multimedia (2004)
6. Nahrstedt, K., Yu, B., Liang, J., Cui, Y.: Hourglass multimedia content and service composition framework for smart room environments. Journal on Pervasive and Mobile Computing 1(1), 43–75 (2005)
7. Basu, P., Wang, K., Little, T.D.C.: Dynamic Task Based Anycasting in Mobile Ad Hoc Networks. Journal Mobile Networks and Applications (2003)
8. Gu, X., Nahrstedt, K.: On Composing Stream Applications in Peer-to-Peer Environments. IEEE Trans. on Parallel and Distributed Systems 17(8), 824–837 (2005)
9. Mukhtar, H., Belaïd, D., Bernard, G.: A Graph-Based Approach for Ad hoc Task Composition Considering User Preferences and Device Capabilities. In: GLOBECOM Workshops. Current version (2009)
10. Kalasapur, S., Kumar, M., Shirazi, B.A.: Dynamic Service Composition in Pervasive Computing. IEEE Transactions on Parallel and Distributed Systems 18(7) (2007)
11. Dutra, R.G., Martucci Jr., M.: Dynamic Adaptive Middleware Services for Service Selection in Mobile Ad-Hoc Networks. In: Cai, Y., Magedanz, T., Li, M., Xia, J., Giannelli, C. (eds.) Mobilware 2010, Part IV. LNICST, vol. 48, pp. 189–202. Springer, Heidelberg (2010)
12. Atrey, P.K., Hossain, M.A., El Saddik, A.: A Method for Computing the Reputation of in Multimedia Services through Selection and Composition. Journal Mobile Networks and Applications 13(6) (2008)
13. Pisinger, D.: An Exact algorithm for Large Multiple Knapsack Problems. European Journal of Operational Research 114 (1999)
14. Chakraborty, D., Joshi, A., Finin, T., Yesha, Y.: Service Composition for Mobile Environments. Mobile Network and Applications 10(4), 435–451 (2005)
15. Karmouch, E., Nayak, A.: A Distributed Protocol for Virtual Device Composition in Mobile Ad Hoc Networks. In: IEEE International Conference on Communications (2009)

16. Mukhtar, H., Belaïd, D., Bernard, G.: User Preferences-Based Automatic Device Selection for Multimedia User Tasks in Pervasive Environments. In: 5th Conference on Networking and Services (2009)

17. Zhang, B., Shi, Y., Xiao, X.: A Policy-Driven Service Composition Method for Adaptation in Pervasive Computing Environment. The Computer Journal 53(2), 152–165 (2007)

18. Perttunen, M., Jurmu, M., Riekki, J.: A QoS Model for Task-Based Service Composition. In: Workshop on Managing Ubiquitous Communications and Services (2007)

19. Hossain, M.A., Atrey, P.K., El Saddik, A.: Gain-based Selection of Ambient Media Services in Pervasive Environments. Springer Journal Mobile Networks and Applications (2008)

20. Karmouch, E., Nayak, A.: A Distributed Constraint Satisfaction Problem for Virtual Device Composition in Mobile Ad Hoc Networks. In: Global Telecommunications Conference, GLOBECOM (2009), Current Version (2010)

21. Jiang, S., Xue, Y., Schmidt, D.: Minimum Disruption Service Composition and Recovery in Mobile Ad hoc Networks. The International Journal of Computer and Telecommunication Networking 53(10) (2009)

22. Schuster, M., Domene, A., Vaidya, R., Arbanowski, S., Kim, S.M., Lee, J.W., Lim, H.: Virtual device Composition. In: 8th International Symposium on Autonomous Decentralized Systems (2007)

23. Senthivel, K., Kalasapur, S., Kumar, M.: PerSON: A Framework for Service Overlay Network in Pervasive Environments. In: Kuo, T.-W., Sha, E., Guo, M., Yang, L.T., Shao, Z. (eds.) EUC 2007. LNCS, vol. 4808, pp. 671–682. Springer, Heidelberg (2007)

24. Park, H., Park, J.-H., Kim, N.: A Framework for Interoperability of Heterogeneous Devices in Ubiquitous Home. In: 2nd Conference on Advances in Future Internet (2010)

25. Ibrahim, N., Le Mouël, F.: A Survey on Service Composition Middleware in Pervasive Environments. International Journal of Computer Science Issues, IJCSI (2009)

26. Lee, J.W., Kim, S.M., Lim, H., Schuster, M., Domene, A.: A Software Architecture for Virtual Device Composition and Its Applications. In: Ichikawa, H., Cho, W.-D., Satoh, I., Youn, H.Y. (eds.) UCS 2007. LNCS, vol. 4836, pp. 150–157. Springer, Heidelberg (2007)

27. Grigoras, D., Riordan, M.: Service Driven Mobile Ad Hoc Networks Formation and Management. In: 4th Symposium on Parallel and Distributed Computing (2005)

28. Gu, X., Nahrstedt, K.: Distributed Multimedia Service Composition with Statistical QoS Assurances. IEEE Transactions on Multimedia 8(1), 141–151 (2006)

29. Jafarpour, H., Hore, B., Mehrotra, S., Venkatasubramanian, N.: CCD: Efficient Customized Content Dissemination in Distributed Publish/Subscribe. In: Bacon, J.M., Cooper, B.F. (eds.) Middleware 2009. LNCS, vol. 5896, pp. 62–82. Springer, Heidelberg (2009)

30. Qian, Z., Guo, M., Zhang, S., Lu, S.: Service-Oriented Multimedia Delivery In Pervasive Space. In: IEEE Wireless Communications & Networking Conference (2009)

31. Xu, C., Muntean, G.-M., Fallon, E., Hanley, A.: Distributed Storage-Assisted Data-driven Overlay Network for P2P VoD Services. IEEE Transactions on Broadcasting (2008)

32. Nahrstedt, K., Balke, W.-T.: Towards Building large Scale Multimedia Systems and Applications: Challenges and Status. In: ACM International Workshop on Multimedia Service Composition (2005)

33. The Spontaneous Virtual Network (SpoVNet), http://www.spovnet.de

34. Kim, J.W., Han, S.W., Yi, D.-H., Kim, N., Kuo, C.-C.J.: Media-Oriented Service Composition with Service Overlay Networks: Challenges, Approaches and Future Trends. Journal of Communications (2010)

35. Buford, J.F., Yu, H., Lua, E.K.: P2P Networking and Applications. Morgan Kaufmann (2009)

User Centric Replication Approach to Maintain Data Availability in MANET

Zeina Torbey[1], Nadia Bennani[1], David Coquil[2], and Lionel Brunie[1]

[1] Université de Lyon, CNRS, LIRIS,
Lyon, France
{zeina.torbey,nadia.bennani,lionel.brunie}@insa-lyon.fr
[2] Chair of Distributed Information Systems
University of Passau, Passau, Germany
{david.coquil}@uni-passau.de

Abstract. The deployment of applications in mobile networks is hindered by limited resources and frequent network disconnection. Data replication can improve data availability in mobile networks but also introduces the challenge of adequately disseminating data without abusing user and network resources. In this context, we present CReaM, a user-Centric REplicAtion Model for mobile environment that gives priority to the users by letting them determine the amount of resources they assign to the system. In this paper, we focus on CReaM's autonomic behavior that generates replication requests based on resource monitoring and user settings. Then, we present a simulation-based evaluation of CReaM, which shows its efficiency comparing with a periodical model; indeed, CReaM gives the same rate of data availability while it causes 50 less overhead.

Keywords: Mobile Ad-Hoc network, Replication, User centric, Data availability, Simulation.

1   Introduction

A mobile Ad hoc NETwork (MANET) consists of nodes that communicate in an autonomous way without any centralized server. Most often, these networks are deployed on devices with limited resources. Moreover, MANETs have to face the problem of frequent networks topology changes that may lead to unanticipated network partitioning and cause incomplete data transfers between the nodes. These characteristics make it difficult to guarantee data availability, hindering the widespread deployment of distributed applications over MANETs. In this context, a possible solution is the use of data replication techniques.

However, applying data replication in MANETs is not a trivial task for several reasons: (1) the network topology changes frequently and unexpectedly. (2) The data to be replicated must be carefully selected because of the limited storage space of the devices. (3) The data may be updated so mechanisms for maintaining data consistency are necessary. In addition, (4) the devices have limited power, which means that

N. Venkatasubramanian et al. (Eds.): Mobilware 2011, LNICST 93, pp. 195–208, 2012.

efficient methods must be adopted to reduce the communication between nodes. In view of all these issues, specific data replication mechanisms for MANETs are required.

Previously proposed MANET replication models replicate data by taking into account resource availability and the access frequency of the data items. Most of them replicate periodically the important data items and place the replica on the devices with the most available resources. Such top-down approaches may lead to an abuse of user resources, as in the worst case they might use all of a user's resources in order to achieve their goal. To the contrary, we feel that users should be at the center of the systems. We propose a user-centric approach in which users are in control of the amount of resources that they share; these resources are then used to enhance data availability, while the rest of the resources are reserved for the users to be able to accomplish their tasks.

To illustrate the motivation of our work, let us consider the following scenario: Marie, a journalist, is in a stadium. She connects to the local MANET, which provides a data sharing service. Marie records interviews with the players and takes photos of them on her notebook. Other users are interested in such photos, but as they sit in the back rows of the stadium, they cannot take them themselves, and thus send requests for such data to the data sharing service. The service connects them to Marie. However, after a while, the load on Marie's device becomes too high and she cannot answer any more requests. We can see here how a system that automatically creates copies of the data when the load on one device becomes too high due to other users' requests would be useful. Indeed, by copying on other devices of the MANET, it would provide relief to Marie as the next requests would be directed to those devices rather than to hers. Let us assume that such a system is in place; when creating a replica, it must decide on which node to place it. According to the criteria of existing replication model of the literature, the device of George (another journalist covering the event) would be selected, because his device has the highest capability. However, from another point of view, the mobile phone of another spectator may be a better choice, simply because it is currently not used, whereas George needs the resources of his device to accomplish his work. But later on, if the spectator needs his resources to accomplish a task, the replication mechanism should again evolve cleverly by dynamically choosing another target device(s) to hold the replica.

Several challenges need to be overcome to develop such a system. First, the system must react dynamically to the resources' consumption on each node to keep all users satisfied. However, reacting each time a change occurs might be ineffective. It is therefore necessary to identify the right factors on which to react as well as the right granularity of reaction. Furthermore, if the system reacts starting from the users' needs, another challenge appears: the system must take local decisions to satisfy these needs, but it must also consider the interest of the whole system. Finding a balance between these two factors is necessary to avoid problems such as replica duplication, network saturation and free riding.

To address these issues, we propose the user Centric REplicAtion Model (CReaM). This model places users in the centre by letting them define their level of participation in the system. Thus, the model operates with respect to the user desire; it replicates automatically when the user is overloaded and places replicas on other users' devices that can support the load instead. The system is therefore driven by the wishes of the users, which is, in our view, a key requirement of a realistic approach. To do so, our model is based on a monitoring mechanism that periodically gathers the consumption of features such as memory, battery, etc, and attributes a status to the peer that reflects the user activity level implied by the monitored values. Each status conditions the peer's local decision about whether to accept or reject other peers' replica demands, whether to generate replication requests, and if need be about which data to replicate.

The paper is organized as follows. Section 2 is an overview of related work. In section 3 we present the proposed model CReaM; we introduce some definitions, and detail the model itself. Section 4 contains the performance evaluations. Finally, we conclude the paper and present directions of future work in section 5.

2   Related Work

Several replication strategies have been proposed to increase data availability in mobile environment. A first criterion to categorize them is the level of autonomy of the peers. In this regard, one can distinguish between centralized (requiring a fixed host) and decentralized solutions. We focus on the latter which can be further divided into group-based and fully decentralized strategies.

From the group based strategies, [7] proposes an economic model for dynamic allocation in M-P2P networks where the price of a data item depends on its access frequency among other values; the solution deploys a super-peer architecture where groups are formed and each group is managed by a service provider that collects information and makes the replication decision. In [1], the replication is done periodically based on the access frequency. Three methods are proposed: in the first one, the most accessed data item is replicated in priority, while the other two reduce replica duplication among neighboring hosts or those in stable groups. In [4], the replica allocation methods are extended, by considering the correlation among data items; correlated data items are replicated together in one node. All these techniques have the drawback of requiring that all hosts have a global view on the available data items and the corresponding access frequencies. Such an assumption is not adapted to highly mobile environments; it requires that all nodes broadcast information to all other nodes, which will cause significant undesirable network traffic overhead. DRAM [8] is also a group based replication solution where the group mobility is studied to avoid the broadcast of information to all nodes. Examples of fully decentralized strategy are REDMAN [9], and [15]; [9] presents a middleware that manages, retrieves, and distributes replicas and maintains approximately the desired resource replication degree. However, this solution is restricted to dense MANETs where the number of connected node in a region is high. The solution proposed in [15] distributes the storage, bandwidth and energy load through a resource-efficient adaptive caching scheme; each node flags a data item to be replicated when it discovered high bandwidth utilization for that data item. The primary difference between [15] and our method is the consideration of the user needs as a trigger for the replication process.

From another point of view, replication strategies need a trigger to start the process and criteria to decide where to place the replicas. In [1, 2, 3, 4], the replication is performed periodically at specific time points, at which all nodes identify the most accessed data of last period and decide to replicate them on suitable hosts. Moussaoui et al. [11] propose two replication processes: *primary replication,* for new data items, and *dynamic replication,* executed periodically to relocate replicas near the interested nodes. Tsuchida et al. [10] handle location-dependant queries in their method *Skip Copy*; the data are replicated on hosts within a specific area using the protocol Geocast. Other research works [2, 12, 9, 13] consider other criteria to choose data items to replicate and the target hosts such as the stability of the radio link, the available storage space, the remaining power, and so on. Boulkenafed et al. [12] calculate the expected time within the group. They use it in addition to the available storage space and the available energy, to avoid weak hosts. Hara et al. extend their work presented in [1] by considering the network partitioning and the host's battery power. In [2], if the radio link between two nodes is weak, the nodes are not considered as neighbors and are allowed to hold replicas of the same data item. In [4], the idea is to decrease the data transmission by increasing the number of replicas but in the same time the methods do not place replicas on nodes with low battery. Chen et al. [13] use advertising messages to communicate available data. These messages include some parameters that can assist the choice of replica holders, e.g., the free storage space, the remaining energy, the processor idle time, etc.

The replication solution proposed in this paper is a fully decentralized solution without any fixed point and does not require regular communication between neighbors. Replication decisions are made locally by each peer. We argue that this strategy is more suitable for highly mobile and dynamic environments where the communication between neighbors is not always possible. In addition, our model is user-centric. The users are in control of their level of participation in the replication process and of the amount of resources that they make available. Then the replication system acts automatically to keep them satisfied; it adapts to the user's needs by replicating when resource consumption exceeds the chosen limit. In this paper, we will first present our model then an overall view of the architecture with a focus on its main component (PSM) that implements the key ideas of our model. In a second part, we will present our experiments that validate and confirm the efficiency of our model with good level of user satisfaction.

3   CReaM: User-Centric Replication Model

In this section, we describe our user-Centric REplicAtion Model for mobile environments (CReaM). CReaM is a decentralized user-centric replication that takes replication decisions at the node level with the goal of increasing data availability. The model is user-centric as it is driven by user-chosen threshold to decide when to replicate. Indeed, the model depends on monitoring the consumption of three resources: the CPU, the battery and the storage. If CReaM notices some decreases in the available resources that are unacceptable with respect to the user level of satisfaction, it acts to decrease the resource consumption. The reaction is to replicate data in order to reduce the load on the peer. CReaM is also decentralized as it takes its decision based on local information: the consumption of the above mentioned resources, the user-specified thresholds, but also the requests observed by the node. It uses this information to select the data to be replicated and requests other peers to hold it. CReaM also manages incoming replication requests in a user-centric way by deciding whether to accept replica placement depending on its effect on user satisfaction with respect to the consumption of its resources. Before detailing the model, we first define some important concepts that are related to it.

3.1   Definitions

Access Frequency (AF). It indicates the number of requests received by a specific node for a specific data item. It is an accumulation starting from zero and increased by 1 after each received request. It is initiated when the data item is created on the node.

Temperature Degree (TD). It indicates the current importance of a data item; the importance is defined for a given time period and from the point of view of neighbor nodes. TD starts from 0; it is updated periodically at specific time points based on a predefined time window. If AF increased during the last time interval, TD increases by the same value. However, if AF remained at the same level, TD starts decreasing to reflect the fact that the data item is important but not requested with the same intensity. At time T_i, TD is updated based on the following rules: (1) TD increases by X if AF increased by X during the time interval $[T_{i-1}, T_i]$. (2) TD decreases by a parameter Y if AF remains unchanged between T_{i-1} and T_i.

In some cases, the data item might still be important to the nodes even if AF starts to be constant. To avoid decreasing TD too rapidly, we define a third rule as follows: TD remains unchanged at T_i if AF starts to be stable at T_{i-1}.

However, in all cases, when AF remains stable for more than two consecutive time periods, TD starts decreasing. In the following illustrative example (Fig. 1), AF remains at 7 between T_4 and T_6, but TD decreasing by Y=1 at T_5 until T_7 when AF starts increasing again.

The Threshold α. It is a numeric value related to TD used to identify important data items: when a data item DI has a TD value that reaches α, it is considered as hot on this node $TD(DI) \geq \alpha$.

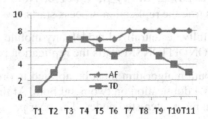

Fig. 1. Example of evolution of AF and TD over time

The Tolerance Thresholds. These thresholds represent the allowed level of resource consumption specified by the user. We define three thresholds: β, the allowed load level on the node's CPU, μ, the allowed level of remaining battery, and δ, the allowed level of remaining storage space.

These thresholds will be used to monitor the peer's status and take the replication decisions; for example when the remaining battery reaches μ, outgoing replication requests will be generated, and when the remaining storage space reaches δ incoming replica placement requests will no longer be accepted.

3.2   The User Centric Replication Model

As any replication model, CReaM answers the following questions: (1) **who** starts the replication process, (2) **when** to start it (3) **what** data to replicate and (4) **where** to place the replica. Let us consider a MANET consisting of *n* mobile nodes: MANET = $\{M_1, M_2 \ldots M_n\}$: $n \in N$.

When. The replication model starts the replication process depending on the peer's status (its available resources, the temperature of data items held by the node). Node M_i ($1 \leq i \leq n$) must verify at least one of the following conditions in order to start the replication process:

- *Condition 1*: a DI_i becomes hot for node M_i. In this case replicating DI will increase its availability.

- *Condition 2*: the user becomes unsatisfied from the availability of its resources. We define three functions to calculate the consumption of the three previously mentioned resources (CPU, battery, storage). The output of these functions is compared to the tolerance thresholds μ, δ and β respectively, to determine whether a user should be unsatisfied with the level of his/her resource. If this is the case, the system reacts to improve the situation. For this purpose, we define the function $NoR(T_{i-1}, T_i)$ that returns the number of requests processed by the node during time interval $[T_{i-1}, T_i]$ that corresponds to the CPU load, the function $BL(T)$ that returns the remaining battery at time T, and the function $SS(T)$ that returns the available storage space at time T.

The answer to the "when" question depends on the set of the conditions named $CONDITIONS_M = \{TD(DI) \geq \alpha, BL(T) \leq \mu, SS(T) \leq \delta, NoR(T_{i-1}, T_i) \geq \beta\}$. When at least one condition becomes true the replication process starts.

Who. CReaM being a fully decentralized model, any mobile node that has at least one verified condition in CONDITIONSM starts the replication process.

Where. A good distribution algorithm must be applied in order to properly distribute the replicas and avoid DI duplication on two neighbors. At the same time, the replicas must be placed near the most interested nodes. The peer participates also in the replica placement process; the system makes the decision to place/refuse the replicas using the tolerance thresholds configured according to the user needs. We are currently working on an algorithm including all these aspects to take the replica placement decision.

What. The data item that must be replicated depends on the condition that has triggered the replication process (i.e. true conditions among the set CONDITIONS$_M$). Thus, several cases need to be considered. For example, if $NoR(T_{i-1}, T_i) \geq \beta$, then the appropriate solution is to replicate the most requested DI in order to decrease the requests coming to the node, consequently decreasing the CPU load and satisfying the user desire. In another example, if a DI becomes hot, it should be replicated in order to increase its availability.

We classify the DI(s) of each node into several categories; a DI may belong to one or more categories at the same time. These categories are defined as follow:

DI_α: includes the hot DI(s). A DI joins this category when its TD becomes equal or greater than the threshold α and leaves it when it is no longer *hot*.

DI_β: contains the requested DI(s) of the last period of time. It is constructed periodically each time T by adding the DI(s) with modified AF during last period of time.

DI_r: includes the rare DI(s) that are important but rarely found on the peers; we are interested to consider such category in order to prevent the data lost occurred when the nodes containing such rare items disconnect.

DI_o: includes "not important" DI(s). A DI which its TD reaches zero is added to this category, and removed from it when its TD starts increasing.

As stated above, an action is initiated in case the user is unsatisfied i.e. a condition from CONDITIONS$_M$ becomes true. Below, each resource is studied separately in order to define what actions to take when necessary:

The CPU: when the number of requests exceeds the threshold β, the node selects a DI to replicate in order to share the load of requests with other nodes and to reduce its NoR. The candidate DI (**cdi**) must be a hot DI that was requested during last period (**cdi** $\in DI_\alpha \cap DI_\beta$). If this set is empty, the best choice is to select an element from DI_β that causes the load regardless if the elected element is hot or not.

$$cdi \in DI_\alpha \cap DI_\beta \text{ if } DI_\alpha \cap DI_\beta <> \{\} \text{ else } cdi \in DI_\beta \qquad (1)$$

However, if the load of the CPU keeps increasing, it would not be appropriate to keep replicating endlessly; instead, the node needs to take more radical actions in order to immediately preserve its resources. Therefore, we define two values for the threshold β, *soft* value β_1 and *hard* value β_2 ($\beta_1 < \beta_2$). If the *soft* threshold is exceeded ($NoR(T_{i-1}-T_i) \geq \beta_1$) the node replicates a DI as explained in (1). If the number of requests reaches the *hard* threshold ($NoR(T_{i-1}-T_i) \geq \beta_2$), the node will stop responding to any request.

The Storage space: following the same logic, we define two values for the threshold δ. If the available storage space becomes less than the soft threshold ($SS(T) \leq \delta_1$) the node accepts only the incoming urgent replication requests; the requests' urgency is evaluated in terms of data importance and requestor nodes' availability. If the hard threshold is exceeded ($SS(T) \leq \delta_2$), the node removes a DI from the set DI_o by applying one of the well known cache replacement algorithms.

The Battery: As with the other resources, it is necessary to define also two values for the threshold μ. Then, if the remaining battery becomes less than the soft threshold

$(BL(T){\leq}\mu_1)$, the same action is applied as defined in (1). If the hard threshold is exceeded $(BL(T){\leq}\mu_2)$ the probability of disconnections becomes high, thus, it is more appropriate to replicate one or more rare DI from the set DI_r in order to avoid data loss. However, unnecessary replication may occur, if each node replicates a rare DI and loads the network by data that might be unhelpful to the remaining nodes. To avoid this situation, we give priority to a DI from the set $DI_a{\cap}DI_r$ that is rare and hot at the same time.

In addition, a node might prevent critical situations of disconnection by reacting when noticing rapid battery consumption even before the thresholds (soft or hard) are reached. Thus, we define an additional value μ_3 for the threshold μ. The battery consumption between T_{i-1} and T_i is calculated using the function $\mathbf{BC} = BL(T_{i-1}) - BL(T_i)$. When BC becomes less than the threshold μ_3, the node reacts preemptive by replicating data items according to formula (1).

Table 1 summarizes all cases. It contains the conditions, the peer's status and the executed actions. We proposed architecture to implement the model of CReaM; the details of this architecture are presented in details in [14].

Table 1. Summary of the peer's status

Condition	Peer's status	Action
$NoR(T_{i-1},T_i) \geq \beta_1$	CPU-Overloaded	Replicate from $DI_a{\cap}DI_\beta / DI_\beta$
$NoR(T_{i-1},T_i) \geq \beta_2$	CPU-Scarce	Stop responding
$SS(T) \leq \delta_1$	S-Overloaded	Response just to urgent RQ
$SS(T) \leq \delta_2$	S-Scarce	Delete replicas from DI_o
$BL(T) \leq \mu_1$	B-Overloaded	Replicate from $DI_a{\cap}DI_\beta / DI_\beta$
$BL(T) \leq \mu_2$	B-Scarce	Replicate from $DI_a{\cap}DI_r$
$BC \leq \mu_3$	HB-Consumption	Replicate from $DI_a{\cap}DI_\beta / DI_\beta$

4   Performance Evaluations

4.1   Simulation Design

In this section, we present the simulation that was carried out in order to validate the key functionalities of our proposed model and to evaluate its performance. The simulator has been developed using the OMNet++ and INETMANET frameworks[1].

The experimental scenario is the following. A fixed set of nodes (100) interact for a given period of time; each node runs CReaM. The nodes move according to a given mobility model (see below) within a predefined region (square region of 1500m x 1500m). Each node is initialized with a set of data items chosen from a predefined list of 75 to 150 documents. The size of a data item is fixed at 1,5 kB. The interaction consists in nodes issuing requests for documents according to a requests generation model detailed below. As the nodes run CReaM, replication requests are also generated and processed during the simulation. The communication layer is simulated using AODV [19] to route requests and data, UDP broadcast to transmit all messages

---

[1] http://www.omnetpp.org

and IEEE802.11n in the MAC layer. The bandwidth is set at 2 Mbit/s. For the parameters of CReaM, we have fixed the tolerance thresholds as summarized in Table 2, the number of replicas is determined experimentally to 2 after each PSM's reaction; and finally the selection of the replica holders has been done randomly, in the meantime of implementing the Replica Distributer behavior.

Table 2. CReaM's Parameters

Threshold of tolerance	β_1= 4R, β_2= 10R, μ_1=60%, μ_2=75%
Threshold Alfa	30
Time period for PSM	7s
Time life for each query	3s

In the following, we explained successively, the mobility model of connected nodes, the data generation and distribution model, and finally the query distribution model.

Mobility Model: The nodes move according to the *Random Way Point* model which is widely used in MANETs simulations and as it seems to be the closest to typical movement patterns of the real mobile nodes. The moving speed of each mobile host v was chosen randomly in the range 0..3 m/s and pause time was 3 seconds. The initial position of each host was also set randomly.

Data Generation Model: The number of data items on the network changes during simulation runs in order to study its impact on the different measurements. The data items are distributed on all mobile nodes in the beginning of the simulation based on the Zipf distribution[2], which has been frequently used to model non-uniform distribution.

Data Requests Generation Model: Is based on the Poisson model [19] with a mean of 4 requests each 2s. The packet length of a request message is 128 bytes including UDP and IP header. Periodically, the simulator selects randomly mobile nodes to send the requests and the subjects (DI) of the requests. The selected requestor nodes broadcast the requests to their neighbors and wait for responses. When a mobile host that receives a request message holds a replica of requested data item, it sends back a response message containing the replica. The response message may be simply forwarded to requesting node by unicast reply using the reverse route of the request. The size of all reply messages was set to 1500 bytes including replying route in our simulations. Each requested host copies the replica to its local storage after it receives the replica. Actually, we assume the new-copied replicas are read-only.

4.2   Experimental Results

As explained before, CReaM starts the replication process on an ad-hoc basis, when the resources consumption exceeds the levels specified by the user. This is different

---

[2] http://www.nslij-genetics.org/wli/zipf

from most existing works, in which each node periodically decides whether to replicate some of its (hot) data items. Thus, to validate our model, we have developed a simulation with the goal of comparing it to a periodical replication model. Three metrics were defined for these experiments, namely data availability, overhead, and user satisfaction. For each particular setting, the simulation was executed 25 times. We now define each metric then, present and analyze the corresponding simulation results.

Data Availability (DA): This metric represents the rate of data availability during the simulation (i.e.) the ratio of successful requests. Formally, it is defined by the following formula: DA=(NoSR/NoTR)*100, where NoSR and NoTR are respectively the number of successful requests and the total number of requests during the simulation. The replication system's goal is to increase the DA as much as possible.

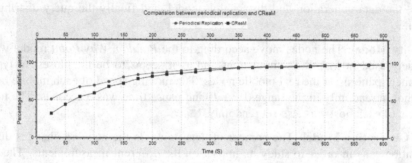

Fig. 2. Data availability with time

Some experiment studies of the positive effects of CReaM and the influence of the data item's number on DA were done; indeed, CReaM increases the data availability in a significant manner and it was proven experimentally that making two replicas in each replication request gives a compromise between the overhead and the augmentation in DA.

Fig. 2 shows the obtained results of comparing CReaM with a periodical replication system with respect to the time. We see here that the periodical replication model increases the data availability better than CReaM in the beginning of the simulation; but with time, CReaM increases also the DA as the periodical replication does. In other words, CReaM gives the same performance with time, because the replicas on the network are created only when it's needed. From other point of view, because CReaM creates the replicas when needed, it causes less overhead. From here the second metrics *overhead* is necessary to show the utility of CReaM.

Overhead (OVH): This metric represents the total number of exchange messages needed for the replication system during the simulation time. Formally, it is defined as OVH=$\sum_{i=1}^{n}$ NoMi where NoMi is the total number of messages needed for the replication system and sent from node i and n is the number of nodes in the system. The aim of any replication system is to decrease the overhead as much as possible.

A comparison between the overhead caused by CReaM and by the periodical replication was done. Fig. 3. shows that during the simulation, CReaM causes much less overhead than the periodical model. This is because CReaM only sends replication requests when one of the conditions monitored by the PSM is reached. We are planning to further study this when the component Replica Distributer will be ready. Indeed we are designing to this end an algorithm that does not require many additional messages to select the replica holders and expect that appropriate replica placement will contribute to maintain the overhead caused by our replication system low as possible with better data dissemination according to requests origins.

In a second series of experiments, we have studied the influence of the number of data items on the overhead created by CReaM. In Fig. 4, we can observe very different results between the overhead caused by CReaM and by the other model. Moreover, we note that the positive effect of CReaM on the overhead gets more significant as the number of data items increases. At the same time, as shown in Fig. 5 the global rates of data availability are similar in all cases. For example, when the number of data item is equal to 150, CReaM causes less than half overhead than the other model while they provide the same rate of data availability.

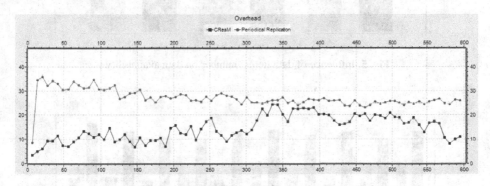

Fig. 3. Overhead with time

User satisfaction US: This metric aims to determine the fraction of simulation time during which a user remained satisfied from their resources' consumption; indeed, the idea of maintaining resource consumption within user defined boundaries is at the centre of the design of our model, as it distinguishes it from other replication models. Thus, user success is a critical criterion to evaluate the success of the approach. Formally, the metric is defined for each user as $USi = (NoTSi/T)*100$, where $NoTSi$ is the total time during which the ith user remains satisfied over the whole simulation, and T is the duration of the simulation.

Fig. 6 shows individual results for a sample of 10 users. We can note that CReaM increases the user satisfaction. This tends to show that CReaM has the desired effect of better distributing the load of data requests on less busy nodes, which helps keeping the user satisfied.

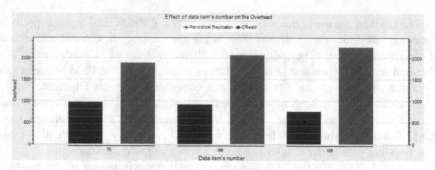

Fig. 4. Influence of data items' number on Overhead

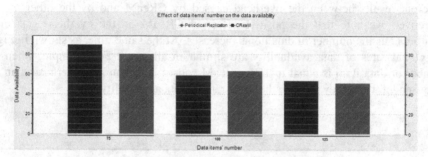

Fig. 5. Influence of data items' number on data availability

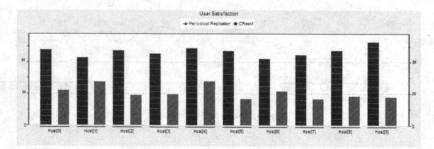

Fig. 6. User Satisfaction

In addition to the US, we define the Total User Satisfaction (TUS) to observe the effect of CReaM on the whole network. It is defined as the $TUS=\Sigma_t(NoUS_t)$, where the NoUS is the number of satisfied users during time period T. Fig. 7 shows that with CReaM the number of satisfied users is higher than with the periodical replication model that not care in the user satisfaction but rather resources availability. That confirms the results obtained for 10 nodes; thus, considering the whole set of users, with time, CReaM also has the desired effect of distributing the load of data requests on all connected nodes, thus keeping the users satisfied.

To summarize, we can conclude from this experimental study that CReaM maintains data availability at level comparable to those of periodical replication systems but with an overhead that is significantly lower than that of the adversary.

This enable CReaM to reach its goal and save the available resources (network and devices resources) for the applications deployed on the MANET. At the same time, it keeps the users satisfied of the level of consumption of their resources, a point that is hardly considered by other replication systems, whereas we argue that this is a crucial and more realistic feature that a real large-scale system should provide.

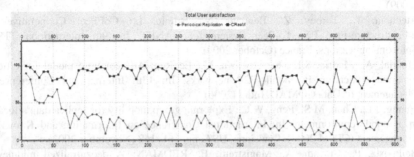

Fig. 7. The total user satisfaction

5 Conclusion and Future Work

In this paper we have presented CReaM, a user-centric replication model for MANETs. CReaM addresses the important problem of maintaining data availability in mobile environments. The model is user-centric, as each node only contributes under the condition that doing so does not cause excessive resource consumption. In this paper, we have focused on the autonomous behavior of the nodes, according to which each node bases on its user needs and available resources to trigger replication requests. This process is based on settings chosen by the user and on monitoring of the resources that are at the user's disposal. CReaM has been evaluated using a simulation-based implementation using the OMNet++ simulation environment. The experimentations show that CReaM increases the data availability in a significant way, with high rate of user satisfaction and low level of overhead.

Another series of experimentations are currently in progress. Their goal is to determine experimentally the best values for the tolerance thresholds that are important parameters of the model. In addition, we are working on the *Replica Distributer* component; our objective is to design it so that it also enhances proactively the data availability from a semantic point of view and the user satisfaction by a better choice of nodes that can hold new replicas, taking into account data distribution.

References

1. Hara, T.: Effective replica allocation in ad hoc networks for improving data accessibility. In: Proceedings of IEEE INFOCOM Conference, pp. 1568–1576 (April 2001)
2. Hara, T., Loh, Y.H., Nishio, S.: Data replication methods based on the stability of radio links in ad hoc networks. In: Proc. of International Workshop on Mobility in Databases and Distributed Systems (MDDS 2003), Prague, Czech Republic, pp. 969–973 (September 2003)

3. Hara, T., Murakami, N., Nishio, S.: Replica allocation for correlated data items in ad hoc sensor networks. ACM SIGMOD Record 33(1), 38–43 (2004)
4. Shinohara, M., Hara, T., Nishio, S.: Data replication considering power consumption in ad hoc networks. In: International Conference on Mobile Data Management, Germany (2007)
5. Nawaf, M.M., Torbey, Z.: Replica update strategy in mobile ad hoc networks. In: International Workshop on Management of Emergent Digital EcoSystems, Lyon-France (2009)
6. Atechian, T., Torbey, Z., Bennani, N., Brunie, L.: CoFFee: Cooperative and InFrastructure-Free Peer-To-Peer System for VANET. In: 9th International ITS of Telecommunications, France (October 2009)
7. Mondal, A., Madria, S.K., Kitsuregawa, M.: EcoRep: An economic model for efficient dynamic replication in mobile-P2P networks. In: 13th International Conference on Management of Data COMAD, India (2006)
8. Huang, J.L., Chen, M.S., Peng, W.C.: Exploring group mobility for replica data allocation in a mobile environment. In: International Conference on Information and Knowledge Management (CIKM 2003), Louisiana, USA, pp. 161–168 (November 2003)
9. Bellavista, P., Corradi, A., Magistretti, E.: REDMAN: A decentralized middleware solution for cooperative replication in dense MANETs. In: 3th IEEE Internationl Conference on Pervasive Computing and Communications Workshops PerCom, pp. 158–162 (2005)
10. Tsuchida, G., Okino, T., Tamori, M., Watanabe, T., Mizuno, T., Ishihara, S.: Replica distribution of data associated with location on wireless ad hoc networks. Electronics and Communications in Japan (Part I: Communications) 90(10), 67–80 (2007)
11. Moussaoui, S., Guerroumi, M., Badache, N.: Data Replication in Mobile Ad Hoc Networks. In: Cao, J., Stojmenovic, I., Jia, X., Das, S.K. (eds.) MSN 2006. LNCS, vol. 4325, pp. 685–697. Springer, Heidelberg (2006)
12. Boulkenafed, M., Issarny, V.: A Middleware Service for Mobile Ad Hoc Data Sharing, Enhancing Data Availability. In: Endler, M., Schmidt, D.C. (eds.) Middleware 2003. LNCS, vol. 2672, pp. 493–511. Springer, Heidelberg (2003)
13. Chen, K., Nahrstedt, K.: An integrated data lookup and replication scheme in Mobile ad hoc networks. In: SPIE International Symposium on the Convergence of Information Technologies and Communications, pp. 1–8 (2001)
14. Torbey, Z., Bennani, N., Coquil, C., Brunie, L.: CReaM: User-Centric Replication Model for Mobile Environments. In: The International Workshop on "Mobile P2P Data Management, Security and Trust (M-PDMST 2010)", pp. 348–353. IEEE, Kansas City (2010) ISBN 978-1-4244-7075-4
15. Harsch, D., Madria, S.: A Resource-Efficient Adaptive Caching Scheme for Mobile Ad Hoc Networks. In: The 29th IEEE International Symposium on Reliable Distributed Systems (October 2010)
16. Hara, T., Madria, S.: Consistency Management Strategies for Data Replication in Mobile Ad Hoc Networks. The IEEE Transactions on Mobile Computing 8(7), 950–967 (2009)
17. Kanzaki, A., Sawai, Y., Shinohara, M., Hara, T., Nishio, S.: Quorum-Based Consistency Management for Data Replication in Mobile Ad Hoc Networks. In: The International Workshop for Ubiquitous Networking and Enablers to Context-Aware Services, Turky, Finland, pp. 357–360 (July 2008)
18. Ad hoc On Demand Distance Vector, http://www.ietf.org/rfc/rfc3561.txt
19. Rodriguez, G.: Poisson Models for Count Data (September 2007)
20. http://www.nslij-genetics.org/wli/zipf/

An Adaptive Smoothing Method for Sensor Noise in Augmented Reality Applications on Smartphones

Rifat Ozcan[1,*], Fatih Orhan[1], M. Fatih Demirci[2], and Osman Abul[2]

[1]AnelARGE, Hacettepe Teknokent, Ankara, Turkey
{rifat.ozcan,fatih.orhan}@anelarge.com
[2]Computer Eng. Dept., TOBB University of Economics and Technology, Ankara, Turkey
{mfdemirci,osmanabul}@etu.edu.tr

Abstract. Handling inaccurate and noisy sensor readings are among important challenges while implementing augmented reality applications on smartphones. As a result, we need to smooth the sensor readings for steady operation. However, no smoothing algorithm performs best in all cases as there is an inherent tradeoff. On one hand, excessive smoothing slows down the effect of device movements, hence makes applications less responsive. On the other hand, insufficient smoothing causes objects on the screen to constantly move back and forth even while the device is steady, hence makes applications too responsive. Clearly, both of the extremes cause augmented reality applications to be less effective in terms of human-computer interaction performance. In this paper, we propose an adaptive smoothing method based on the rate of change in device view direction. Basically, the method adjusts the smoothing level adaptively based on the phone movement. Our experimental results show that our adaptive approach, in comparison to previous proposals, achieves a better smoothing for various cases of phone movements.

Keywords: Augmented reality, sensors, noise, smoothing.

1 Introduction

An Augmented Reality (AR) system combines real and virtual objects in a real environment, registers (aligns) real and virtual objects with each other, and runs interactively, in three dimensions, and in real time [1, 2]. Even though initial work on AR systems started in 70's, functional and practical systems appeared in 90's [7]. These elements required for AR systems, such as displays, sensors, batteries and computers were too bulky, heavy and expensive for mobile or everyday use. Starting with the new millennium, the mobile device display units enhanced and grew in size and capability. Moreover, variety of sensors, cameras, GPS receivers, accelerometers, and magnetometers were integrated into smartphones. The sensor integrations and other enhancements provided the necessary components for the realization of AR systems on smartphones [11, 3]. After the introduction of iPhone and Android

---

* Corresponding author.

N. Venkatasubramanian et al. (Eds.): Mobilware 2011, LNICST 93, pp. 209–218, 2012.

devices, the concept became hype and many applications popped-up one after another. Layar[1] and Wikitude[2] are two popular AR applications among many others. In our company, we also developed a similar AR browser that mainly presents points of interests (POIs) (i.e., restaurants, clubs, cinemas, pharmacies etc.) around user location, and capable of automatic POI filtering based on user context.

An important problem in AR is to track the user or object movements so that virtual and real objects can be aligned properly. This is also referred as the registration problem. The methods can be categorized into two: (i) computer vision based approaches [6], and (ii) sensor based approaches. Computer vision based approaches track the manually placed markers in the scene and determine the position and orientation of the camera. Clearly, this prevents AR systems to be used in outdoor applications. This approach is not well-suited to smartphones, since limited memory and CPU processing capabilities of these devices may not allow costly computer vision based tracking methods to be applied in real time. For the mentioned reason, AR systems on smartphones use the sensor based approaches. Magnetic field and accelerometer sensors together with GPS receivers are used to determine the orientation of the camera. Even though this approach does not require manual markers and enables outdoor usage, noise in mobile phone's magnetic field and accelerometer sensors adversely affect the quality of AR applications, and this fact adds another challenge into the problem [5].

In the literature, various smoothing techniques are applied in different fields, including signal processing [8, 10], statistics [9], and information retrieval [12, 4] in order to remove noise from the data. These methods vary in complexity and accuracy. To the best of our knowledge, Gotow et al. [5] presents a pioneering work towards this problem in the context of AR systems and smartphones. The authors propose *compass filter algorithm* to smooth the readings from magnetic field sensor. This algorithm identifies outliers in the noisy sensor readings based on a deviation threshold parameter. If the deviation of a new sensor measurement from the mean of sample is higher than the deviation threshold, then this measurement is interpreted as outlier.

In this paper, we propose an adaptive smoothing method for sensor noise cancellation. The main contributions of this study are as follows:

- We first analyze the noise in sensor readings for various cases of phone movements such as phone-stationary at hand and phone-rotating about an axis.
- We propose an adaptive smoothing method which adjusts the level of smoothing to the phone movement. This is achieved by monitoring the change in phone view direction.
- We show in our experiments that the proposed approach provides us with far better results over the three previous methods, simple, exponential, and compass filter [5] smoothing algorithms.

The rest of this paper is organized as follows: In the next section, we present the alternative smoothing methods in the literature, which are applicable to smartphones.

---

[1] http://www.layar.com/
[2] http://www.wikitude.org/

This section also introduces our adaptive smoothing method. Later, we evaluate and compare the proposed approach and alternative smoothing algorithms in the experimental section. We close the paper with our conclusions.

2   Smoothing Methods

In this section we present three smoothing approaches (namely, simple moving average, exponential moving average and compass filtering algorithm) that are applicable to smartphones from the literature, and describe our adaptive smoothing method afterwards.

In a typical mobile augmented reality application, the objective is to present the nearby points of interests (POIs). This requires a mapping of 3D object locations to the 2D smartphone screen. It is trivial to find nearby POIs given the locations of the device and POIs. However, the exact location of POIs on the smartphone screen changes based on the phone orientation. The orientation is computed using the values read from magnetic field and accelerometer sensors. However, the noise in these sensors causes the location of the POI to be noisy which in turn results in POI to be going back and forth even though the device is steady at hand. This causes a frustrating user interface especially when the user wants to click the POI for further detailed information.

We apply smoothing for magnetic field and accelerometer sensor values using a history of measured values. Let S_i to be the ith measurement from a sensor (For the sake of simplicity, we will assume one sensor measuring one value. It is straightforward to extend this to the case where a sensor giving a vector in 3D.). We define the history array of sensor measurements as follows, where HL denotes the length of the measurement history array:

$$H = [S_0, S_1, ..., S_{HL-1}]$$

Each time we get a new value from the sensor, the history array shifts by one position; causing the least recent measurement (in this case, S_0) to be forgotten, and the new measurement to become the most recent measurement (in this case, S_{HL-1}). Finally, the smoothed value is computed based on the smoothing function (f_s) and history array (H).

2.1   Simple Moving Average

This approach simply takes the mean of the recent measurements as follows:

$$f_s = \frac{\sum_{i=0}^{HL-1} H[i]}{HL} \tag{1}$$

The drawback of simple moving average is that it incurs a significant lag to the latest data point. The lag duration is directly proportional to the length, HL, of the history array. The computation complexity of this approach is $O(1)$ assuming that the current sum is kept and constantly updated.

2.2   Exponential Moving Average

The simple moving average assigns the same weight to all recent data points independent of the time of the measurement. However, in some cases, it is desirable that more recent measurements should have higher weights in comparison to older measurements. Exponential moving average achieves this criterion by giving exponentially decreasing weights to older data points [9]. The formula for this smoothing function is given below:

$$f_s = \alpha \sum_{i=0}^{HL-1} (1-\alpha)^{((HL-1)-i)} H[i] \tag{2}$$

The drawback of this method is the need to tune the parameter alpha, a fraction between 0 and 1. The value of alpha needs to be close to 1 when phone is rotating and making sharp moves, but when the phone is stationary choosing a value closer to 0 is better as this selection assigns the same weight to all history values. Therefore, no magic alpha value can cover all the use cases. Moreover, the method is relatively costly, especially on smartphones, since the formula requires many floating point operations.

2.3   Compass Filtering Algorithm

Gotow et al. [5] discuss that noise reduction in smartphone sensors as one of the challenges for augmented reality applications, and as a result they propose a custom smoothing algorithm. The main idea behind their method, called compass filtering algorithm, is to identify outliers in the noisy sensor values. The outliers are detected based on a deviation threshold parameter. If the deviation of a new sensor measurement from the mean of sample is below the deviation threshold, then this data is interpreted as a non outlier, and inserted into the data buffer. Otherwise, it is tagged as outlier and put into another buffer, called outlier buffer. The simple average of values in the data buffer is returned as the smoothed sensor value (see [5] for the details of the algorithm).

2.4   Adaptive Smoothing Method

Our smoothing method is adaptive in the sense that the rate (level) of smoothing is dynamically adapted to the smartphone rotation. The basic idea is to use prolonged history values when the device is stationary and not rotating, and otherwise focus on only the most recent values. This achieves the smoothing of noisy values and prevents POIs to be appearing going back and forth constantly even the device is stationary at hand. If the phone is rotating or making sharp moves, we use fewer history values in order to respond to the rapid changes in the POI location in a reasonable time so as to diminish the lag time as much as possible. We first describe how we identify that the phone is rotating, and then present the details of our algorithm.

For our method, we need to introduce rotation matrix (R) which is calculated based on values from magnetic field and accelerometer sensors (Note that this rotation matrix performs the projection of object location in world coordinates to phone coordinate system). We re-compute R each time we have a new sensor reading. The third row of a rotation matrix gives the phone view direction of the camera. We call this row vector as the view vector (V). Suppose that R_p denotes the rotation matrix computed in the previous sensor update, and V_p is the view direction based on R_p. Then, the rate of change (C) in the view direction is computed by the magnitude of the view difference vector computed as follows:

$$C = \left| \vec{V} - \vec{V_p} \right|$$

We measure the rate of the change value for different phone movements such as phone-stationary at hand, and phone-rotating about an axis. More details on this will be provided in the next experimental section. In the light of our experiments, we determine a value, C_{thr}, for the threshold parameter. If the rate of change value is below this threshold then the phone is predicted to be stationary, otherwise it is assumed rotating. Our smoothing algorithm is based on this decision.

The main idea in our method is to keep a virtual history length (VHL) that changes based on the phone movement. Whenever we read raw sensor values M_{raw} and A_{raw}, from magnetic field and accelerometer sensors, respectively, we store these values in history arrays H_{Mag} and H_{Acc}. We determine the phone rotation based on threshold value (C_{thr}) and rate of change (C) computed as described previously. If the device is predicted as stationary, we increase VHL by α, otherwise we decrease it by β. Finally, we restrict the value of VHL to change between a lower, HL_{min}, and an upper, HL_{max}, bound. Then, the sensor value is smoothed by the simple moving average of last VHL values in the respective history array (H_{Mag} or H_{Acc}). This way, we achieve an adaptive smoothing based on phone movement.

3   Experiments

To demonstrate our approach to noise removal in an AR application, we experiment with an HTC G1 smartphone running Android operating system. The phone has a magnetic field sensor and an accelerometer sensor. In the experiments, we configure sensors in order to get the data as fast as possible. According to our measurements, in this mode, magnetic field and accelerometer sensors output about 50 and 40 readings per second, respectively. In the following, we first present the experimental results for the detection of the phone rotation. Then, we compare three smoothing algorithms against our method.

Our experiments consist of four different phone movement scenarios. First, we leave the phone steady on the table and read the sensor values. Next, we hold the phone at hand but do not move it at all. In the third and fourth cases, we rotate the phone about X and Y axis, respectively around ±90 degrees. The experimental results obtained with this setup are presented in the following. We present figures for only two most representative and relevant of these four cases, namely phone is steady at hand and phone is rotating about Y axis (Other two cases show similar trends).

3.1   Detection of the Phone Rotation

In this section, the objective is to measure the rate of change value (C) in the view direction for different phone movements. We empirically fixed the value for the threshold parameter C_{thr}. The plot in Fig.1a shows the value of C when the smartphone is steady at hand. In this case, the values are noisy and the value of C varies considerably. However, we observe that there is a minor movement while the phone is at hand, therefore the absolute value may exceed 0.0020. Fig.1b shows the case when the phone is rotated about Y axis. The results show that C increases up to the range [0.015-0.020]. The reason for the decrease is that we first rotate the phone in some direction and we stop at some point for a while, and then rotate the phone back to its original orientation, i.e. like a swing move.

The experimental results are used to estimate the threshold value for the rate of change in the view direction. In particular, this value is set to 0.0020 such that if C is less than this value, the device is predicted to be stationary. Otherwise it is rotating.

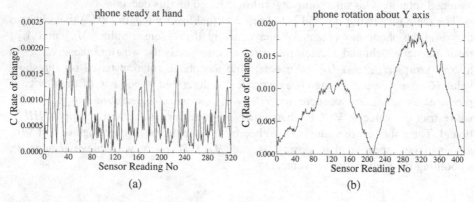

Fig. 1. Rate of change in phone view direction when a) phone is steady at hand, and b) phone is rotating about Y axis

3.2   Comparison of Smoothing Methods

In this section, we first evaluate our method for different phone movement scenarios. Then, we compare our approach against the other smoothing techniques. In the experiments, we set the value of HL_{max} to 120 (representing roughly two seconds of sensor data) in order to ensure that when the phone is stationary, and thus the POIs will not move back and forth. We do not allow the VHL value to decrease to one so that it does some sort of smoothing but only relies on last 20 values (HL_{min}). It is observed that considering the last 20 sensor values does not cause any distracting delay for users. The threshold value for view vector change (C_{thr}) is experimentally tuned and found to be 0.003 which gives the best case. We experimented with different values for α and β parameters. If we set α (the increase factor for VHL if we detect that the phone is stationary) to a value bigger than 1, it is observed that the sensor value fluctuates even though the device is kept stationary. We conjecture that the reason for this behavior is that when we increase the *VHL* value larger than 1, this causes the history values to include raw sensor values that belong to the time when the phone is rotating. This causes the smoothed value to be fluctuating even though the device is stationary for some time. Therefore we set both α and β parameters to 1 in order to handle this case. This ensures that when we increase the *VHL* value, we always grow the history array towards the new values (future direction) instead of old values (past direction).

Fig2 presents how the proposed approach performs for smoothing original sensor values. In particular, Fig. 2a shows the smoothing when the phone is stationary at hand. The curves named "original" and "adaptive" correspond to the original and our smoothed sensor values, respectively. We also show the virtual history length (VHL) values based on the secondary Y axis on the right side of the plot. As it is expected, VHL values remain to be the maximum history length (HL_{max} = 120), and our smoothing algorithm stabilizes the sensor values as much as possible. This achieves POIs to be left almost stationary on the phone screen without affected by the sensor noise. Fig. 2b shows the case when the phone is rotating about Y axis. We see that VHL value peacefully responds to the change in sensor values and adapts the smoothing accordingly. Note that there are peaks in VHL values in Fig. 2b. This is due to the fact that, as we mention previously, when we rotate the phone about an axis for some degree, we stop at that point for a while, and then rotate back to the original position. This causes the change in sensor values (so does the change in phone view direction) to remain minimal for that small time period. This increases the VHL value for a while (since the phone is stationary at that time) but later the change becomes larger than the threshold and VHL recovers itself.

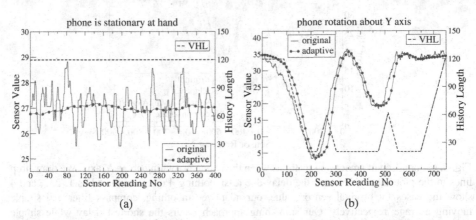

Fig. 2. Our smoothing algorithm and virtual history length (VHL) value when a) phone is steady at hand; and b) phone is rotating about Y axis

Secondly, we compare our smoothing algorithm with simple moving average and compass filter algorithms. The results are plotted in Fig. 3. Note that compass filter algorithm proposed in [5] requires two parameters: a) data buffer length (like history length in some sense), b) the deviation threshold to determine outliers. We examine with different parameter values, and observe that it behaves like a simple moving average method in the sense that if you increase the value of data buffer size, it makes more smoothing but when the phone is rotating it incurs more delay as depicted in Fig. 3. We set the buffer size to 60 and the deviation threshold value to 1 for compass filter smoothing. In order to show the delay due to smoothing, we draw drop lines in the plot where the sensor value reaches to its maximum after the rotation (Points numbered as 1, 2, 3, and 4 show the cases for original sensor value, our adaptive smoothing, compass filter and simple moving average, respectively). We observe that our adaptive approach incurs the shortest delay due to smoothing while simple moving average has the longest delay. The smoothing delay can be computed quantitatively as follows: For example, the number of sensor readings between points 1 and 2 is divided by the number of sensors readings per second (in our case, this is approximately 90 values per second, for both sensors, in total). This computes the delay due to smoothing. According to our measurements, the delay between original and our adaptive method is only 130 msec, while compass filter and simple moving average smoothing incurs 330 msec and 800 msec delays, respectively. Note that this same behavior is also observed when sensor value drops to its local minimum points (sensor readings around 200-250, and around 500-550). In this way, our AR application can respond to phone rotations quickly and change the POI locations without any distracting delay. Furthermore, we repeat this experiment 10 times and observe the same typical trend as in Fig.3.

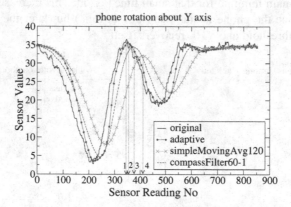

Fig. 3. Comparison of smoothing methods when the phone is rotating about Y axis. We draw drop lines in the plot in order to show the delay due to smoothing. Points numbered as 1, 2, 3, and 4 show the cases for original sensor value, our adaptive smoothing, compass filter and simple moving average, respectively. Our smoothing approach incurs the shortest delay while simple moving average has the longest delay.

Finally, we compare our approach with exponential smoothing method in Fig. 4. The plot in Fig. 4a, shows the case when the phone is rotating about Y axis. As we previously mention, the alpha value in exponential smoothing must be tuned for different cases. For example, we tune this parameter to 0.1 when phone is rotating and the result seems that exponential smoothing does better than our approach because it does not incur any delay. However, this value of alpha does not work when phone is stationary as shown in Fig. 4b. In this case, the exponential smoothing algorithm cannot handle the noise in sensor values unlike our algorithm. Therefore, it is impractical to select a single value for alpha which works in all cases. Compass filter smoothing incurs slightly more fluctuation of sensor values than our approach. Note that, when the phone is stationary, simple moving average exhibits exactly the same behavior as our approach. In order to show the smoothing quantitatively when the phone is stationary, we use the linear least squares fit of a straight line to the sensor values (since we expect the sensor values to be almost the same when the phone is stationary as shown in Fig.2.a) and measure the root mean square error from the fitted line. According to the results, the original, exponential smoothing, compass filter smoothing, and the proposed adaptive smoothing have 0.66, 0.36, 0.17, and 0.09 error rates, respectively. The results reveal that our approach achieves far better results compared to the alternative methods.

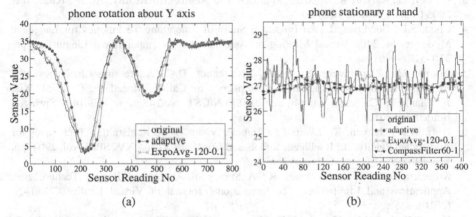

Fig. 4. Comparison of our smoothing approach and exponential smoothing when a) phone is rotating about Y axis, and b) phone is steady at hand. It is observed that it is possible to tune the exponential smoothing for the case of phone rotation as in a), but this tuning does not perform well if the phone is stationary as in b). However, our smoothing approach is a good compromise between these two extreme cases and adapts itself to the device movement.

4   Conclusions

Noise reduction in smartphone sensors is one of the challenges for AR applications. In this paper, we propose an adaptive smoothing approach, which is movement-aware in the sense that it adapts the level of smoothing based on the phone movement behavior. We conducted experiments based on real sensor values read from a smartphone for various phone movement cases (e.g. steady at-hand and rotation). Our results show that even though it is possible to tune alternative smoothing techniques to perform well in specific cases, our adaptive smoothing method achieves a better smoothing performance in the overall case. Although our approach was applied on a

HTC G1 phone, we expect the same smoothing performance on other smartphones. In the future, we will evaluate the performance on other smartphones especially for Apple's iPhone. In addition, we plan to provide a general method to determine the value of the C_{thr} threshold as it was determined experimentally in this paper.

Acknowledgments. This work is supported by the Scientific and Technological Research Council of Turkey (TÜBÝTAK) by the grant number 7100183.

References

1. Azuma, R.: A Survey of Augmented Reality. Presence 6(4), 355–385 (1997)
2. Azuma, R.T., Baillot, Y., Behringer, R., Feiner, S.K., Julier, S., MacIntyre, B.: Recent Advances in Augmented Reality. IEEE Computer Graphics and Applications 21(6), 34–47 (2001)
3. Bimber, O., Raskar, R.: Modern Approaches to Augmented Reality. ACM SIGGRAPH 2005 Courses, Article 1 (2005)
4. Chen, S.F., Goodman, J.: An Empirical Study of Smoothing Techniques for Language Modeling. In: 34th Annual Meeting on Association for Computational Linguistics, pp. 310–318 (1996)
5. Gotow, J.B., Zienkiewicz, K., White, J., Schmidt, D.C.: Addressing Challenges with Augmented Reality Applications on Smartphones. In: Cai, Y., Magedanz, T., Li, M., Xia, J., Giannelli, C. (eds.) Mobilware 2010. LNICST, vol. 48, pp. 129–143. Springer, Heidelberg (2010)
6. Hoff, W.A., Nguyen, K., Lyon, T.: Computer Vision-based Registration Techniques for Augmented Reality. In: Intelligent Robots and Computer Vision XV. SPIE, vol. 2904, pp. 538–548 (1996)
7. Krevelen, D.W.F., van Poelman, R.: A Survey of Augmented Reality Technologies, Applications and Limitations. The International Journal of Virtual Reality 9(2), 1–20 (2010)
8. Ngo, T.B., Le, H.L., Nguyen, T.H.: Survey of Kalman Filters and their Application in Signal Processing. In: ICAI 2009, vol. 3, pp. 335–339 (2009)
9. NIST/SEMATECH e-Handbook of Statistical Methods, http://www.itl.nist.gov/div898/handbook/
10. Orfanidis, S.J.: Introduction to Signal Processing. Prentice Hall (1995)
11. Schmalstieg, D., Wagner, D.: Experiences with Handheld Augmented Reality. In: 6th IEEE and ACM International Symposium on Mixed and Augmented Reality, ISMAR 2007, pp. 1–13 (2007)
12. Zhai, C., Lafferty, J.: A Study of Smoothing Methods for Language Models Applied to Ad Hoc Information Retrieval. In: SIGIR 2001, pp. 334–342 (2001)

Mobile Architecture for Dynamic Generation and Scalable Distribution of Sensor-Based Applications

Marco Picone[1], Marco Muro[1], Vincenzo Micelli[2],
Michele Amoretti[1], and Francesco Zanichelli[1]

[1] Distributed Systems Group - Università degli Studi di Parma, Parma, Italy
{picone,muro}@ce.unipr.it,
{michele.amoretti,francesco.zanichelli}@unipr.it
http://www.dsg.ce.unipr.it
[2] RimLab - Università degli Studi di Parma, Parma, Italy
micelli@ce.unipr.it

Abstract. The widespread and ubiquitous nature of mobile devices makes them attractive as providers of information collected from their rich equipment of sensors (camera, microphone, GPS, etc.), and also from external sensors (placed on persons, or in the environment). Thus, we envision large-scale sensor networks that use mobile devices as raw data sources, but also aggregated information producers - merging basic data coming from sensors distributed in the environment.

In this paper we propose an architectural framework for agile development and deployment of mobile cloud applications, harvesting heterogeneous sensor data. The novelty of the architecture is the possibility to dynamically manage multiple internal and external sensors, and generate graphical user interfaces to collect user inputs and present semantically integrated information, in a cloud-based personalized fashion.

Keywords: context-aware networking, cross platform development, mobile cloud.

1 Introduction

Recent years have seen the relentless market success of mobile devices (PDAs, smart-phones, MIDs, PMPs, net-books, etc.), whose ever increasing capabilities make them attractive to a growing number of network applications in business and infotainment domains, that now can be fully experienced in mobility.

At the same time, the widespread and ubiquitous nature of mobile devices makes them attractive as providers of information collected from their rich equipment of sensors (camera, microphone, accelerometers, compass, GPS), and also from external sensors (placed on persons, or in the environment). Thus, we envision large-scale sensor networks that use mobile devices as raw data sources, but also aggregated information producers - merging raw data coming from sensors distributed in the environment. There are several important challenges in

N. Venkatasubramanian et al. (Eds.): Mobilware 2011, LNICST 93, pp. 219–232, 2012.

realizing such types of distributed applications, *e.g.* providing efficient methods for sensor nodes to make their data available to the network, allowing data access from potentially disconnected and highly mobile devices, ensuring that privacy constraints are met, and allowing application developers to build modular, service-oriented applications.

With the growing of the mobile application market, new solutions for software distribution have been recently introduced, with the dominance of online application stores (such as AppStore and Android Market). These virtual marketplaces have solved many problems to developers and common users, allowing for easy dissemination and installation of apps with specific security and update management policies. If on one hand this approach allows for widespread distribution of applications, on the other hand it appears to quite unsuitable for highly dynamic scenarios where application needs may change very frequently within a week or even the same day, according to user credentials, location or purposes [5].

In this context, we propose an architectural framework for agile development and deployment of mobile cloud applications, harvesting heterogeneous sensor data. The novelty of the architecture is the possibility to dynamically manage multiple internal and external sensors, and generate graphical user interfaces to collect user inputs and present semantically integrated information, in a cloud-based personalized fashion.

The proposed architecture is characterized by two main functional modules, namely the *service platform* and the *mobile platform*. The former is characterized by a semantic service engine, that allows for dynamic composition of sensed data, to be presented to mobile users in a personalized fashion. The latter is a lightweight mobile application that is able to manage sensors and interact with the service platform for storing/retrieving data. The mobile platform is designed for running over different mobile operating systems (such as iOS, Symbian/RIMM, Windows Mobile and Android) and tolerating the rapid obsolescence of technologies and, consequently, of devices that are frequently substituted by models with different features and functionalities. Its flexibility support the "install once, run forever" paradigm, thus solving the previously discussed software distribution issue.

The paper is structured as follows. Section 2 presents the state of the art in the field of sensor-based mobile architecture. Section 3 specifies the proposed architecture. Section 4 introduces two example scenarios and describes the first prototype of a demo application we are developing. Finally, section 5 concludes the paper summarizing achieved results and proposing some future developments.

2   State of The Art

Integration of mobile devices and sensor networks for context awareness is a hot topic in the field of distributed systems. Context-aware computing is a mobile computing paradigm in which applications can discover and take advantage of contextual information (such as user location, time of day, nearby people and devices, and user activity). In their recent work [12], Soylu *et al.* integrate and extend fundamental and promising theoretical and technical approaches for the development of adaptive, context-aware software systems. Moreover, they present an interesting view point for context-aware pervasive application development, particularly based on higher abstraction where ontologies and semantic web activities, also web itself, are of crucial importance. The long and short of it is that perception, adaptivity, interoperability and standard compliance are key enablers of pervasive computing.

Perception means (especially) sensing the environment. In [4], Bednarz *et al.* present a multi-sensor XML-based communication protocol, called Human System Integration Protocol (HSIP). Hard-wired or wireless sensors are assumed to be connected to a data server to which, after registration, they to transmit information.

Sensor networks consist of tiny low-powered computing devices with extremely restricted computational, communication and battery capabilities. Each device may be equipped with a physical sensor for reading temperature, sound, pressure or other physical phenomena and can operate both as a sensor and a wireless router. One of the major tasks of sensor networks is the distributed collection and processing of sensor readings over extended periods of time. Scalability, self-configuration, ease of deployment and low cost have made sensor networks a very attractive solution for a wide range of environmental monitoring, distributed surveillance, healthcare and control applications. In many situations, collecting data at a certain fixed location is neither possible nor practical. Having mobile collectors (that collect data and transfer messages between individual sensors [8]) can be the only way to solve the problem - a thesis that we support in this paper.

Another approach, suggested by Kansal *et al.* [9], is to implement a sensor network of mobile phones, to be provided as a shared system, as opposed to a system where a single application owns and uses a dedicated set of mobile devices carried by users or vehicles. Using mobile devices as sensors has a significant advantage over unattended wireless sensor networks in that deploying the sensing hardware and providing it with network and power is already taken care of. Secondly, mobile phones can provide coverage where static sensors are hard to deploy and maintain. Thirdly, each mobile device is associated with a human user, whose assistance can sometimes be used to enhance application functionality. For instance, a human user may help by pointing the camera appropriately at the target object to be sensed.

On the problem of creating device-independent interfaces, in literature we found some interesting works. Among others, in [10] Nichols *et al.* present the *Personal Universal Controller (PUC)*, an approach for improving the interface to complex appliances by introducing an intermediary graphical or speech interface. A PUC engages in two-way communication with everyday appliances, first downloading a specification of each appliance's function, and then automatically creating an interface for controlling that appliance.

3   Proposed Architecture

We propose a mobile device -centric approach for sensor-based distributed applications. The main idea (sketched in figure 1) is that mobile nodes collect data from sensors (their own ones, or those placed in the surrounding environment), and share such data within the network, by means of cloud services [7]. Authorized users can visualize data thanks to mobile web applications (that are independent from the mobile platform) and dynamically compose the user interface according to currently selected data visualization services, to context and to user profiles.

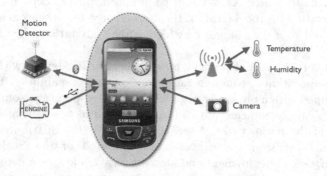

Fig. 1. Mobile device -centric approach

As we know, mobile terminals such as smart-phones and tablets allow to collect a huge amount of data from local and external inputs and sensors connected by multiple interfaces such as Bluetooth, WiFi or USB. Concurrently, user inputs may contribute to enhance the quality and effectiveness of the application, by enriching collected data before they are shared within the network.

Such a mobile device -centric approach has a number of advantages over the centralized approach for sensor data collecting, namely:

- *Energy efficiency* In a mobile scenario, sensors will store data locally and provide them to mobile collectors. Data can be sent directly when the appropriate connection is available, or in a subsequent time, according to user preferences and always trying to preserve sensor battery lifetime.
- *Improved availability of sensor networks* Mobile devices may act as gateways for sensor networks that, for some reasons, are disconnected from the Internet.
- *Ubiquity* Users can query the network and collect data from any location.

Figure 2 illustrates the global architecture, where the following elements are highlighted:

- Mobile Device (MD) - Is the principal entity of the system, interacting with external sensors to collect data, exchanging them with the cloud, and allowing user to enter extra information.

- The Cloud - Provides personalized environments with services for storing information generated by MDs, as well as mobile Web user interfaces (UIs).
- External Modules (EMs) - Represent external software entities that, according with their authorization level, can interact with the Cloud to consume its services, or to provide new ones, for example to integrate multi-source data and provide new information.
- MD Communication Layer - Allows the communication between the Cloud and the MD in terms of login procedures, data exchange, UI specification transmission and notifications pushing to the device.
- EM Communication Layer - Allows the communication between the Cloud and EMs to transmit and receive data.

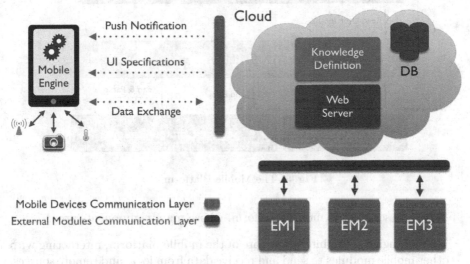

Fig. 2. The proposed architecture

In the following we describe the mobile platform that runs over the MD, and the service platform used by the Cloud and EMs.

3.1   Mobile Platform

On the mobile side, there is the necessity to communicate with different types of external sensors and to generate a rich user interface to collect user input. To these purposes, a cross-platform solution (*e.g.* HTML-based, such as PhoneGap [11]), for the development of the mobile engine, may not be efficient (not providing thread management and synchronization mechanisms). Similarly, a mobile code solution, where software pieces are transferred between systems (*i.e.* transferred across a network or via a USB flash drive) and executed by the recipient on a local system, has several issues, related to runtime generation of the user interfaces on multiple platforms, and also to the management of different sensors.

For these reasons, in our opinion the mobile platform need to be developed using native programming languages - such as Java, C++ or Objective-C - for each platform, and provided with the ability to automatically generate, starting from a standardized UI Specification Language, all user interfaces for interacting with available sensors in the environment, and accessing remote services. This approach allows for reduced complexity of the mobile platform dissemination and update process, too (the mobile platform needs to be downloaded once, for example from an app store). This approach is also highly scalable, allowing for real-time, context-driven adaptation of the application, *e.g.* taking into account user location, environment settings, etc.

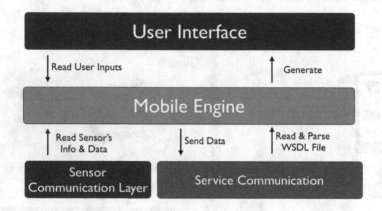

Fig. 3. The Mobile Platform

Figure 3 describes the mobile platform, whose main components are:

- Mobile Engine - The intelligent core of the mobile platform, interacting with other mobile modules to send and receive data from local and remote sources, and dynamically generating the GUI that allows the user to enrich sensor data with other useful knowledge.
- Sensor Communication Layer - Middleware enabling the communication with internal and external sensors/inputs through different channels, according to the device profile.
- Service Communication Layer - Middleware allowing the interaction with the Cloud to discover services, test their QoS, send/retrieve data, etc.

Aggregated sensor data are presented to the user on his mobile device by the service platform in a personalized fashion, by means of a Web-based application.

3.2   Service Platform

Mobile devices exchange data with the Cloud, that is enabled by a service platform (illustrated in figure 4) provided with the following components:

- Semantic Service Engine - The core of the service platform, managing all available modules in order to provide different types of services to final users.

- Database Communication Layer - A middleware for storing and retrieving data and information from system databases.
- Service Ontology - A Web 3.0 knowledge base encompassing all the characteristics of each service, user, sensor and inputs.
- Client Communication Layer - A middleware that enables mobile devices to connect transmit and receive data.
- Security Layer - A middleware that provides protocols for securing the communication between service platform and mobile clients.
- Web Interface Builder - A component that builds dynamic Web pages for showing real-time or cached data in personalized fashion, according to user needs, profile and credentials.

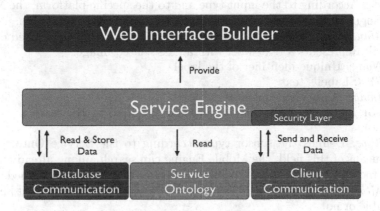

Fig. 4. The Service Platform

Services exposed by the Cloud have specific input parameters (representing sensor data). The Mobile Engine discovers such information at runtime. A service can be used only if the Mobile Engine is able to provide all needed sensor data. The service description should be something like:

- **Service.** Defines a specific functionality with different UI sections and a list of required sensors with the following parameters.
  - *Name:* Unique identifier of the service.
  - *Storing Type:* Defines the storing procedure of input and sensor data. The service may enable immediate or delayed data transmission (the latter would require that the Mobile Engine temporarily stores data in a local file) - possible parameters being REMOTE and LOCAL. This dual opportunity allows the user, once the service description has been retrieved, to execute the service offline, by caching data and uploading the locally stored file later, when connectivity is available.
  - *Storing Location:* In case of a remote storage procedure, this tag contains the service endpoint; otherwise, in case a local storage on the mobile device, it contains the filename.

- **UI-Section:** Defines a single section of service's UI allowing the designer to divide data entry in different slices, that may be either mandatory or not, and may contain labels and figures to show useful information, or input fields.
  - *Name:* Unique identifier of the section.
  - *Description:* Short text containing general information about presented data, or the instructions about required data.
  - *Mandatory:* Boolean field to specify whether the section can be skipped or not.
- **Input:** Represents a generic input for the data entry.
  - *Name:* Unique identifier of the field.
  - *Type:* Defines the type of requested data, *e.g.* string, numeric, list, boolean etc. According to the input type and to the specific platform, the Mobile Engine will properly generate the UI to simplify data collection.
  - *Mandatory:* Boolean field to specify if the section must be filled or not.
- **Label:** Represents a text label with an associated image.
  - *Name:* Unique identifier of the label.
  - *Text:* Label's text.
  - *Image:* Associated image.
- **Sensor List :** Contains the list of sensors required by the service.
- **Sensor**
  - *Type:* Defines the sensor type according to the Service Ontology. By means of this field, the Mobile Engine can search among already discovered and bound sensors to verify if service needs can be satisfied.
  - *Mandatory:* Boolean field that specifies whether the sensor must be available or not.
  - *Working Frequency:* Specifies the sampling rate of the sensor's data.
  - *Reading Limit Type:* Defines if the sampling of sensor data will stop after a specific time, or upon reaching a specific number of collected samples (possible parameters are TIME and SAMPLES).
  - *Reading Limit Value:* Represents the amount of seconds or the number of samples after which the sampling of sensor data will stop.

The Mobile Engine reads and shows to the user the list of available services. Once a service has been selected, the operator can choose among available and bound sensors which he/she wants to use for the service. If more than one sensor of the same type are available, the user can select which of them must be used. Similarly, if one or more mandatory sensors are no more available, the engine shows an error message and prevents next interaction. After the sensor selection phase, the Web Interface Builder dynamically generates the required UI according to service description allowing the user to add manual inputs associated with the data that could be retrieved from the sensors.

Dynamic UI generation for data visualization is provided by the Web Interface Builder of the service platform, and published to the mobile client as a personalized Web interface. Using platform-specific CSS sheets, such a Web interface can be customized. Finally, the Security Layer allows to visualize information only to users that are provided with the right credentials.

3.3   QoS and QoI Management

In the proposed mobile device -centric architecture, quality of service (QoS) management is very important. Each service may specify a minimum guaranteed quality of service, defined in terms of transmission rate, packets error, computational power, connection type, etc. During the connection establishment phase, the server could ask to the client to check if it is able to send data with the requested QoS. This kind of test could be also repeated periodically during the data delivery phase, to identify possible lowering of performance and QoS.

Another important aspect we took into account is the quality of information (QoI), that refers to the ability to figure out if available information coming from sensors is fit-for-use for a particular service. Let us consider a scenario in which several PDAs want to use services that require sensors provided by a Wireless Sensor Network (WSN). Each service has to execute tasks that need resources from the network. QoI management provides mechanisms for investigating new task admission and resource utilization, for controlling the individual QoI provided to new and existing tasks. This can be done using real-time feedback-based monitoring systems. The QoI can be characterized by a set of quality attributes, such as accuracy, latency, and spatio-temporal relevancy. To this purpose, as suggested in [13], we can consider three key design elements: (a) the QoI satisfaction index of a task, which quantifies the degree to which the required QoI is satisfied by the WSN; (b) the QoI network capacity, which expresses the ability of the WSN to host a new task with specific QoI requirements without sacrificing the attained QoI levels of other existing tasks, and (c) an adaptive, negotiation-based admission control mechanism that reconfigures and optimizes the usage of network resources in order to optimally accommodate the QoI requirements of all tasks.

4   Analyzed Scenarios and Prototype

In this section we analyze two appealing scenarios that perfectly match with our dynamic architecture. The first scenario is related to an industrial environment where one or more operators make an inspection of different production line, whereas the second one is associated to an e-Health system that collects information about patients through sensor interaction and user feedbacks. The important aspect is that both scenarios can be realized with the same mobile engine implementation, without specific development or efforts on the mobile side, thus reducing costs, focusing on service characteristics and increasing scalability. We have started the development of applications for both scenarios. In the last subsection we describe those being implemented for the industrial one.

4.1   Industrial Scenario

Mobile applications have become an important means for improving industrial service processes [2] [3]. Since their increasing complexity should not reduce usability, the personalized UI approach we propose appears to be highly suitable.

Let us consider a small/medium company whose core business is to bottle any type of drink, from water to wine. A large amount of this business is based on the perfect functioning of the production line, that is costly in terms of safety and security. Periodic controls and ordinary maintenance are very important to prevent accidents and to assure the correct working of the system.

Each industrial machine endows one or more sensors that collect status information, allowing to detect potential problems all along the production line. Traditional plants have pipelined machines, each one being cabled with a computer that stores data sent by the machine, and operates on the machine's actuators. Usually the software running on master machines is not standard-based, for which it is difficult to collect and integrate data from several machines, unless they are made by the same vendor.

Our approach would require a unique server running the Service Platform, and a set of mobile devices running the Mobile Engine. Company operators would perform machine maintenance according to the following procedure:

- collect sensor data using a smartphone;
- check bottlers' status by evaluating received data;
- eventually discover any change in the composition and structure of the machines;
- make interviews with workers of the warehouse, to investigate any questioning or difficulty concerning machines, and to enrich gathered data;
- immediately update all collected information.

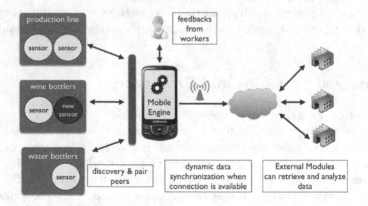

Fig. 5. Industrial scenario

Suppose that the company has started a new, more efficient bottling line. The chief operator notifies this change to the operations centre, by adding the sensors of the new line to the list of monitored ones, using his smartphone. The chief operator may also collect feedbacks from workers in order to enrich sensed information provided to the operations centre. The mobile device can also work in offline mode, by locally storing important information and uploading them as soon as a connection is available.

4.2   e-Health Scenario

The proposed architecture can be used in a number of healthcare scenarios. In particular, some diseases require to monitor the status of patients that follow specific treatments, assigned by their doctors. Patient monitoring may be very costly, when manually performed by a specialist. Our architecture can help simplifying this process, by automating patient monitoring. Figure 6 shows a scenario we plan to address, related to individuals with walking disabilities, provided with Ankle-foot orthoses (AFOs) to aid in their walking (we prepared and published online an AFO demonstrative video [1]).

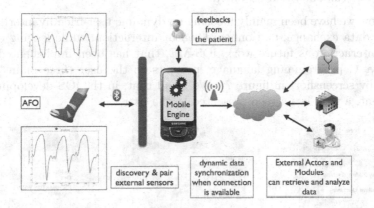

Fig. 6. e-Health scenario

Despite the widespread use of AFOs, their performance is not well evaluated, because the quantitative assessment is currently limited to short-term in-clinic observation. To better understand how AFOs perform in aiding individuals with walking disabilities and further enhance the AFO efficacy, a continuous, non-invasive measurement method is necessary. After a careful investigation by Gait analysis experts, ankle angle is selected as a primary Gait parameter for assessing the efficacy of AFO.

Our RimLab is working on a sensor-provided AFO, able to collect data about the ankle angle. Thus, a patient could use her/his PDA to send AFO data and insert additional qualitative information (*e.g.* how much the AFO is comfortable). The Doctor may access such collected data to monitor the patient and to evaluate the effectiveness of the proposed treatment.

The AFO case study can be generalized, considering any set of sensors, targeting different diseases. The PDA is used to access services that allow to send sensed data, to manually insert additional information, and to get treatment updates, doctor's feedbacks, etc. Similarly, the doctor uses services to read information coming from sensors or user inputs, to define new inputs that the patient has to insert, and to modify the treatment.

4.3   Prototype

In order to evaluate our architecture and our approach we have designed and developed a first prototype of the system and a demo application (a video is available at [6]). Main developed components are:

- Semantic Service Engine based on PhP technology to provide the list of available services and their description.
- Database and associated Communication Layer to parse, store and retrieve data.
- Mobile Engine prototype on the iOS platform (namely, iOS-ME) in order to test its scalability and usability.

Up to now we have been mainly focusing on dynamic user-friendly interface generation, data exchange, and onboard sensor interaction, while leaving external sensor interaction as future work. iOS-ME, that has been implemented in the Objective-C programming language, presents to the user three main "views" (shown by screenshots in figure 7). We recall that, in the iOS development environment, a view is a screen presented to the user.

(a) Service list.

(b) Sensor discovery and pairing

(c) Filling Machine needed sensors

(d) Filling Machine input fields

(e) Data exchange interface

(f) Remote data visualization

Fig. 7. iOS Mobile Engine Prototype

The "Setting" tab emulates external sensor management and is used by the Sensor Communication Layer to show discovered external devices and already paired sensors. The "Services" section allows to discover Cloud services, with associated description, and to visualize them in a table structure. When clicking on an available service, iOS-ME shows a summary of required sensors, and the list of those that are already available or missing. The user is allowed to select sensors that she/he wants to use for the specific service. After that, the user can move to the next "view" - the one devoted to data entry. As described before, each UI-section contains both mandatory and not mandatory fields, differently highlighted (red and black). Until all mandatory fields are correctly filled, the engine prevents the user from moving to next view. After that, when all user data are collected and sensors are correctly configured, iOS-ME starts the data exchange with the server and shows a report about each operation in order to show possible communication errors to the user. This task continues until the user clicks the stop button, that ends the uploading procedure. The last application tab is related to data visualization, that (as described in section 3) is based on a mobile Web technologies, with an appropriate style sheet for each device type.

5   Conclusion

In this paper we have illustrated a novel architecture for agile development and deployment of mobile, sensor-based applications. The distinctive feature of such an architecture is the mobile device -centric approach, for which mobile devices are providers of information collected from their rich equipment of sensors (camera, microphone, GPS, etc.), and also from external sensors (placed on persons, or in the environment). We have illustrated two significant example scenarios, and a prototype we have developed and tested.

As future work, we are going to complete the development of the Service Platform, improving the semantic service engine. Moreover, we are going to develop versions of the Mobile Engine for other platforms than iOS - *e.g.* Android and BlackBerry.

References

1. AFO demontrative video, http://rimlab.ce.unipr.it/Research.html
2. Aleksy, M., Stieger, B., Vollmar, G.: Case Study on Utilizing Mobile Applications in Industrial Field Service. In: IEEE Conf. on Commerce and Enterprise Computing, Vienna, Austria (2009)
3. Aleksy, M., Stieger, B.: Supporting Service Processes with Semantic Mobile Applications. In: 8th ACM-SIGMM International Conference on Advances in Mobile Computing & Multimedia (MoMM 2010), Paris, France (November 2010)
4. Bednarz, T.P., Caris, C., Thompson, J., Wesner, C., Dunn, M.: Human-Computer Interaction Experiments. In: 24th IEEE International Conference on Advanced Information Networking and Applications (2010)

5. Das, T., Mohan, P., Padmanabhan, V.N., Ramjee, R., Sharma, A.: PRISM: Platform for Remote Sensing using Smartphones. In: MobiSys 2010, San Francisco, California, USA (June 2010)
6. Video of the demo application, http://dsg.ce.unipr.it/?q=node/51
7. Dikaiakos, M.D., Katsaros, D., Mehra, P., Pallis, G., Vakali, A.: Cloud Computing: Distributed Internet Computing for IT and Scientific Research. IEEE Internet Computing 13(5) (September-October 2009)
8. Dyo, V.: Middleware Design for Integration of Sensor Network and Mobile Devices. In: 6th ACM International Middleware Conference, Grenoble, France, pp. 49–54 (November 2005)
9. Kansal, A., Goraczko, M., Zhao, F.: Building a Sensor Network of Mobile Phones. In: 6th IEEE International Symposium on Information Processing in Sensor Networks, Cambridge, Massachusets (2007)
10. Nichols, J., Myers, B.A., Higgins, M., Hughes, J., Harris, T.K., Rosenfeld, R., Pignol, M.: Generating Remote Control Interfaces for Complex Appliances. In: UIST 2002, Paris, France (October 2002)
11. PhoneGap homepage, http://www.phonegap.com
12. Soylu, A., De Causmaecker, P., Desmet, P.: Context and Adaptivity in Pervasive Computing Environments: Links with Software Engineering and Ontological Engineering. Journal of Software 4(9), 992–1013 (2009)
13. Liu, C.H., Bisdikian, C., Branch, J.W., Leung, K.K.: QoI-Aware Wireless Sensor Network Management for Dynamic Multi-Task Operations. In: 7th IEEE Conference on Sensor Mesh and Ad Hoc Communications and Networks, SECON (2010)

Verification and Validation
of Smartphone Sensor Networks

Hamilton Turner and Jules White

Dept. of Electrical and Computer Engineering
Virginia Tech
Blacksburg, VA, 24060, USA
{hturner0,julesw}@vt.edu

Abstract. This paper introduces a subset of mobile wireless sensor networks, called smartphone sensor networks, where large numbers of smartphone devices cooperate to perform sensing tasks. While these emerging networks show high potential, little work has been done on design-time verification and validation to ensure that a designed system will meet the specified goals. This paper introduces Empower, a simulation environment for smartphone sensor networks that simulates smartphone-specific properties of a sensor network, such as data collection policies, and outputs high-level system metrics, such as coverage of the environment being monitored. Experimentation is used to demonstrate that Empower's ability to derive system design parameters, such as the minimum number of smartphones required for proper operation, or the most appropriate data collection policy for the production environment.

Keywords: smartphones, mobile wireless sensor network, simulation.

1 Introduction

From 2009 to 2010, smartphones sales increased by 96% worldwide [1]. The resultant rise in the number of available smartphones has generated interest in the area of smartphone sensor networks, where consumer-owned smartphone devices are utilized as sensing platforms, and sensing results are aggregated into a coherent final product, such as a map of noise pollution in an urban environment. The primary motivations for using smartphones as sensor network nodes include: available sensing hardware such as GPS chipsets and modern cameras, significant local storage and processing power, access to a network infrastructure, end-user maintenance and upkeep, frequent battery recharging, and ubiquitous deployment platforms for dispersing applications to end-users [2]. Moreover, the natural distribution and mobility of end-users provides an ideal environment for data collection.

Numerous smartphone sensor networks have been developed, such as applications to track and analyze CO_2 emissions [3], detect traffic accidents and provide situational awareness services to first responders [4, 5], measure traffic [6], and monitor cardiac patients [7]. Additionally, citizens living in the Gulf Coast region have been using smartphone sensors, such as cameras and GPS, to enter

N. Venkatasubramanian et al. (Eds.): Mobilware 2011, LNICST 93, pp. 233–247, 2012.
© Institute for Computer Sciences, Social Informatics and Telecommunications Engineering 2012

data on the ecological impact of the Gulf Oil spill, thus providing scientists with a wealth of field data on this disaster that can then be used to generate impact analysis and recommendations [8]. A key challenge, however, is that verification and validation of smartphone-powered sensor networks is hard. As shown in Figure 1, there are a large number of components contained in a smartphone sensor network, including the smartphones and their associated properties (e.g., movement, location accuracy at a given time and location, available battery life), the environment being monitored, the algorithms to aggregate the incoming sensor data, and other components.

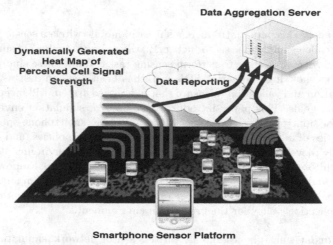

Fig. 1. Architecture of a Smartphone-based Cellular Coverage Mapping Application

Open Problem ⇒ Emergent and context-dependent aspects of smartphones make verification and validation challenging.

Because smartphone sensor networks rely on end-user smartphones, then introduce challenges that are not present in a more traditional wireless sensor network model, including complex system properties such as system adoption rate and cellular network infrastructure, context-dependent aspects such as unanticipated smartphone reconfiguration, and emergent system properties. Due to these issues, it is tough for smartphone sensor network developers to have confidence that the chosen system architecture, protocols, and policies will work as expected and desired in the environment being monitored. Additionally, the costly nature of changing software system designs late in the development cycle motivates making good system design decisions as early as possible.

Verification and validation of systems early in the development is critical to reduce the overall system cost, and critical to ensure successful creation of a smartphone sensor network that will properly monitor the environment of interest. Typical verification and validation of a sensor network (SN) is done either through formal methods, using tools such as Real-Time Maude [9], or model checking, using tools such as SPIN [10]. Neither of these approaches are feasible for verifying and validating smartphone sensor networks because they fail to account for the context-dependent aspects of smartphones, such as movement of the smartphone by its end-user. Moreover, wireless sensor networks have primarily been investigated in the context of small, very low-power sensors communicating through an ad hoc network, usually not interacting with an end-user, and with very limited computing resources.

Solution Approach ⇒ Simulation of smartphone data collection systems to enable design-time verification and validation. To address the need to verify and validate smartphone sensor networks, we present a platform for the *E*valuation of *M*obile *Ph*One *W*ireless *E*nvironmental data *R*eporting, or 'Empower'. Empower allows design time verification and validation of smartphone sensor networks, ensuring the system meets specifications and fulfills the posed systems goals, taking into account complex system parameters and policies, such as rate of change in the number of participating smartphones, run-time smartphone context changes, and data collection/reporting policies. In Section 5 we present empirical data showing Empower can also be used to identify emergent properties of smartphone sensor networks.

This paper provides the following contributions to the study of smartphone sensor networks:

- we introduce and describe Empower, which is a simulation environment for smartphone sensor networks,
- we describe Empower's formal simulation model,
- and we present emperical data from experiments from using Empower to verify and validate a smartphone-based sensor network for dynamically mapping cellular coverage

The remainder of this paper is organized as follows: Section 2 describes a continuous map of cellular network coverage, which we use as a motivating example throughout the paper; Section 3 discusses the challenges that are faced when attempting to verify the effectiveness of a designed smartphone data collection system; Section 4 covers the Empower framework; Section 5 presents empirical results from analyzing multiple designed smartphone data collection systems and demonstrates Empower identifying system failures and bottlenecks; and Section 7 presents concluding remarks and lessons learned.

2   Motivating Example: Continuous, Accurate Measurement of Cellular Network Coverage

In order to motivate the challenges associated with verifying and validating smartphone sensor networks, we present a motivating smartphone application for dynamically mapping cellular network coverage using end-user smartphones. In order to create a smartphone sensor network that accurately monitors cellular network coverage and conforms rapidly to any changes in coverage, there are a number of needed system components, many of which were shown in Figure 1.

First, a smartphone application must be programmed and deployed to numerous smartphones, which are preferably well geographically distributed. As smartphones are moved geographically, they use the built-in cellular chipsets to sample the cellular coverage in their region. Figure 2 shows Empower visualizing the simulated real cellular network coverage map. When a smartphone's internet connection is enabled, these coverage readings, along with meta information describing the location and time of each reading, the network chipset on the smartphone, and the particular operating system being run, can be transmitted to a centralized cloud-based data aggregation server. As readings are entered, data aggregation algorithms are used to combine the data into a smaller format that can then be represented as a coverage map. Figure 3 shows a cellular coverage map Empower has generated by aggregrating the incoming network coverage readings. System policies can be used to control various aspects of the process, such as the rate of data collection, the speed at which data becomes outdated, or the method used to aggregate the incoming data.

3   Challenges of Verifying and Validating Smartphone Wireless Sensor Networks

Smartphone wireless sensor networks (WSN) have a large number of potential applications, such as real-time traffic monitoring, accurate weather monitoring, or rapid network analysis after a disaster. Unfortunately, it is difficult to ensure that a set of smartphone data collection policies will meet the desired objectives, as the success of these systems is heavily dependent on emergent properties of end-user smartphones. For example, the number, distribution, and movement of smartphones influences coverage, the properties of the network being used to transmit data impact timeliness of data reporting, and the change in the environment heavily impacts the rate at which data ages. When developing system policies to deal with these and other issues, developers face a number of challenges.

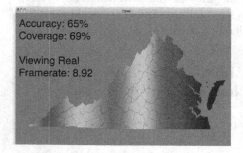
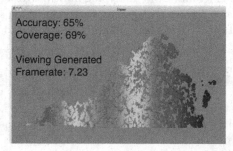

Fig. 2. Empower Visualization of Simulated Real Cellular Network Coverage

Fig. 3. Empower Visualization of Generated Cellular Network Coverage Map

3.1   Challenge 1: Unpredictable Smartphone Availability Makes It Hard to Estimate the Minimum Number of Nodes Required to Ensure System Goals Are Reached

The availability of nodes e.g. smartphones in a smartphone sensor network is highly unpredictable, as smartphones may appear and disappear rapidly from the network in a complex fashion dictated by their end-users, and the overall trend in system adoption can follow different patterns. While the number of smartphones participating in a smartphone WSN clearly has an impact on the probability of system success, it is tough to know how significant the impact is. Additionally, it is hard to know the number of smartphones required, on average, for the system to meet a specific goal, such as acquiring 80% coverage of the environment.

For example, a key verification and validation challenge of building a smartphone WSN to dynamically map a cellular network is determining how many smartphones are needed on average to generate a coverage map that is 80% accurate. Given the number of complex factors included in determining the exact number of smartphones available to participate in generating a map of the cellular network, such as population measurements and adoption studies, it is critical that system designers have a concrete number for the minimum density of participating smartphones required in order to assess the risk of system failure.

3.2   Challenge 2: The Complex and Emergent Properties of Smartphone Based Opportunistic Sensing Systems Make Determining the Impact of Various Policy Decisions Difficult

In order to verify and validate a smartphone powered WSN, it is important to understand the impact of system policies, such as data collection controls, on system metrics, such as the accuracy of incoming data or the utilization of system resources. The complex relationship between system policies, system parameters, and emergent properties makes it difficult to know what system policies should be used in which situations, or even which policies can be used without violating system constraints.

For example, if a system to map cellular network coverage was powered by postal service workers carrying smartphones, a data collection and reporting policy that took too many superfluous readings and wasted battery power could be expensive or cause premature battery exhaustion during the workday. Further, if the data collection policy only collects a limited set of measurements each day, a policy that chooses optimal locations for data readings may have a direct impact on the system success or failure. However, verifying and validating that the location selection method is efficient and selects the appropriate data samples across thousands of phones is hard. Section 4.3 describes how Empower aids validating these design decisions by allowing system designers to plug and simulate custom data collection and reporting policies across thousands of smartphones.

4 Empower: A Simulation Environment for Verifying and Validating Smartphone Sensor Networks

To address the need to verify and validate smartphone sensor networks, we present Empower, a simulation environment for the Evaluation of Mobile PhOne Wireless Environmental data Reporting. As shown in Figure 1, smartphone powered opportunistic sensing systems contain multiple configurable components. Empower can be used to model various aspects of these systems, including: the smartphones in an environment, the network being used to transmit information between the data collection server and the clients, various system-level policies such as data collection and reporting policies, the algorithms used for data evaluation, system-level metrics, and system goals.

Figure 4 shows an overview of the Empower application, including the visualization that Empower uses to represent a given environment, the formal model that is used to back the executing simulation, the output (which si both shown on-screen and logged), as well as small visualizations for each smartphone object. In section 4.2 we discuss how Empower can be used by developers to derive critical system design parameters, focusing on the minimum number of smartphones required to achieve system goals as a design parameter of interest. In section 4.3, we discuss Empower's approach to system-level policies, such as data collection frequency and data reporting decisions, and show how Empower can be used to identify the most appropriate policies for various operational environments.

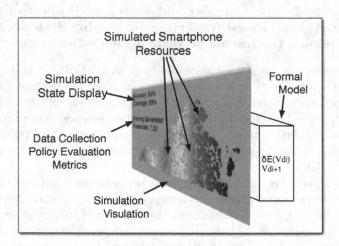

Fig. 4. Overview of Empower Software

4.1 Empower Formal Simulation Model

Empower uses a simulation engine based on a formal model for smartphone-based opportunistic sensing. The model is based on the 8-tuple:

$$M = < E, D, \boldsymbol{V e_0}, V d_0, \delta E(\boldsymbol{V e_i}), \delta D(V d_i), O(V e_i, V d_{ij}), M(V e_i, \omega_i) > \quad (1)$$

$$|E| = |Ve_i| \qquad (2)$$

$$\forall \boldsymbol{V}\boldsymbol{d}_{ij} \in Vd_i, |\boldsymbol{V}\boldsymbol{d}_{ij}| = |D| \qquad (3)$$

$$\delta E(\boldsymbol{V}\boldsymbol{e}_i) = \boldsymbol{V}\boldsymbol{e}_{i+1} \qquad (4)$$

$$\delta E(\boldsymbol{V}\boldsymbol{d}_i) = \boldsymbol{V}\boldsymbol{d}_{i+1} \qquad (5)$$

$$O(Ve_i, Vd_{ij}) = \boldsymbol{\omega}_{ij} \qquad (6)$$

$$M(Ve_i, \omega_i) = \boldsymbol{Met}_i \qquad (7)$$

where:

- E is the set of parameters or variables that describe the environment that the smartphones are operating in.
- D is the set of parameters that describe each smartphone in the simulation.
- Vd_i is a set of vectors containing the parameter values describing the state of each smartphone at time i.
- $\boldsymbol{V}\boldsymbol{d}_{ij} \in Vd_i$ is a vector describing the state of the j_{th} smartphone at time i.
- $\delta E(Vd_i)$ is a function that maps the state of every smartphone at time i, Vd_i, to their new states at time $i+1$, Vd_{i+1}.
- $\delta D(\boldsymbol{V}\boldsymbol{e}_i)$ is a function that maps the state of the environment at time i, $\boldsymbol{V}\boldsymbol{e}_i$, to its new state at time $i+1$, $\boldsymbol{V}\boldsymbol{e}_{i+1}$.
- ω is a set of metric outputs, such as the overall coverage and accuracy of the perceived network, at time i.
- $O(Ve_i, Vd_{ij})$ is the smartphone sensor sampling function which determines the sensor values, ω_{ij}, read by the j_{th} smartphone at time i. The sensor values that are produced are a function of the state of the smartphone, Vd_{ij}, and the state of the environment, Ve_i.
- ω_i is the set of all smartphone sensor value vectors at time i.
- $M(Ve_i, \omega_i)$ is a function that, based on the current state of the environment and set of sensor outputs from all smartphones, calculates the values, $\boldsymbol{Met}_i$, for the verification and validation metrics of interest. For example, the overall accuracy of the perceived cellular signal strength map versus the actual cellular signal strength map could be an output metric.

The core of the formal simulation model are the functions $\delta E(Vd_i)$ and $\delta D(\boldsymbol{V}\boldsymbol{e}_i)$. These functions evolve the states of the smartphones and the environment over the course of the simulation. Empower includes implementations of the functions that are optimized for modeling environments that change based on geographic coordinates and the movement of smartphones through those areas. Both functions can be customized or replaced for simulations that do not focus on sensor data collection that is tied to the geolocation of a smartphone. Section 4.2 discusses the parameters and operation of these functions.

In order to verify and validate a set of data collection and reporting policies in a specific smartphone scenario, developers must be able to incorporate their application-specific policies into the Empower formal model. The function $O(Ve_i, Vd_{ij})$ is designed to be configured by the user to accurately model the data collection and reporting policies of the application. At each time step,

$O(Ve_i, Vd_{ij})$ determines what data is sampled, based on the sampling policy of the application. Moreover, $O(Ve_i, Vd_{ij})$ also determines which of these samples are actually reported to the aggregation system by the smartphone by limiting the values that are output into ω_{ij}. For example, although the data collection policy may determine that a particular sensor is sampled at a given timestamp, $O(Ve_i, Vd_{ij})$ may not output that sensor value until a later time step to simulate buffering of data on the phone. The base implementation of $O(Ve_i, Vd_{ij})$ is described in Section 4.3.

The final critical aspect of the formal model is the set of metrics that are calculated by Empower and used for verification and validation. The function $M(Ve_i, \omega_i)$ can be adjusted to calculate any metrics that are a function of the environment state, smartphone state, or sensor values.

4.2   Solution 1: Using Simulation of Smartphones to Derive System Design Parameters

Section 3.1 introduces the system design parameter of minimum required number of nodes. In order to assist system designers in identifying the minimum number of smartphones required to ensure that system goals are met, Empower allows designers to vary the minimum number phones in a smartphone sensor network, and then simulate the system to determine the probability of system goals being reached. By varying simulation parameters, developers can identify a baseline for the minimum number of smartphones required to achieve the system goals that is specific to the future production environment of their smartphone sensor network, such as a highly-dynamic environment with a low density of highly mobile smartphones that frequently input data readings.

Empower allows design time control of the following smartphone properties:

- **Initial number of smartphones** in the system. System designers specify this as a constant number. For some situations, such as a mandatory adoption policy, this number can be significantly high. For other systems, the rate of adoption (discussed below) is more important.

- **Rate of Adoption** determines how many smartphones are participating in the opportunistic system at various times. This is controlled by a designer-specified function that accepts time, which is tracked by the simulation environment and used to relate the simulation results to a real-world timescale, and returns the approximate number of smartphones that should currently be inside of the data collection system. By implementing the rate of adoption function, a designer can arbitrarily control the number of smartphones in the system at any given time.

- **Smartphone Properties and Settings**, such as smartphone location or network connectivity enabled versus disabled, can be specified by the system designer using high-level functions. Empower controls configuring individual smartphone objects, ensuring that overall distributions match the desired settings. For example, a developer can specify that 60% of the smartphones in a network should initially have their GPS chip enabled. Designers can control each smartphone property by specifying a function that accepts time as a parameter and returns the appropriate distribution of that property at the given time.

- **Frequency and Magnitude of Smartphone Movement** can be controlled via developer-specified functions. Developers can input high-level values specifying how frequently smartphones move during the simulation execution, and how significant each move is in terms of meters travelled per movement. This is a fairly simple model of movement, and the authors are actively attempting to build a more flexible movement function that would allow integration of research on human movement patterns, with a goal of allowing system developers to simply select a pre-defined movement pattern which has been vetted by prior research.

By testing numerous property configurations, system designers can understand which properties are most critical to data collection and reporting policy success and take steps to ensure that those properties are met. For example, Empower can allow a system designer to pinpoint the minimal number and diversity of smartphones required for the system to achieve the metrics of interest by modifying these configuration parameters and executing the simulation. This information is quite valuable for the successful deployment of such a system.

4.3   Solution 2: Exposing Policy Decisions As a Configurable Simulation Property

As Section 3.2 outlines, the complex parameters and emergent properties of a smartphone-powered opportunistic sensing system make it difficult to understand the effects of system-level policy decisions. To address this issue, Empower allows various system-level policies to be configured, both at the beginning of the simulation and during the simulation execution. This enables system designers to verify that their chosen policies will improve metrics of interest under the conditions they believe most likely to occur in the operational environment. By testing these different policies with various parameter combinations, system designers are able to determine the most optimal policy for different operational environments. Moreover, it is possible to identify various emergent properties and understand the impact of those properties on system metrics.

Empower currently allows two system-level policies to be specified:

- **A Data Collection Policy** for the smartphones in the system can be specified. This policy determines which smartphones attempt to collect data, based on the properties of each smartphone. In the experiments outlined in Section 5, we compare a data collection policy that favors highly-mobile smartphones for data collection over less mobile phones to a mobility-independent data collection policy. System designers can specify the data collection policy by creating a function which accepts as input the properties of a smartphone (current location, available sensors, mobility frequency and magnitude) and returns a boolean value indicating if that smartphone should attempt to collect data.

- **A Data Reporting Policy** determines how smartphones report data back to the central server. Interesting issues that this policy aims to address are the limited network connectivity on smartphone platforms (both in terms of network availability and network throughput), the rate at which data becomes useless after it has been collected, and the amount of available persistent storage on individual smartphones. System designers can specify a function that receives the amount of available storage, the current network connectivity, and all other smartphone properties. Based on these properties, the function can return that data should be discarded, cached, or sent to the data collection server.

5 Using Empower to Determine System-Level Policies

In this section we present results from experiments performed using Empower that evaluate the impact of data collection policy decisions in the smartphone-based cellular network mapping example from Section 2, such as data collection policy, on overall system properties such as accuracy and wastefulness. Additionally, we perform experiments to derive system design parameters, such as the minimum number of smartphones required to achieve system goals. These results show that Empower can be used to verify the design of a smartphone sensor network by ensuring that system goals are met. Moreover, these results show that Empower can be used to determine critical system design parameters.

5.1 Experimental Platform

These experiments were performed on a 2.66 GHz Intel Core i7 machine with 4 GB of 1067 Mhz DD3 ram, running the Mac OS X 10.6.6 operating system. Empower is written with Java, and the Eclipse IDE was used to both aid development and to run the simulations.

5.2 Experiment 1: Measuring the Combined Impact of Smartphone Quantities and Data Collection Policy Decisions on System Accuracy

Sections 3.1 and 3.2 discuss the challenges that arise due to unpredictable smartphone counts and system policy decisions. In particular, it is tough for a system developer to determine the minimum number of smartphones required to ensure system goals are met. Additionally, it is tough to determine the effect of system policies due to the complex nature of the system properties and the potential for emergent properties. In order to measure the effect of system policy decisions, while also considering system properties, we simulate multiple system policies in conjunction with multiple combinations of system properties of environment topology and smartphone quantities. The simulated policy for each iteration is one of two possible data collection policies, where the first policy is a constant data collection policy in which smartphones are taking readings as rapidly as possible, and the second is a context-aware policy where more mobile smartphones collect data more frequently.

Hypothesis: A Constant Data Collection Policy Will Result in Minimum 20% Higher Accuracy For all System Property Permutations. We expect that the constant data collection policy, given the much higher number of inputs, would yield significantly higher accuracy. Additionally, we believe our results will allow a clear determination of the minimum number of smartphones required to a system accuracy of 80%.

Experiment 1 Results. Figure 5 shows, for a static environment and various smartphone counts, the accuracy over time for each of the two chosen data collection policies. Figure 6 shows, for a dynamic environment and various smartphone counts, the accuracy over time achieved by the two data collection policies.

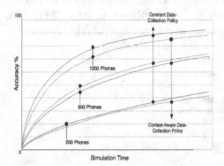
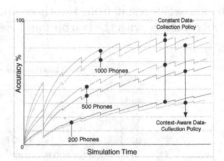

Fig. 5. Measuring the effect of smartphone count on the accuracy in static environments

Fig. 6. Measuring the effect of smartphone count on the accuracy in a dynamic environment

Figure 6 shows multiple dips in accuracy, which we identified as being the times at which we changed the real environment, and therefore the current perceived environment is incorrect. The magnitude of these dips noticeably decreases over time, which is discussed in Section 5.4. As expected, the constant data collection policy does result in a small, but notable, increase in accuracy for both types of environments. However, the acceptable performance of the context-aware data collection policy was unexpected. The context-aware system policy did not result in a significant loss in accuracy, indicating that our hypothesis was incorrect. However, it is easily discernible, for each type of represented environment, the minimum number of smartphones required in order to ensure that 80% accuracy is achieved. For both of the environments tested, independently of the type of data collection policy, 80% accuracy cannot be achieved within 1460 simulation hours without a minimum of 900-1000 smartphones.

5.3 Experiment 2: Determining the Wastefulness of Various Data Collection Policies

Given that Experiment 1 has shown that a context-aware data collection policy is acceptable under some circumstances, the next logical experiment was to attempt to determine, for a given circumstance, if a context-aware policy was acceptable. Experiment 1 has already shown data on the slight increase in accuracy that a constant data collection policy results in, and therefore we choose to measure the wastefulness of each of the policies. In order to do this, we counted the number of data readings that resulted in absolutely no change in the accuracy of the system, and accumulated those numbers over time.

Hypothesis: Constant Data Collection Is Accurate But Wasteful. Our hypothesis for this experiment is that a constant data collection policy e.g. having each smartphone constantly collect data would be accurate but also notably wasteful of system resources.

Experiment 2 Results. Figure 7 therefore represents the difference between the constant data collection policy and the context-aware data collection policy. The six series result from the three options for smartphone counts (200, 500, 1000) combined with the two options for environment topology (static, dynamic).

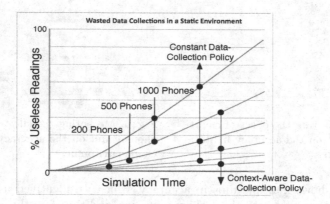

Fig. 7. The number of wasted readings for constant versus mobility-based data collection

As expected, the constant data collection policy resulted in higher number of wasted readings, with more smartphones resulting in a larger difference.

5.4   Analysis of Results

The experimental data provided both expected and unexpected results. For Experiment 1, we were able to determine the minimum number of smartphones required to ensure that system goals were met for each operational environment we tested. However, our experimental hypothesis was ultimately proved incorrect, as the context-aware data collection policy resulted in much higher accuracy than was expected. In Experiment 2, we were able to show relative wastefulness of a constant data collection policy versus a context aware data collection policy.

One interesting result was the unexpected significance of our metric implementations. For example, transitioning from having no knowledge to having some (potentially incorrect) knowledge makes it difficult to approximate the accuracy of the overall simulation. In our experiments, we chose to count regions where we knew no information as the absolute worst possible values (e.g. the values far-thest from the real network). This in turn had significant implications - the effect of an unknown region on overall accuracy was very bad, and therefore coverage had a significant relation to accuracy. Essentially, all values that were input re-garding a region, no matter how incorrect, were likely to be better than the worst possible value. This effect was determined to be responsible for the reduction in magnitude of the dips shown in Figure 6 as the simulation progressed.

6   Related Work

This section compares Empower with related research from two key areas. First, significant research has been performed in the area of mobile sensor networks. Second, prior research in opportunistic sensing discusses some of the issues present with this paradigm.

Mobile Wireless Sensor Networks. While smartphone sensor networks have many differences from conventional mobile wireless sensor networks, such as a reduced need for ad hoc networking, some similarities do exist. Much mobile wireless sensor network research focuses on methods for networking and power reduction in mobile ad hoc networks. For example, Jain et al. show that by exploiting mobile nodes as intermediate data carriers it is possible to significantly reduce the amount of power required to transmit information between remote sensors and base stations [11]. However, smartphone sensor network nodes can be assumed to have fairly regular direct connection to the Internet, and are regularly recharged.

Mainwaring et al. explores building a wireless sensor network to perform habi-tat monitoring, because "the connection with its immediate physical environ-ment allows each sensor to provide localized measurements, [...] integration of local processing and storage allows nodes to perform complex filtering, [...] and ability to communicate allows information to be retrieved and nodes to be retasked in the field" [12]. However, methods of system-level verification and val-idation are not addressed, and there are no guarantees that such as system can meet its described goals. Most verification and validation research for wireless sensor networks has been done in the context of individual nodes, and little work has been done in full-system verification and validation.

Opportunistic Sensing. Research in opportunistic sensing has been increasing in popularity as sensors rise in availability. However, much of this research has been preliminary, and has not had a focus on the overall success of the oppor-tunistic network. Lilien et al. describe a framework standard, intended to allow components to be added and removed from any opportunistic network during the system production [13]. This may be a promising future approach, but in our research we have simply allowed mobile applications and previously-established standards, such as Hyper text transport protocol, to manage the interactions between opportunistic sensing components. Eisenman et al. discuss techniques for implementing intelligent network in a network largely consisting of mobile nodes [14]. Our research focuses on smartphone systems, which typically have an available network connection. However, in disaster scenarios this ad hoc networking would become invaluable, and therefore Empower allows the network components of the simulation to be handled by third party network driver software. This allows other researchers to integrate the work done with Empower and work being performed in the area of ad hoc networks.

7   Concluding Remarks and Lessons Learned

In this paper we discussed the emerging importance of smartphone-based data collection systems. We described the current problems with building these systems, which largely arise because the properties of these systems are highly emergent. This makes verification and validation of these systems at design time quite difficult.

In order to address this issue, we developed a simulation environment titled Empower that allows smartphone based data collection systems to be simulated. This simulation allows smartphone-specific system properties, such as data collection policies and smartphone count, to be specified, and provides system-level metrics that can be used to identify if the system achieved the goals of interest. By simulating the system with different properties, system designers can have informed opinions on the effectiveness of their system during the production phase. From our research on simulating smartphone sensor network data collection systems, we learned the following important lessons:

1. **Smartphone-based Data Collection Systems have Very High Potential.** Through our research, we were able to realize that smartphone-based data collection systems, when properly focused and directed, can have an enormous impact with a very small user base. While we have only performed initial research on quantifying these values, further work in this area is likely to be very promising.
2. **Calculation of Metrics for Data Collection Systems is Hard.** In our research the environments were divided into discrete regions, enabling us to perform system metrics much more simply than if we had truly continuous environments. This had significant impacts on many parts of the system, such as inputting data readings, speed of execution, and accuracy of calculations. In future work we plan to investigate continuous environments in order to address this gap.

Empower and data from the experiments described in this paper are available in opensource form from `https://github.com/crabpot8/Empower`.

References

1. Gartner says worldwide mobile phone sales grew 35 percent in third quarter 2010; smartphone sales increased 96 percent (November 2010),
   `http://www.gartner.com/it/page.jsp?id=1466313`

2. Turner, H., White, J., Thompson, C., Zienkiewicz, K., Campbell, S., Schmidt, D.: Building Mobile Sensor Networks Using Smartphones and Web Services: Ramifications and Development Challenges. In: Handbook of Research on Mobility and Computing, Hershey, PA (2009),
   http://www.cs.wustl.edu/~schmidt/PDF/hamilton-book-chapter.pdf
3. Froehlich, J., Dillahunt, T., Klasnja, P., Mankoff, J., Consolvo, S., Harrison, B., Landay, J.: UbiGreen: investigating a mobile tool for tracking and supporting green transportation habits. In: Proceedings of the 27th International Conference on Human Factors in Computing Systems, pp. 1043–1052. ACM (2009)
4. Thompson, C., White, J., Dougherty, B., Schmidt, D.: Optimizing Mobile Application Performance with Model-Driven Engineering. In: Proceedings of the 7th IFIP Workshop on Software Technologies for Future Embedded and Ubiquitous Systems (2009)
5. Jones, W.: Forecasting traffic flow. IEEE Spectrum 38(1), 90–91 (2001)
6. Rose, G.: Mobile phones as traffic probes: practices, prospects and issues. Transport Reviews 26(3), 275–291 (2006)
7. Leijdekkers, P., Gay, V.: Personal heart monitoring and rehabilitation system using smart phones. In: Proceedings of the International Conference on Mobile Business, p. 29. Citeseer (2006)
8. Gahran, A.: Reporting on the gulf oil spill from your cell phone, 2010, this is an electronic document, June 11 (2010), http://articles.cnn.com/2010-06-11/tech/oil.spil.app_1_cell-phones-apps-geotagged?_s=PM:TECH (date retrieved January 12, 2010) (date last modified: date unavailable)
9. Ölveczky, P.C., Thorvaldsen, S.: Formal Modeling and Analysis of the OGDC Wireless Sensor Network Algorithm in Real-Time Maude. In: Bonsangue, M.M., Johnsen, E.B. (eds.) FMOODS 2007. LNCS, vol. 4468, pp. 122–140. Springer, Heidelberg (2007)
10. Sharma, O., Lewis, J., Miller, A., Dearle, A., Balasubramaniam, D., Morrison, R., Sventek, J.: Towards Verifying Correctness of Wireless Sensor Network Applications Using Insense and Spin. In: Păsăreanu, C.S. (ed.) Model Checking Software. LNCS, vol. 5578, pp. 223–240. Springer, Heidelberg (2009)
11. Jain, S., Shah, R., Brunette, W., Borriello, G., Roy, S.: Exploiting mobility for energy efficient data collection in wireless sensor networks. Mobile Networks and Applications 11(3), 327–339 (2006)
12. Mainwaring, A., Culler, D., Polastre, J., Szewczyk, R., Anderson, J.: Wireless sensor networks for habitat monitoring. In: Proceedings of the 1st ACM International Workshop on Wireless Sensor Networks and Applications, pp. 88–97. ACM (2002)
13. Lilien, L., Gupta, A., Yang, Z.: Opportunistic networks for emergency applications and their standard implementation framework. In: IEEE International Performance, Computing, and Communications Conference, IPCCC 2007, pp. 588–593. IEEE (2007)
14. Eisenman, S.B., Lane, N.D., Campbell, A.T.: Techniques for Improving Opportunistic Sensor Networking Performance. In: Nikoletseas, S.E., Chlebus, B.S., Johnson, D.B., Krishnamachari, B. (eds.) DCOSS 2008. LNCS, vol. 5067, pp. 157–175. Springer, Heidelberg (2008)

Author Index